LOVE ENAMORED AND DRIVEN MAD

The Other Voice in Early Modern Europe:
The Toronto Series, 72

Medieval and Renaissance
Texts and Studies

Volume 567

The Other Voice in
Early Modern Europe:
The Toronto Series

SERIES EDITORS Margaret L. King *and* Albert Rabil, Jr.
SERIES EDITOR, ENGLISH TEXTS Elizabeth H. Hageman

Previous Publications in the Series

MADRE MARÍA ROSA
Journey of Five Capuchin Nuns
Edited and translated by Sarah E. Owens
Volume 1, 2009

GIOVAN BATTISTA ANDREINI
Love in the Mirror: A Bilingual Edition
Edited and translated by Jon R. Snyder
Volume 2, 2009

RAYMOND DE SABANAC AND SIMONE ZANACCHI
Two Women of the Great Schism: The Revelations *of Constance de Rabastens by Raymond de Sabanac and* Life of the Blessed Ursulina of Parma *by Simone Zanacchi*
Edited and translated by Renate Blumenfeld-Kosinski and Bruce L. Venarde
Volume 3, 2010

OLIVA SABUCO DE NANTES BARRERA
The True Medicine
Edited and translated by Gianna Pomata
Volume 4, 2010

LOUISE-GENEVIÈVE GILLOT DE SAINCTONGE
Dramatizing Dido, Circe, and Griselda
Edited and translated by Janet Levarie Smarr
Volume 5, 2010

PERNETTE DU GUILLET
Complete Poems: A Bilingual Edition
Edited by Karen Simroth James
Translated by Marta Rijn Finch
Volume 6, 2010

ANTONIA PULCI
Saints' Lives and Bible Stories for the Stage: A Bilingual Edition
Edited by Elissa B. Weaver
Translated by James Wyatt Cook
Volume 7, 2010

VALERIA MIANI
Celinda, A Tragedy: A Bilingual Edition
Edited by Valeria Finucci
Translated by Julia Kisacky
Annotated by Valeria Finucci and Julia Kisacky
Volume 8, 2010

Enchanted Eloquence: Fairy Tales by Seventeenth-Century French Women Writers
Edited and translated by Lewis C. Seifert and Domna C. Stanton
Volume 9, 2010

GOTTFRIED WILHELM LEIBNIZ, SOPHIE, ELECTRESS OF HANOVER AND QUEEN SOPHIE CHARLOTTE OF PRUSSIA
Leibniz and the Two Sophies: The Philosophical Correspondence
Edited and translated by Lloyd Strickland
Volume 10, 2011

The Other Voice in Early Modern Europe: The Toronto Series

SERIES EDITORS Margaret L. King *and* Albert Rabil, Jr.
SERIES EDITOR, ENGLISH TEXTS Elizabeth H. Hageman

Previous Publications in the Series

In Dialogue with the Other Voice in Sixteenth-Century Italy: Literary and Social Contexts for Women's Writing
Edited by Julie D. Campbell and Maria Galli Stampino
Volume 11, 2011

SISTER GIUSTINA NICCOLINI
The Chronicle of Le Murate
Edited and translated by Saundra Weddle
Volume 12, 2011

LIUBOV KRICHEVSKAYA
No Good without Reward: Selected Writings: A Bilingual Edition
Edited and translated by Brian James Baer
Volume 13, 2011

ELIZABETH COOKE HOBY RUSSELL
The Writings of an English Sappho
Edited by Patricia Phillippy
With translations by Jaime Goodrich
Volume 14, 2011

LUCREZIA MARINELLA
Exhortations to Women and to Others If They Please
Edited and translated by Laura Benedetti
Volume 15, 2012

MARGHERITA DATINI
Letters to Francesco Datini
Translated by Carolyn James and Antonio Pagliaro
Volume 16, 2012

DELARIVIER MANLEY AND MARY PIX
English Women Staging Islam, 1696–1707
Edited and introduced by Bernadette Andrea
Volume 17, 2012

CECILIA DEL NACIMIENTO
Journeys of a Mystic Soul in Poetry and Prose
Introduction and prose translations by Kevin Donnelly
Poetry translations by Sandra Sider
Volume 18, 2012

LADY MARGARET DOUGLAS AND OTHERS
The Devonshire Manuscript: A Women's Book of Courtly Poetry
Edited and introduced by Elizabeth Heale
Volume 19, 2012

ARCANGELA TARABOTTI
Letters Familiar and Formal
Edited and translated by Meredith K. Ray and Lynn Lara Westwater
Volume 20, 2012

PERE TORRELLAS AND JUAN DE FLORES
Three Spanish Querelle *Texts:* Grisel and Mirabella, The Slander against Women, *and* The Defense of Ladies against Slanderers*: A Bilingual Edition and Study*
Edited and translated by Emily C. Francomano
Volume 21, 2013

The Other Voice in Early Modern Europe: The Toronto Series

SERIES EDITORS Margaret L. King *and* Albert Rabil, Jr.
SERIES EDITOR, ENGLISH TEXTS Elizabeth H. Hageman

Previous Publications in the Series

BARBARA TORELLI BENEDETTI
Partenia, a Pastoral Play: A Bilingual Edition
Edited and translated by Lisa Sampson and Barbara Burgess-Van Aken
Volume 22, 2013

FRANÇOIS ROUSSET, JEAN LIEBAULT, JACQUES GUILLEMEAU, JACQUES DUVAL AND LOUIS DE SERRES
Pregnancy and Birth in Early Modern France: Treatises by Caring Physicians and Surgeons (1581–1625)
Edited and translated by Valerie Worth-Stylianou
Volume 23, 2013

MARY ASTELL
The Christian Religion, as Professed by a Daughter of the Church of England
Edited by Jacqueline Broad
Volume 24, 2013

SOPHIA OF HANOVER
Memoirs (1630–1680)
Edited and translated by Sean Ward
Volume 25, 2013

KATHERINE AUSTEN
Book M: A London Widow's Life Writings
Edited by Pamela S. Hammons
Volume 26, 2013

ANNE KILLIGREW
"My Rare Wit Killing Sin": Poems of a Restoration Courtier
Edited by Margaret J. M. Ezell
Volume 27, 2013

TULLIA D'ARAGONA AND OTHERS
The Poems and Letters of Tullia d'Aragona and Others: A Bilingual Edition
Edited and translated by Julia L. Hairston
Volume 28, 2014

LUISA DE CARVAJAL Y MENDOZA
The Life and Writings of Luisa de Carvajal y Mendoza
Edited and translated by Anne J. Cruz
Volume 29, 2014

Russian Women Poets of the Eighteenth and Early Nineteenth Centuries: A Bilingual Edition
Edited and translated by Amanda Ewington
Volume 30, 2014

JACQUES DU BOSC
L'Honnête Femme: The Respectable Woman in Society *and the* New Collection of Letters and Responses by Contemporary Women
Edited and translated by Sharon Diane Nell and Aurora Wolfgang
Volume 31, 2014

The Other Voice in Early Modern Europe: The Toronto Series

Previous Publications in the Series

LADY HESTER PULTER
Poems, Emblems, and *The Unfortunate Florinda*
Edited by Alice Eardley
Volume 32, 2014

JEANNE FLORE
Tales and Trials of Love, Concerning Venus's Punishment of Those Who Scorn True Love and Denounce Cupid's Sovereignity: A Bilingual Edition and Study
Edited and translated by Kelly Digby Peebles
Poems translated by Marta Rijn Finch
Volume 33, 2014

VERONICA GAMBARA
Complete Poems: A Bilingual Edition
Critical introduction by Molly M. Martin
Edited and translated by Molly M. Martin and Paola Ugolini
Volume 34, 2014

CATHERINE DE MÉDICIS AND OTHERS
Portraits of the Queen Mother: Polemics, Panegyrics, Letters
Translation and study by Leah L. Chang and Katherine Kong
Volume 35, 2014

FRANÇOISE PASCAL, MARIE-CATHERINE DESJARDINS, ANTOINETTE DESHOULIÈRES, AND CATHERINE DURAND
Challenges to Traditional Authority: Plays by French Women Authors, 1650–1700
Edited and translated by Perry Gethner
Volume 36, 2015

FRANCISZKA URSZULA RADZIWIŁŁOWA
Selected Drama and Verse
Edited by Patrick John Corness and Barbara Judkowiak
Translated by Patrick John Corness
Translation Editor Aldona Zwierzyńska-Coldicott
Introduction by Barbara Judkowiak
Volume 37, 2015

DIODATA MALVASIA
Writings on the Sisters of San Luca and Their Miraculous Madonna
Edited and translated by Danielle Callegari and Shannon McHugh
Volume 38, 2015

MARGARET VAN NOORT
Spiritual Writings of Sister Margaret of the Mother of God (1635–1643)
Edited by Cordula van Wyhe
Translated by Susan M. Smith
Volume 39, 2015

The Other Voice in Early Modern Europe: The Toronto Series

SERIES EDITORS Margaret L. King *and* Albert Rabil, Jr.
SERIES EDITOR, ENGLISH TEXTS Elizabeth H. Hageman

Previous Publications in the Series

GIOVAN FRANCESCO STRAPAROLA
The Pleasant Nights
Edited and translated by Suzanne Magnanini
Volume 40, 2015

ANGÉLIQUE DE SAINT-JEAN ARNAULD D'ANDILLY
Writings of Resistance
Edited and translated by John J. Conley, S.J.
Volume 41, 2015

FRANCESCO BARBARO
The Wealth of Wives: A Fifteenth-Century Marriage Manual
Edited and translated by Margaret L. King
Volume 42, 2015

JEANNE D'ALBRET
Letters from the Queen of Navarre with an Ample Declaration
Edited and translated by Kathleen M. Llewellyn, Emily E. Thompson, and Colette H. Winn
Volume 43, 2016

BATHSUA MAKIN AND MARY MORE WITH A REPLY TO MORE BY ROBERT WHITEHALL
Educating English Daughters: Late Seventeenth-Century Debates
Edited by Frances Teague and Margaret J. M. Ezell
Associate Editor Jessica Walker
Volume 44, 2016

ANNA STANISŁAWSKA
Orphan Girl: A Transaction, or an Account of the Entire Life of an Orphan Girl by way of Plaintful Threnodies in the Year 1685: *The Aesop Episode*
Verse translation, introduction, and commentary by Barry Keane
Volume 45, 2016

ALESSANDRA MACINGHI STROZZI
Letters to Her Sons, 1447–1470
Edited and translated by Judith Bryce
Volume 46, 2016

MOTHER JUANA DE LA CRUZ
Mother Juana de la Cruz, 1481–1534: Visionary Sermons
Edited by Jessica A. Boon and Ronald E. Surtz. Introductory material and notes by Jessica A. Boon. Translated by Ronald E. Surtz and Nora Weinerth
Volume 47, 2016

CLAUDINE-ALEXANDRINE GUÉRIN DE TENCIN
Memoirs of the Count of Comminge *and* The Misfortunes of Love
Edited and translated by Jonathan Walsh
Volume 48, 2016

The Other Voice in
Early Modern Europe:
The Toronto Series

SERIES EDITORS Margaret L. King *and* Albert Rabil, Jr.
SERIES EDITOR, ENGLISH TEXTS Elizabeth H. Hageman

Previous Publications in the Series

FELICIANA ENRÍQUEZ DE GUZMÁN, ANA CARO MALLÉN, AND SOR MARCELA DE SAN FÉLIX
Women Playwrights of Early Modern Spain
Edited by Nieves Romero-Díaz and Lisa Vollendorf
Translated and annotated by Harley Erdman
Volume 49, 2016

ANNA TRAPNEL
Anna Trapnel's Report and Plea; or, A Narrative of Her Journey from London into Cornwall
Edited by Hilary Hinds
Volume 50, 2016

MARÍA VELA Y CUETO
Autobiography and Letters of a Spanish Nun
Edited by Susan Laningham
Translated by Jane Tar
Volume 51, 2016

CHRISTINE DE PIZAN
The Book of the Mutability of Fortune
Edited and translated by Geri L. Smith
Volume 52, 2017

MARGUERITE D'AUGE, RENÉE BURLAMACCHI, AND JEANNE DU LAURENS
Sin and Salvation in Early Modern France: Three Women's Stories
Edited, and with an introduction by Colette H. Winn. Translated by Nicholas Van Handel and Colette H. Winn
Volume 53, 2017

ISABELLA D'ESTE
Selected Letters
Edited and translated by Deanna Shemek
Volume 54, 2017

IPPOLITA MARIA SFORZA
Duchess and Hostage in Renaissance Naples: Letters and Orations
Edited and translated by Diana Robin and Lynn Lara Westwater
Volume 55, 2017

LOUISE BOURGEOIS
Midwife to the Queen of France: Diverse Observations
Translated by Stephanie O'Hara
Edited by Alison Klairmont Lingo
Volume 56, 2017

CHRISTINE DE PIZAN
Othea's Letter to Hector
Edited and translated by Renate Blumenfeld-Kosinski and Earl Jeffrey Richards
Volume 57, 2017

The Other Voice in Early Modern Europe: The Toronto Series

Previous Publications in the Series

MARIE-GENEVIÈVE-CHARLOTTE THIROUX D'ARCONVILLE
Selected Philosophical, Scientific, and Autobiographical Writings
Edited and translated by Julie Candler Hayes
Volume 58, 2018

LADY MARY WROTH
Pamphilia to Amphilanthus *in Manuscript and Print*
Edited by Ilona Bell
Texts by Steven W. May and Ilona Bell
Volume 59, 2017

Witness, Warning, and Prophecy: Quaker Women's Writing, 1655–1700
Edited by Teresa Feroli and Margaret Olofson Thickstun
Volume 60, 2018

SYMPHORIEN CHAMPIER
The Ship of Virtuous Ladies
Edited by Todd W. Reeser
Volume 61, 2018

ISABELLA ANDREINI
Mirtilla, A Pastoral: *A Bilingual Edition*
Edited by Valeria Finucci
Translated by Julia Kisacky
Volume 62, 2018

MARGHERITA COSTA
The Buffoons, A Ridiculous Comedy: *A Bilingual Edition*
Edited and translated by Sara E. Díaz and Jessica Goethals
Volume 63, 2018

MARGARET CAVENDISH, DUCHESS OF NEWCASTLE
Poems and Fancies *with* The Animal Parliament
Edited by Brandie R. Siegfried
Volume 64, 2018

MARGARET FELL
Women's Speaking Justified *and Other Pamphlets*
Edited by Jane Donawerth and Rebecca M. Lush
Volume 65, 2018

MARY WROTH, JANE CAVENDISH, AND ELIZABETH BRACKLEY
Women's Household Drama:
Loves Victorie, A Pastorall, *and* The concealed Fansyes
Edited by Marta Straznicky and Sara Mueller
Volume 66, 2018

The Other Voice in
Early Modern Europe:
The Toronto Series

Previous Publications in the Series

ELEONORA FONSECA PIMENTEL
From Arcadia to Revolution: The Neapolitan Monitor *and Other Writings*
Edited and translated by Verina R. Jones
Volume 67, 2019

CHARLOTTE ARBALESTE DUPLESSIS-MORNAY, ANNE DE CHAUFEPIÉ, AND ANNE MARGUERITE PETIT DU NOYER
The Huguenot Experience of Persecution and Exile: Three Women's Stories
Edited by Colette H. Winn
Translated by Lauren King and Colette H. Winn
Volume 68, 2019

ANNE BRADSTREET
Poems and Meditations
Edited by Margaret Olofson Thickstun
Volume 69, 2019

ARCANGELA TARABOTTI
Antisatire: *In Defense of Women, against Francesco Buoninsegni*
Edited by Elissa B. Weaver
Volume 70, 2020

MARY FRANKLIN AND HANNAH BURTON
She Being Dead Yet Speaketh: The Franklin Family Papers
Edited by Vera J. Camden
Volume 71, 2020

LUCREZIA MARINELLA

Love Enamored and Driven Mad

Edited and translated by

JANET E. GOMEZ AND MARIA GALLI STAMPINO

Iter Press
Toronto, Ontario

ACMRS Press
Tempe, Arizona

2020

Iter Press
Tel: 416/978-7074 Email: iter@utoronto.ca
Fax: 416/978-1668 Web: www.itergateway.org

ACMRS Press
Tel: 480/965-5900 Email: acmrspress@asu.edu
Fax: 480/965-1681 Web: acmrspress.com

Printed in Canada.

Library of Congress Cataloging-in-Publication Data

Names: Marinella, Lucrezia, 1571–1653, author. | Gomez, Janet, editor, translator. | Stampino, Maria Galli, editor, translator.

Title: Love enamored and driven mad / Lucrezia Marinella ; edited and translated by Janet E. Gomez and Maria Galli Stampino.

Other titles: Amore innamorato et impazzato. English

Description: Toronto, Ontario : Iter Press ; Tempe, Arizona : Arizona Center for Medieval and Renaissance Studies, 2020. | Series: The other voice in early modern Europe: the Toronto series ; 72 | Includes bibliographical references. | Translated into English from Italian. | Summary: "English translation of a lengthy poem by Italian author Lucrezia Marinella, composed in 1598, elaborating the classical motif of the enamored Cupid with religious allegorization and pro-woman themes"--Provided by publisher.

Identifiers: LCCN 2019028719 (print) | LCCN 2019028720 (ebook) | ISBN 9780866986250 (paperback) | ISBN 9780866987585 (ebook)

Classification: LCC PQ4627.M84 A8313 2019 (print) | LCC PQ4627.M84 (ebook) | DDC 851/.5--dc23

LC record available at https://lccn.loc.gov/2019028719

LC ebook record available at https://lccn.loc.gov/2019028720

Cover illustration:
Detail from *The Abduction of Helen* (c.1626–31; oil on canvas) / Reni, Guido (1575–1642) / Louvre, Paris, France / The Bridgeman Art Library XIR122659.

Cover design:
Maureen Morin, Information Technology Services, University of Toronto Libraries.

Typesetting and production:
Iter Press.

Contents

Acknowledgments

The fact that it is habitual to include a list of people whose support and help have bolstered one's work should not detract from the fact that each project stems from a myriad of ideas and interactions, without which it would not exist. Our translation is no exception to this (providential!) rule.

Maria would like to first thank Janet for asking to work with her on this project, and for helping her refine her grasp of her homegrown Italian-Cuban/Cuban-Italian dictionary. Janet would like to thank Maria for meeting her that fateful day at a Nordstrom Bistro during a seasonably hot Christmas break in Miami, where Maria accepted to partner with, at the time, a meek and daring second-year graduate student and thus saving her from a Marinellian *via smarrita*!

The idea for this translation would not exist without Al Rabil and Margaret King, whose series has helped revolutionize early modern studies. We thank them for their support and encouragement. Professor King was particularly helpful and patient with us on this project. Also, we would like to thank Virginia Cox for suggesting that this text deserves its place among the others in the series.

Maria needs to spend a few lines to mention her family: Robert (Tino) has shared work and faced all sorts of emergencies and crises with unfailing coolness and understanding. Lawrence and Beatrice appreciate (and were originally a bit surprised) that their mom had "written a book!" For this, and for their subsequently being boundlessly proud, they deserve a special commendation.

Dean Leonidas Bachas, Sr. Associate Deans Angel Kaifer and Doug Fuller, colleagues Athena Sanders, Leonard Clemons, Gylla Lucky, Maggie Pertierra, Nadieska González-Miranda, Rose Glemaud, and Ana Garcia are part of Maria's work community: they have enriched (and simplified!) her life while serving in the Dean's Office in the College of Arts & Sciences at the University of Miami.

At UM, Maria was lucky to have Francesca Filanti as research assistant. She spent many hours valiantly looking up all manners of classical references that found their ways in our footnotes. For this and for her enthusiasm she deserves appreciation and kudos. In addition, colleagues in the Early Modern (now: Medieval and Early Modern) Research Group (operating under the ægis of the Center for the Humanities) have provided insights, feedback, and many probing questions throughout the years. Anne J. Cruz, Karl Gunther, Mary Lindemann, Frank Palmeri, and Mihoko Suzuki deserve special mention—plus Perri Lee Roberts, whose mentorship as a scholar and an educator has literally touched Maria's UM experience from her first day on campus.

In the profession at large, Jane Tylus continues to teach Maria a whole lot about dedication to our work—as faculty, scholar, mentor, and member of the university community.

At Johns Hopkins University, Janet would like to thank Walter Stephens for his continuous feedback, unwavering support, and finally realizing that she would, perplexingly, only finish her dissertation in six years if she had 300 simultaneous projects. At the University of Florida, a special thanks goes out to Associate Dean, Professor, Ironman, and Torontonian, Mary A. Watt, who among many things reminds Janet to go for a run and *riveder le stelle* every chance she would get. That this is published in the Toronto Series is uncanny. Finally, Janet thanks all the friends and family who have been very supportive, patient, and have given her food for thought through the creation of this edition, including but not limited to, Francesco Caruso, Mrs. Anne Hopkins, and Bella the dog.

Lastly, Cheryl Lemmens, editor extraordinaire, made the final translation much stronger. Margaret English-Haskin was instrumental in shepherding our work from file to book format, and we thank her for her support and patience.

In his pivotal study *After Babel*, George Steiner writes that "Translation is an exemplary case of metamorphosis" (273). We hope to have not disappointed Lucrezia Marinella, whose courage in taking up other authors' stories and ideas and working her own metamorphoses is an example for us, translators.

Introduction: Classical Topoi Tell a Woman's Story

The Other Voice

As a prolific author whose writings were published over a span of some fifty years, and encompassing a wide variety of topics and styles from heroic verse to hagiography, Lucrezia Marinella was already a remarkable "other voice" in the patriarchal culture of early modern Italy. She is probably best known today for her lengthy treatise *Le nobiltà, et eccellenze delle donne, et i difetti, e mancamenti de gli huomini* (*The Nobility and Excellence of Women and the Defects and Vices of Men*, 1600), written as a response to a virulently misogynistic tract. Less well known, but no less a statement of feminine strength and humanity, is *Amore innamorato et impazzato* (*Love Enamored and Driven Mad*, 1618), a poem largely based on the story of Cupid and Psyche yet utterly unlike it. In this work, published at the midpoint of her writing career, Marinella exhibits her intellectual independence and progressive standpoint by adopting a well-known plot from classical antiquity—with a twist. While ensuring its relevance to her day and age by interpreting it in allegorical fashion, consistent with prevailing religious concerns, she modifies the story so that it remains a vehicle for pious entertainment even as readers simultaneously become aware of another point of view—a woman's—concerning the plot.

The story of Cupid and Psyche, which forms the narrative kernel of *Amore innamorato et impazzato,* is found in Apuleius's *Metamorphoses* (or *The Golden Ass*), written in the second century CE. Apuleius's female characters—from the inexperienced, passive Psyche and her petty, envious sisters to the self-absorbed and viciously misogynistic Venus—are hardly role models. The male characters, conversely, are compassionate and attentive; Cupid saves Psyche from death, searches for her after she flees, and implores Jupiter to allow them to marry, while the powerful Jupiter grants Cupid's request with benevolent mercy.

Marinella's poem turns this plot—and its gendered character traits—upside down. Proud and rebellious, Cupid decides he is greater than all the other gods, and Jupiter in turn resolves to punish him by making him feel the pains he inflicts on humans and deities alike, sending Mercury to set things in motion. Not only does Cupid fall in love, but he goes mad and becomes violent, destructive, even murderous in his irrationality. By contrast, the main female characters, Ersilia and Venus, offer behaviors that at the time would have been considered as positive: the virginal young woman who protects her chastity, and the devoted mother who travels to the end of the known world to recover her son. Minor female mythological figures such as the Graces and nymphs are portrayed as kind, compassionate, helpful, and observant. Even as she follows the prevailing moral and ideological compass of Counter-Reformation Italy, then, Marinella presents situations and characters that stray from traditional narratives and illuminate how women contribute to the workings and harmony of families and other groups.

Marinella's Life and Works

Lucrezia Marinella was one of the most prolific women writers in early modern Italy, aided in part by her longevity. We know relatively little about her life, in spite of attempts to find manuscripts of her work (none have surfaced, to date) and other documents about her (some of which have come to light, as we will see below). She was born in Venice, circa 1571,[1] to Giovanni Marinelli, whose family origin is uncertain.[2] Marinelli was a physician and a scholar of natural philosophy who also published several works, some of which were aimed specifically at women.[3] Although he had not been born in Venice,[4] his family belonged to the stratum of the *cittadini*, which included between five and eight percent of all Venetians who had never practiced an *arte meccanica* (any job involving manual labor); lower than the patriciate, they were nevertheless crucial to the city as they supplied civil servants and administrators to the *scuole*, charitable institutions central to social life in Venice.[5] Lucrezia had two older brothers: Curzio, a physician who graduated from the Paduan *Studio* in April 1587,[6] and who himself published in

1. On how scholar Girolami Tiraboschi established the date of her birth, see Susan Haskins, "Vexatious Litigant, or the Case of Lucrezia Marinella? New Documents Concerning Her Life (Part One)," *Nouvelles de la république des Lettres*, 25, no. 1 (2006), 84.

2. He was born in Modena, but sources report his coming from Naples and from Mola, near Bari, in Apulia. See Laura Benedetti, "Introduction," in *Exhortation to Women and to Others if They Please*, by Lucrezia Marinella, ed. and trans. Laura Benedetti (Toronto: Iter Inc. and Centre for Reformation and Renaissance Studies, 2012), 7.

3. Among them are *La copia delle parole* [*The Abundance of Words*] (Venice, 1562), extolling the richness of the Italian vernacular and offering lists of synonyms; *Gli ornamenti delle donne* [*Women's Ornaments*] (Venice, 1562), concerning hygiene and beauty remedies; and *Le medicine pertinenti alle infirmità delle donne* [*Medicines Pertaining to Women's Illnesses*] (Venice, 1563; revised and reprinted, Venice, 1674). See Maria Luisa Altieri Biagi, Clemente Mazzotta, Angela Chiantera, and Paola Altieri, *Medicina per le donne nel Cinquecento: Testi di Giovanni Marinello e di Girolamo Mercurio* (Turin: Strenna UTET, 1992), introduction, 7–40, and selection from *Le medicine*, 45–64.

4. Nor is his name "listed in the catalogue of graduations from the Studio di Padova [i.e., the closest university to Venice] or that of the Venetian College of Physicians." See Haskins, "Vexatious Litigant (Part One)," 87.

5. Ibid., 89.

6. Ibid., 88.

the fields of medicine and history;[7] and Angelico, a priest who died after 1630.[8] She also had a sister, Diamantina, who married a doctor from Belluno and was dead by 1620.[9] We do not know how Lucrezia acquired her considerable learning, although, as Sarah Ross pithily states, she "certainly read Latin."[10]

In 1607, Lucrezia married Girolamo Vacca, also a physician. At approximately thirty-six years old, she was much older than the average Venetian spouse, as was he (forty-eight); as Haskins notes, he "may have been a widower."[11] Her dowry, negotiated by Curzio, amounted to 3,500 ducats, whose source is unknown.[12] She had at least two children: her 1645 will mentions a son, Antonio, and a daughter, Paulina, who by 1648 had had a daughter, Angioletta.[13] No documentation has been found concerning their birth or baptism in Venice; this, and other ties between Vacca and Padua, suggest that "Marinella may well have lived in or near [that city] for some time after her marriage."[14] Before and after her marriage, Lucrezia enjoyed a comfortable life in financial terms, as evinced by the documents assembled by Susan Haskins.[15] Vacca died in September 1629, at the age of seventy,[16] and she outlived him by many years. She died of a recurring fever, possibly malaria, on October 9, 1653, and was buried in her parish church of San Pantalon.[17] Her tomb is no longer extant, presumably a victim of the radical rebuilding that took place later in the seventeenth century, when the floor plan of the church was rotated by 90 degrees.[18]

7. Françoise Lavocat mentions Curzio's annotations to Paolo Giovio and to Livy, as well as his *Discorso nel quale si scrive il modo di studiar l'Historie per reggere stati* [*Discourse on the Way to Study History to Lead States*], published in 1580 alongside Francesco Guicciardini's *Storia d'Italia* [*History of Italy*], in which he espouses "un repubblicanismo aristocratico machiavelliano, anti-mediceo ed anti-papale" [a position in favor of aristocratic republics, modelled on Machiavelli, anti-Medici, and anti-pope]. See Lavocat, "Introduzione," in *Arcadia felice*, by Lucrezia Marinella, ed. Françoise Lavocat (Florence: Olschki, 1998), xii. All translations from texts other than *Amore innamorato* are by Maria Galli Stampino.

8. Haskins, "Vexatious Litigant (Part One)," 92.

9. Ibid., 88 and 92.

10. Sarah Gwyneth Ross, *The Birth of Feminism: Woman as Intellect in Renaissance Italy and England* (Cambridge, MA: Harvard University Press, 2009), 202.

11. Haskins, "Vexatious Litigant (Part One)," 93.

12. Ibid., 107 and 109. Documents pertaining to her marriage contract are found at 117–20.

13. Marinella's will is found in Haskins, "Vexatious Litigant (Part One)," 122–23.

14. Susan Haskins, "Vexatious Litigant, or the Case of Lucrezia Marinella? New Documents Concerning Her Life (Part II)," *Nouvelles de la république des Lettres*, 26, nos. 1–2 (2007), 204.

15. Ibid., 208–11.

16. Ibid., 216.

17. Ibid., 225–26.

18. See the history in the Italian Wikipedia entry of the church: <https://it.wikipedia.org/wiki/Chiesa_di_San_Pantalon>.

Works, 1595–1605

While her life is ordinary in several critical aspects, including the paucity of documentation about it, Marinella's writings set her apart from the great majority of her contemporaries. She wrote and published in a variety of genres, and on several different topics, in two separate periods of her life. Between 1595 and 1605, seven works by Marinella circulated in print, some of them in more than one edition, starting with the epic poem on a religious topic *La Colomba sacra, poema eroico* (*The Holy Dove: Heroic Poem*, 1595), in *ottava rima*,[19] her favorite poetic form for narrative works. As would be typical of most of Marinella's production, she selected a female saint from early Christianity and extolled her heroic status. Saint Columba was martyred for her faith by the emperor Aurelian in Sens, a city in modern-day France, in the third century CE. A virgin, she was miraculously protected from rape by a bear, and from certain death by fire when a rain shower extinguished the pyre on which she had been tied; she was then put to death by beheading. In this work, published by Giovanni Battista Ciotti in Venice and dedicated to Margherita Gonzaga d'Este, duchess of Ferrara, two elements are intertwined: a devout topic, and attention to a woman. Two years later, she published another religiously-themed work: *Vita del serafico e glorioso San Francesco. Descritta in ottava rima. Ove si spiegano le attioni, le astinenze e i miracoli di esso* (*Life of the Seraphic and Glorious Saint Francis, in* ottava rima, *in which his actions, asceticism, and miracles are explained*), with the publisher Pietro Maria Bertano and a dedication to Christine of Lorraine, grand duchess of Tuscany. The dedications to noblewomen, the alignment with prevailing Counter-Reformation hagiographic themes, and prefatory sonnets written by notable Venetians point to her "determination to insert herself into a prestigious male literary tradition"[20] even at an early age.

Her next work is the one for which she is best known to twenty-first-century readers: *Le nobiltà, et eccellenze delle donne, et i difetti, e mancamenti de gli huomini* (*The Nobility and Excellence of Women and the Defects and Vices of Men*). Ciotti published it in 1600, then in an expanded version in 1601 with the title *La nobiltà, et l'eccellenza delle donne, co' diffetti, et mancamenti de gli huomini*; it was also published by Giovanni Battista Combi in 1621. Marinella dedicated it to Lucio Scarano, a doctor and *letterato*. Although *La nobiltà* is in many ways least representative of her production, being one of two texts in prose, and polemical in its outlook, it is nevertheless a fundamental work: a long tract in response to

19. *Ottava rima* is composed of stanzas of eight eleven-syllable lines with three rhymes: one connecting the first, third, and fifth lines; a second one tying the second, fourth, and sixth lines; and the third one for the couplet at the end of the stanza, i.e., the seventh and eighth lines.

20. Cox, *The Prodigious Muse.Women's Writing in Counter-Reformation Italy* (Baltimore: Johns Hopkins University Press, 2011), 143. Cox devotes ten pages (141–51) to these two poems.

Giuseppe Passi's virulently misogynist *I donneschi difetti* (*The Defects of Women*, 1599).[21] Widely read and cited in the seventeenth century,[22] *La nobiltà* is a "formally argued academic treatise, setting out its case for the superiority of women to men through a combination of theoretical reasoning and exemplification."[23] Marinella forcefully defends women from Passi's attacks, turning the tables on him by underscoring men's shortcomings.[24] It is, to cite Laura Schnieders, "a hefty work, a compilation built on a thick grid of direct and indirect citations from literary, philosophic, religious works, etc., as well as on numerous, and at times long, lists of *exempla*."[25] Not always a linear text, its strength lies in the quantity of its examples as well as in the force of its argument.[26]

After this foray into polemical writing, Marinella returned to hagiographic topics. In 1602 she published *La vita di Maria Vergine, imperatrice dell'universo* (*Life of the Virgin Mary, Empress of the Universe*), a prose and verse narrative in which Marinella "fleshe[d] out the meager Gospel record" of Mary's life by drawing on "the vast body of apocryphal material that had accumulated around the figure of the Virgin."[27] This was her most appealing work for her contemporaries, judging by the number of editions: it was reprinted in 1604, 1610, and 1617 (the

21. For a helpful introduction to Passi and selected translation from his treatise, see Suzanne Magnanini, with David Lamari, "Giuseppe Passi's Attacks on Women in *The Defects of Women*," in *In Dialogue with the Other Voice in Sixteenth-Century Italy: Literary and Social Contexts for Women's Writings*, ed. Julie D. Campbell and Maria Galli Stampino (Toronto: Iter Inc. and Centre for Reformation and Renaissance Studies, 2011), 143–94.

22. Cox, *The Prodigious Muse*, 364n109.

23. Ibid., 237.

24. In the 1601 edition, as Laura Benedetti has pointed out, Marinella devotes 132 pages to praising women and 192 to criticizing men. She further notes that the English translator, Anne Dunhill, has "overturn[ed] this ratio" [stravolgendo questo rapporto], since her translation offers 106 and 34 pages respectively, depicting Marinella as "more moderate, reasonable, and therefore more acceptable, but overall far from the seventeenth-century Venetian woman" [più moderata, ragionevole e dunque assimilabile, ma in fondo lontana dalla veneziana del Seicento]. See Laura Benedetti, "Tradurre Marinella in America: opportunità e pericoli di una nuova frontiera," in *Conflitti culturali a Venezia dalla prima età moderna ad oggi*, ed. Rotraud von Kulessa, Daria Perocco, and Sabine Meine (Florence: Franco Cesati, 2014), 216.

25. "[U]n'opera molto ampia dal carattere compilativo, costruita su una fitta rete di citazioni dirette o indirette da opere letterarie, filosofiche, religiose etc., nonché su numerose, e in alcuni casi lunghe, liste di *exempla*." See Laura Schnieders, "La polemica dei sessi: Lucrezia Marinella e Giuseppe Passi," in *Conflitti culturali a Venezia dalla prima età moderna ad oggi*, ed. Rotraud von Kulessa, Daria Perocco, and Sabine Meine (Florence: Franco Cesati, 2014), 193.

26. On the connections between *La nobiltà* and Marinella's scientific knowledge, see Meredith K. Ray, *Daughters of Alchemy: Women and Scientific Culture in Early Modern Italy* (Cambridge, MA: Harvard University Press, 2015), particularly 94–100.

27. Cox, *The Prodigious Muse*, 151.

latter is a much expanded and revised version).[28] As Susan Haskins points out, the connections between Mary and Venice were deep, firmly rooted in the history and self-image of the city;[29] this might explain the fact that, in an unusual move, Marinella dedicated the book to the reigning doge, Marino Grimani, and to the senate of the Venetian republic.

The following year (1603), a collection of *Rime sacre* (*Sacred Poems*) appeared in Venice, paid for by its printer, Ascanio Collosini, who dedicated it to Eugenia Ceruti Scaini. It includes sonnets and madrigals, as well as a narrative poem in *ottava rima.*[30] Two works by Marinella were printed in 1605: *Scielta d'alcune rime sacre* (*Selection of some Sacred Poems*), by Comin Ventura of Bergamo, who dedicated it to Cornelia Casale; and *Arcadia felice* (*Happy Arcadia*), by Ciotti, with Marinella's dedication to Eleonora Medici Gonzaga, duchess of Mantua. The latter is a mostly prose text in the pastoral genre, a choice which Françoise Lavocat has rightly dubbed as "original,"[31] with political and mythological sources and a possible reading connected to contemporary events.[32]

To crown this intense period of publication, Marinella provided "learned annotations and an allegory" for an edition of Luigi Tansillo's *Le lagrime di San Pietro ... poema sacro, et heroico* (*St. Peter's Tears, A Sacred and Heroic Poem*), which appeared in Venice in 1606. Her role, noted on the title page and on the cover of the volume, "strikingly" inverted the convention of men as literary annotators, and in fact her annotations were commissioned by the book's publisher, Barezzo Barezzi, "on the strength of the learning and intellect that made her universally admired." As Virginia Cox notes, Marinella's role as annotator "mark[ed] the high point of women's erudite performance in this period."[33]

28. Susan Haskins has translated the prose portion on the basis of the 1610 edition: "Lucrezia Marinella's *Life of the Virgin Mary, Empress of the Universe,*" in *Who is Mary? Three Early Modern Women on the Idea of the Virgin Mary*, ed. and trans. Susan Haskins (Chicago: University of Chicago Press, 2008), 119–246.

29. Ibid., 122.

30. A brief analysis of the stylistic innovations of this collection is in Cox, *The Prodigious Muse*, 54–55. On the figure of the Virgin Mary in Marinella's religiously-themed verses, see Leonardo Giorgetti's essay "'Colei che 'l mondo e 'l cielo empie di luce': Mary's Glorification and Poetic Fame in Lucrezia Marinella's Spiritual Poetry," in *Genealogías. Rewriting the Canon: Women Writing in XVI–XVII Century Italy*, ed. Stefano Santossuosso (Seville: ArcCiBel, 2018).

31. Lavocat, "Introduzione," xxi.

32. See ibid., xxv–xli. On the use of prose and poetry, see xli.

33. Virginia Cox, *Women's Writing in Italy, 1400–1650* (Baltimore: Johns Hopkins University Press, 2008), 154.

Works, 1617–1648

After this flurry of work, Marinella's voice goes silent until 1617, when a much expanded version of *La vita di Maria Vergine imperatrice dell'universo*, now including lives of the apostles and of the evangelists, appeared for Barezzi. It was followed by *Amore innamorato et impazzato* in 1618, for Giovanni Battista Combi, bearing Marinella's dedication to Caterina Medici Gonzaga, duchess of Mantua (daughter of Christine of Lorraine, who succeeded her cousin Eleonora as consort to the duke).[34] The reasons for this silence are unknown, but her marriage and motherhood, as well as the decline and ultimate dissolution of the Accademia veneziana, with which Marinella was loosely connected, can be mentioned as possible causes.[35] In this second phase of her creativity, Marinella's works appeared more infrequently: After *Amore innamorato* and the 1621 printing of *La nobiltà* we have *De' gesti heroici e della vita maravigliosa della serafica S. Caterina da Siena* (*Heroic Deeds and Marvelous Life of the Seraphic St. Catherine of Siena*, 1624); *L'Enrico, overo Bisanzio acquistato* (*Enrico, or Byzantium Conquered*, 1635); *Le vittorie di Francesco il serafico, li passi gloriosi della diva Chiara* (*The Victories of the Seraphic Francis and the Glorious Steps of the Blessed Claire*, 1643); *Essortationi alle donne et a gli altri se saranno loro a grado* (*Exhortations to Women and to Others if They Please*, 1645); and lastly *Holocausto d'amore della vergine Santa Giustina* (*Love Sacrifice of the Virgin St. Justine*, 1648). The dedications of these works are remarkable for their ambition: *De' gesti heroici* is dedicated to Maria Maddalena of Austria, grand duchess of Tuscany, widow of grand duke Cosimo II de' Medici and co-regent with Christine of Lorraine between 1621 and 1628;[36] *Enrico* to the ruling doge, Francesco Erizzo, and the Venetian senate; *Le vittorie* to Pope Urban VIII (Maffeo Barberini); *Essortationi* to Gaspar de Teves y Guzmán, Spanish ambassador to Venice; and *Holocausto* to the doge Francesco Molin. Marinella's desire to insert herself within the ranks of the political and cultural intelligentsia in Venice and on the Italian peninsula is evident in these choices.

34. Lavocat gives a publication date of 1598 ("Introduzione," xviii), but draws her citations from the 1618 edition. Panizza does the same: Letizia Panizza, "Introduction to the Translation," in *The Nobility and Excellence of Women and the Defects and Vices of Men*, by Lucrezia Marinella, ed. and trans. Anne Dunhill (Chicago: University of Chicago Press, 1999), 8. Cox's extensive research failed to uncover any copies of this hypothetical first edition; she notes that *Amore* is not included in Ciotti's "otherwise compendious list of Marinella's publications" in his "Avvertenza" to the readers of *Arcadia felice*: Cox, *Women's Writing*, 334n94. It may be significant that Lavocat also refers to a 1622 edition of *Enrico*, which likewise is not found anywhere: Lavocat, "Introduzione," xx, n78.

35. Lavocat, xiii–xiv.

36. As Cox states, Maria Maddalena was "coregent of Tuscany with Christine [of Lorraine] at the time of Marinella's writing": *Prodigious Muse*, 154. Her son Ferdinando II began ruling in his own right after he came of age in 1628.

Leaving aside *Amore innamorato* for the moment, since we will devote more attention to it in due course, we see among these texts a prevalence of hagiographic themes; a different sense of Marinella's self as author; and a different scope of her works. The prose biography of St. Catherine is explicitly connected with the dedicatee, Maria Maddalena, and her marital family: as Virginia Cox explains, its "fifth book … has Catherine experiencing a divinely sent vision of the triumph of the Medici dynasty," and later, "at the moment of her death," she is portrayed "praying … for the protection of her homeland [i.e., Siena] by its future Medici rulers," destined to impending power even beyond Tuscany.[37] Furthermore, as Armando Maggi reveals in the "Introduzione" to his critical edition of this text, Marinella combines four different genres: biography (on the basis of earlier hagiographies); religious writing, aiming at eliciting the reader's emotional response; epic poetry; and panegyric.[38] *Enrico* is notable for its genre, its dedication, its political positions, and its references to Marinella as authoritative point of reference for the history of Venice.[39] Additionally, as Francesca D'Alessandro Behr has shown, *Enrico* is replete with references to and reworkings of classical poetry.[40] *Le vittorie* is not only dedicated to the pope, but it includes philosophy and theology, "the latter incorporated via a dense series of marginal notes," as is also the case in *Holocausto d'amore*.[41]

Among the later Marinella works, *Essortationi* has perhaps garnered the most attention from literary and cultural historians, as it offers strong criticism of Marinella's own earlier pro-woman position. Stephen Kolsky sees it as "a rhetorically charged narrative parallel to *La nobiltà e l'eccellenza delle donne*,"[42] while Virginia Cox considers it as "something of a paradox, in that a work that contains the period's most despondent analysis of women's literary possibilities

37. Ibid. The Medici acquired the Republic of Siena in 1555, while St. Catherine was born in 1347 and died in 1380.

38. Armando Maggi, "Introduzione: Lo sperimentalismo di Lucrezia Marinella," in *De' gesti heroici e della vita maravigliosa della serafica S. Caterina da Siena*, by Lucrezia Marinella, ed. Armando Maggi (Ravenna: Longo, 2011), 11.

39. Maria Galli Stampino, "A Singular Venetian Epic Poem," in *Enrico; or Byzantium Conquered: A Heroic Poem*, by Lucrezia Marinella, ed. and trans. Maria Galli Stampino (Chicago: University of Chicago Press, 2009), 2–3, 7, 12–13, 27, and 61–62. For an analysis of the rhetorical topoi utilized by Marinella to address her narrative persona, see Maria Galli Stampino, "The Woman Narrator's Voice: The Case of Lucrezia Marinella's *Enrico*," *Italian Studies* 69 (2014): 75–94. Laura Lazzari's work also contextualizes *Enrico* with respect to social and cultural references: *Poesia epica e scrittura femminile nel Seicento:* L'Enrico *di Lucrezia Marinelli* (Leonforte: Insula, 2010), in particular 45–52.

40. Francesca D'Alessandro Behr, *Arms and the Woman: Classical Tradition and Women Writers in the Venetian Renaissance* (Columbus: Ohio State University Press, 2018).

41. Cox, *Women's Writing*, 372n250.

42. Stephen Kolsky, "Moderata Fonte, Lucrezia Marinella, Giuseppe Passi: An Early Seventeenth-Century Feminist Controversy," *Modern Language Review* 96 (2001), 984.

is also probably the most confident and wide-ranging female-authored secular didactic text of the age."[43] Paola Malpezzi Price and Christine Ristaino refer to earlier rhetorical *topoi*, particularly "the Greek *paignion*, or a playful exercise ascribed to oratory," connecting it to twentieth-century criticism, and conclude that "Marinella's *Essortationi* are both a prose record of their author's struggle and a documentation of the disconnect among women of the time."[44] Laura Benedetti, the English translator of this treatise, interprets it as a recantation of Marinella's pro-female positions—"a reactionary work, not only because of Marinella's endorsement of conservative views of women but also for her disregard for the contemporary literary scene," in which she "implicitly presents herself as an Amazon, a phoenix, an exception to the rule, established by God and nature, that women should not waste their time in intellectual endeavors."[45] It is difficult to avoid construing *Essortationi* as part of the "backlash" that Virginia Cox sees occurring in seventeenth-century Italy against women writers.[46] Nevertheless, Marinella's incredible range in both forms and topics, and the extensive chronological span of her publications, make her a unique writer within the panorama of early modern Italy, and indeed western Europe.

Historical Context

Amore innamorato would be a difficult text to interpret within the frame suggested by Carlo Dionisotti in 1967. As the earliest scholar to attract attention to the flourishing of women's writing in sixteenth-century Italy, he connected it to Petrarchan poetry and enterprising publishers, particularly in Venice. In his analysis, women only "constituted a group"[47] from 1538, when Vittoria Colonna's *Rime* were first printed, to "around 1560, when, for a variety of economic and sociocultural reasons, the publication of vernacular literature entered a decline."[48] Virginia Cox has since offered a different view, one that moves away from (mostly male) publishers and narrow generic scope, significantly expanding Dionisotti's chronological span.[49] Within this reading *Amore* is in many ways exemplary: it is situated in the most productive period for women writers, and it belongs to a

43. Cox, *Women's Writing*, 224.

44. Paola Malpezzi Price and Christine Ristaino, *Lucrezia Marinella and the "Querelle des Femmes" in Seventeenth-Century Italy* (Madison and Teaneck, NJ: Fairleigh Dickinson University Press, 2008), 154–55.

45. Benedetti, "Introduction," 30 and 32.

46. See Cox, *Women's Writing*, viii.

47. "[F]anno gruppo": Carlo Dionisotti, "La letteratura italiana nell'età del Concilio di Trento," in *Geografia e storia della letteratura italiana* (Turin: Einaudi, 1967), 191.

48. Cox, *Women's Writing*, xx.

49. Cox, *Women's Writing*, xx–xxi.

genre well beyond the lyric poetry that Dionisotti identified as central for female authors.

Marinella's predilection for narrative poetry emerges clearly from the short précis of her writings offered above. In terms of genre, *Amore innamorato* falls squarely within her taste even as it adds two new elements: on the one hand, a source from classical antiquity (rather than hagiography); on the other, allegorical readings of characters and plot. These features present interesting challenges to Marinella, historically and ideologically, while offering significant advantages.

Ovid: Metamorphoseon libri (Metamorphoses)

Proceeding chronologically, Ovid's Metamorphoses (finished in 7 CE) exerts a fundamental influence on *Amore innamorato*, as it had and would continue to do in early modernity throughout western Europe.[50] Whether directly or through other authors (such as Petrarch), Ovid's stories recounting shape-shifting humans due to the will and whim of gods allowed writers (especially women writers) to reimagine and refashion classical antiquity according to their cultural expectations, or against them.

In the case of *Amore innamorato* specifically, Ovid is a point of reference: early on in the poem (Canto 1:41–50) Marinella mentions several of the Ovidian stories, as if to display her knowledge of classical literature. More importantly, the story of Phoebus/Apollo and Daphne, recounted in Book 1 of the *Metamorphoses* (1: 452–567), is a crucial point of reference, one that Marinella turns upside down. Apollo has just killed a monstrous python with his bow and arrows, and, seeing Cupid drawing *his* bow, mocks him: "What hast thou to do with the arms of men, thou wanton boy? … Do thou be content with thy torch to light the hidden fires of love, and lay no claim on my honours."[51] Angered, Cupid replies, "Thy dart may pierce all things else, Apollo, but mine shall pierce thee; and by as much as all living things are less than deity, by so much less is thy glory than mine."[52] Marinella explicitly alludes to this in Canto 1, octave 48; the very placement of this echo in

50. The scholarly literature on this topic is extensive. The following essay collections provide good starting points: *Ovid and the Renaissance Body*, ed. Goran V. Stanivukovic (Toronto: University of Toronto Press, 2001); *Metamorphosis: The Changing Face of Ovid in Medieval and Early Modern Europe* ed. Alison Keith and Stephen Rupp (Toronto: Centre for Reformation and Renaissance Studies, 2007); and, with respect to two national traditions, *Shakespeare's Ovid: The* Metamorphoses *in the Plays and Poems*, ed. A. B. Taylor (Cambridge: Cambridge University Press, 2000); and *Ovid in the Age of Cervantes*, ed. Frederick A. De Armas (Toronto: University of Toronto Press, 2010).

51. Ovid, *Metamorphoses*, ed and trans. Frank Justus Miller, rev. G. P. Goold, 2 vols. (Cambridge, MA: Harvard University Press, 1977), 1: 35. "'quid' que 'tibi, lascive puer, cum fortibus armis?' / … 'tu face nescio quos esto contentus amores / inritare tua, nec laudes adsere nostras!'" Ibid., 1:34.

52. Ibid., 1:35. "'figat tuus omnia, Phoebe / te meus arcus' ait; 'quantoque animalia cedunt / cuncta deo, tanto minor est tua gloria nostra.'" Ibid., 1:34.

Canto 1, mirroring Book 1, is likely to be deliberate. Cupid then shoots a golden arrow at Apollo and a leaden one at Daphne, with predictable results. The god pursues the frightened nymph, calling out to her as she flees: "Oh nymph, O Peneus' daughter, stay! I who pursue thee am no enemy. Oh stay! ... Nay, stop and ask who thy lover is. I am no mountain-dweller, no shepherd I, no unkempt guardian here of flocks and herds. Thou knowest not, rash one, thou knowest not whom thou fleest, and for that reason dost thou flee."[53] Run indeed she does, praying to her father (the river deity Peneus) for help; she has barely finished speaking when she is transformed into the laurel tree. In *Amore innamorato*, Ersilia prays to Diana as she flees Cupid, and Diana covers her with a white cloud into which she disappears (Canto 3, 43–44). Marinella thus takes Ovid's story—in which Cupid has been affronted and avenges himself through the use of the golden and leaden arrows—and turns it around so that Cupid himself, not Phoebus, is the target, so to speak. Furthermore, Cupid blasts Jupiter, who believes himself to be the most powerful god, but does not recognize that Cupid holds sway over him (3.59).

Marinella draws two important themes from Ovid: the arrogance of Cupid on the one hand; and the motif of the chase, which echoes in several Canti, involving—as we will see—references not just to Ovid, but to Petrarch's famous sonnet "Una candida cerva" (190 in *Rerum Vulgarium Fragmenta*, also known as the *Canzoniere*).

Prudentius: Psychomachia (Battle of the Soul)

Prudentius's *Psychomachia* (penned late in the fourth century CE) is usually considered as the earliest allegorical work in Western literature. Like other patristic texts, it was a significant source of rhetorical examples and ideological stances in the early modern *querelle des femmes*, although it was reprinted only rarely, in the original Latin, and mostly north of the Alps (France, Switzerland, and Germany) in post-Reformation Europe. Marinella's knowledge of it, then, was perforce indirect.[54] In the context of *Amore innamorato*, Prudentius embodies all virtues and vices as female, in keeping with the grammatical gender of those terms in Latin (e.g., *Ira* for wrath, *Luxuria* for lust, *Patientia* for forbearance).[55] As Jessamyn

53. Ibid., 37 and 39. "'nympha, precor, Penei, mane! non insequor hostis; / nympha, mane! ... cui placeas, inquire tamen: non incola montis, / non ego sum pastor, non hic armenta gregresque / horridus observo. nescis, temeraria, nescis, / quem fugias, ideoque fugis" Ibid., 36 and 38.

54. Rosa Giorgi points out that the visual theme of psychomachy "returned in the Baroque era as part of the allegorical imagery promoted by the Counter-Reformation": *Angels and Demons in Art*, ed. Stefano Zuffi, trans. Rosanna M. Giammanco Frongia (Los Angeles: The J. Paul Getty Museum, 2005), 125.

55. As Valerie Edden has noted, this stems from two sources: "some of the virtues [he represents] derive directly from Roman deities, such as Fides, Pudicitia and Concordia ... ; others derive from a tradition of personified abstractions which had been popularised particularly by Statius and Claudian."

Lewis has pointed out, it would be reductive to present *Psychomachia* rhetorically as a straightforward misogynistic text, as it includes distinct gender tensions: all these characters are both negatively and positively female.[56] Prudentius is not simply following the position of other Church fathers (to mention but one, Tertullian calls women *diaboli ianua*).[57] He attributes positive aspects to his (female-embodied) virtues, via *virtus* (male-like attributes);[58] moreover, all characters are "'daughters' of God," whether vices or virtues.[59] Also noticeable is the fact that *Psychomachia*'s "highest number of verbal allusions [are] to Vergil's *Aeneid*,"[60] making this text a potentially crucial exemplar for Marinella, whose attraction for the ideology and the form of the epic are well established. In Lewis's words, "Prudentius' relationship with the classical and pagan past, while occasionally critical, is more about re-imagining it and adapting it to a Christian present than it is about destroying it."[61] In this vein, the appreciation for and homage to classical antiquity is in some sense parallel to Dante's undertaking in the *Divina*

See Edden, "Prudentius," in *Latin Literature of the Fourth Century*, ed. J. W. Binns (London: Routledge and Kegan Paul, 1974), 164–65. In other words, what we consider to be an early Christian trait is in fact inherited from classical antiquity. For an in-depth analysis of how Prudentius melds classical and Christian elements, see Jacques Fontaine, *Naissance de la poésie dans l'Occident chrétien: Esquisse d'une histoire de la poésie latine chrétienne du IIIe au VIe siècle* (Paris: Études augustiniennes, 1981), particularly chapter 12.

56. Jessamyn Eva Lewis, "Gender and Violence in Prudentius' *Psychomachia*" (PhD diss., University of California, Los Angeles, 2000), 72.

57. "Tu es diaboli ianua, tu es arboris illius resignatrix, tu es divinae legis prima desertrix": *Q. Septimii Florentis Tertulliani de habitu muliebri liber*, in *Q. Septimii Florentis Tertulliani Opera Volumen Tertium*, ed. Johann Salomo Semler (Halle an der Saale, Germany: Johann Christian Hendel, 1770), 28. "You are the one who opened the door to the Devil, you are the one who first plucked the fruit of the forbidden tree, you are the first who deserted the divine law." Tertullian, *The Apparel of Women*, trans. with an introduction by Edwin A. Quain, in *Disciplinary, Moral, and Ascetical Works*, ed. and trans. Rudolph Arbesmann, Sister Emily Joseph Daly, and Edwin A. Quain (Washington, DC: Catholic University of America Press, 2010), 118.

58. According to *The Concise Oxford Dictionary of English Etymology*, the term "virtue" comes from the Old French *vertu*, modeled, like the Italian *virtù*, on the Latin *virtus* ("valour, worth, merit, moral perfection"), which in turn comes from *vir*, man as leader, emblem of physical and moral courage. *The Concise Oxford Dictionary of English Etymology*, ed. T. F. Hoad (Oxford: Oxford University Press, 1986), online.

59. Lewis, "Gender and Violence," 2. Lewis adds that other works by Prudentius, in particular his *Peristephanon*, are connected with the *Acta* tradition concerning early martyrs, including their focus on women (mothers, wives, and virgins): ibid., 5–6. This is Marinella's own inclination in *Colomba sacra*, although she eschews the dichotomy present in canonical (and male-authored) works, as Laura Benedetti has pointed out in "Saintes et guerrières: L'héroïsme féminin dans l'œuvre di Lucrezia Marinella," *Écritures* 1 (2005), 100–1.

60. Lewis, "Gender and Violence," 8.

61. Ibid., 8–9. Recall Edden's point in note 55, above.

commedia. Psychomachia works as an essential connector between the classical tradition, the *Divine Comedy*, the epic genre, allegory, and Marinella, who utilizes *Amore innamorato*, among other things, to pay homage to Dante.

In his study of *Psychomachia*, James J. Paxson insists on the physicality of bodies presented in the poem; in his words, "the most memorable details of Prudentius' descriptive discourse are the moments of graphic demolition that befall the Vices at the hands of their conquerors," connected with "the Vergilian descriptive tradition of epic battle."[62] Lewis has underscored the gender dimension in the characters doing battle in Prudentius's text:

> The nature of women is viewed as essentially sexual, prone to vice and capable of corrupting men as well. But women who could transcend their feminine natures through continence had a claim to virtue, often conceived in terms of masculinity. Prudentius grounds his allegory in this line of thought and characterizes the psychomachic struggle in ascetically-gendered and sexualized terms.[63]

Whether we choose to emphasize violence or gender, in Prudentius these types are figural, not physical, and devoid of the descriptive richness of early modern epic poems.[64]

Dante: Divina commedia (Divine Comedy)

It is noteworthy that *Amore innamorato* includes sustained references to Dante's *Divine Comedy*, arguably the most well-known allegorical text within the Italian literary canon. Just as Cupid's journey is, in part, motivated by lust, Dante's, too, is similarly propelled by it; it leads them both to a search for their respective lost beloveds. It is on their journeys that they learn they must transform this love from carnal lust to spiritual *caritas*.[65] Structurally, we have Cupid follow the path of the

62. James J. Paxson, *The Poetics of Personification* (Cambridge: Cambridge University Press, 1994), 66.

63. Lewis, "Gender and Violence," 85–86.

64. Or, to quote Paxson (*Poetics*, 66): Prudentius's characters are "abstract universals contained in a narrative continuum."

65. Dante's notion of love is transformed throughout the *Commedia* from the *amor* encountered in his preceding work in *Vita nuova*. The *Vita nuova* follows the genre of courtly love writing, in which the emphasis is on an earthly love, arguably lust, toward a lady. For an example, see Dante's sonnet "Amore e 'l cor gentil sono una cosa" [Love and the noble heart are one and the same] in *Vita Nuova* 20: Dante Alighieri, *Vita Nuova, Digital Dante* edition (New York: Columbia University Libraries and Department of Italian, 2014), <https://digitaldante.columbia.edu/library/la-vita-nuova/#cap20>. In *Inferno* 2, through Virgil's mediation, Beatrice expresses her personal love for Dante: "Love prompted me, that Love which makes me speak" [Amor mi mosse, che mi fa parlare] (*Inferno* 2.72): <https://digitaldante.columbia.edu/dante/divine-comedy/inferno/inferno-2/>. Beatrice's words resonate with

pilgrim—that is, of a man who is lost, descends into hell, climbs a mountain, goes to heaven, and eventually needs a Marian (to wit, female) intercessor in order to complete his transformation. While structurally Marinella has her protagonist, a pagan demigod, follow in the steps of a Christian allegorical journey, her cleverness is in her choice of having the god of love himself conduct the journey. Marinella transforms Cupid from the god of love into a Christ-like figure who embodies the love of the Christian God.

The connection between Marinella and Dante emerges in the strongest terms in Canto 5 of *Amore innamorato*. At the center of her allegorical poem, Marinella has Cupid descend into hell in what appears to resemble Dante's circle of the lustful, Canto 5 of the *Inferno*.[66] Like Dante,[67] Cupid encounters female beings placed here because of their excessive passions, which overrun their reason. However, these are not the passive, pity-seeking victims that we find in the *Inferno*—quite the contrary. As soon as the female shades recognize Cupid, they blame their eternal damnation on him and brutally beat him. In Marinella's poem, women have not only a voice but are given a chance to defend themselves and their reputation by taking an active stance.[68] *Amore innamorato* provides a distinctly pro-woman viewpoint, and an explicit response to one of the earliest (and most important) texts within the Italian literary canon.

Boccaccio: Genealogia deorum gentilium (Genealogy of the Pagan Gods)

One more recognized writer must be mentioned as a possible source of inspiration and model for Marinella: Giovanni Boccaccio. His retelling of Apuleius's story of Cupid and Psyche occupies a short portion of chapter 3 of the second book of

---

Francesca's repetition of *Amor* (*Inferno* 5.100–108), which once again also recalls Dante's own sonnet in *Vita Nuova* 20. Additionally, even as Dante becomes a Pauline figure (*Inferno* 2.32), Dante the pilgrim and readers of the *Inferno* perhaps cannot distinguish the difference between lust and love until later in the *Commedia*. At the end of the *Commedia* the transformation from earthly to spiritual love, or the Pauline notion of *caritas*, is clear when it becomes "the Love that moves the sun and the other stars" [l'amor che move il sole e l'altre stelle] (*Paradiso* 33.145): <https://digitaldante.columbia.edu/dante/divine-comedy/paradiso/paradiso-33/>.

66. The correspondence is too precise to be casual; in other words, Marinella's gesture is certainly metaliterary.

67. While Dante meets male sinners (Paolo, for example, who was equally incontinent), the strongest similarity between Marinella's Cupid and Dante, the pilgrim, is that Dante engages in conversation with a female, Francesca.

68. Reputation was an unmarried woman's most prized trait in early modernity. On this, see in particular chapter 1 of Margaret L. King, *Women of the Renaissance* (Chicago: University of Chicago Press, 1991), and, specifically about Venice in Marinella's time, chapter 7 of Daria Martelli, *Polifonie: Le donne a Venezia nell'età di Moderata Fonte (seconda metà del secolo XVI)* (Padua: Cleup, 2011).

his *Genealogia deorum gentilium* [*Genealogy of the Pagan Gods*], and it includes an allegorical explanation of the various characters it involves.[69] Although, as we mention below, Boccaccio invests his characters with different meanings from the ones in *Amore innamorato*, he must be included as a literary point of reference, as an author who took up striking pro- and anti-woman stances, and finally because Giuseppe Betussi's Italian translation of this work, originally published in Latin, was reprinted several times in Venice in the late sixteenth century.[70] Marinella was obviously well acquainted with Boccaccio's opinions concerning women; she singles him out as one of four authors whose positions she dismantles in *The Nobility and Excellence of Women and the Defects and Vices of Men*,[71] then invokes him in a positive light in her *Exhortations to Women and to Others*.[72] Given his literary renown, his allegorical reading of the Cupid and Psyche story, and his ideological positions, Boccaccio should be considered as an allusion, however implicit or distant, for the text at hand.

Tasso: Gerusalemme liberata (Jerusalem Delivered)

Marinella's use of allegory must also be tied to one of her literary points of reference, Torquato Tasso's *Gerusalemme liberata* (*Jerusalem Delivered*), the first to be called (by its author) "heroic" (just as *La Colomba sacra* and *Enrico* will be).[73] For

69. Additionally, as Salvatore Ussia helpfully summarizes, Apuleius's *Metamorphoses* as a whole influenced Boccaccio in several of his texts: Salvatore Ussia, *Amore innamorato: Riscritture poetiche della novella di Amore e Psiche secoli XV–XVII* (Vercelli: Mercurio, 2001), 11–13.

70. Specifically, in 1545 by Comin da Trino di Monferrato; in 1547 by Pietro de Nicolini da Stabbio; in 1553 "al segno del diamante"; in 1558 by Francesco de gl'Imperatori; in 1564 by Francesco Lorenzini da Turino; in 1569 by G. Sansovino; in 1574 by Giovan Maria Bertano; in 1581 by Fabio and Agostino Zoppini; in 1585 "appresso la Compagnia degli Uniti"; and in 1588 by Marc'Antonio Zaltieri. Salvatore Ussia incorrectly states that Betussi's translation was done in 1585: Ussia, *Amore innamorato*, 13.

71. Alongside those of Ercole Tasso and Arrigo di Namur, Sperone Speroni, and Torquato Tasso. See Marinella, *The Nobility and Excellence of Women and the Defects and Vices of Men*, ed. and trans. Anne Dunhill, introd. Letizia Panizza (Chicago: University of Chicago Press, 1999), 141–45.

72. Lucrezia Marinella, *Exhortations to Women and to Others if They Please*, ed. and trans. Laura Benedetti (Toronto: Iter Inc. and Centre for Reformation and Renaissance Studies, 2012), 71 and 118.

73. Rinaldina Russell, "Margherita Sarrocchi and the Writing of the *Scanderbeide*," in *Scanderbeide: The Heroic Deeds of Georg Scanderbeg, King of Epirus*, by Margherita Sarrocchi, ed. and trans. Rinaldina Russell (Chicago: University of Chicago Press, 2006), 18; and Stampino, "A Singular Venetian Epic Poem," 3. The phrase "poema eroico" was not added to Giovan Giorgio Trissino's *La Italia liberata da Gotthi* until the 1779 London edition. See the title page of the original: Rome: Valerio e Luigi Dorici, 1547. Tasso was not the only antecedent of Marinella's to have appended an allegory to his work; as Letizia Panizza points out, there existed "a distinguished vernacular literary tradition of philosophical love poetry practiced by illustrious vernacular poets like Dante, Lorenzo de' Medici, Benedetto Varchi, and Francesco de' Vieri, who treated a love poem like a sacred text to be expounded by long, densely philosophical commentaries." Panizza, "Introduction to the Translation," 9.

his poem, Tasso selected as its topic the First Crusade—a subject matter endowed with an unambiguously religious character, rather than one derived from classical antiquity as in *Amore innamorato.* After completing it, unsure of whether his treatment was in keeping with the doctrinal tenets of the Catholic Church, Tasso penned a short "Allegory" (1576) in which he offered his interpretation of this rhetorical tool, then invested as many elements of his poem as possible with moral and manifestly religious traits, be they edifying or repellent. As he explains, "Allegory observes passions, opinions, and customs not only in the way in which they appear, but mainly in their intrinsic nature. It represents them with mysterious notes (so to speak), such that only those who know the nature of things can fully understand them."[74] The use of a musical metaphor, which Tasso underscores with his parenthetical aside, is noteworthy: allegory is both clear (to those in the know) and hidden (to the rest). It is therefore necessary to make the core message of an allegorical text explicit to all readers through an explanation—the Allegory appended to *Jerusalem Delivered* after the fact, and the allegories that Marinella attaches at the beginning of her poem and then to each canto. In this way, she can recover and transform a plot from classical antiquity, making it suitable for a woman writer and her readers.[75]

There is another significant connection between Tasso's "Allegory" and Marinella's poem. In order to make a stronger case for his approach and provide it with historical perspective, Tasso draws several examples of allegorical readings from earlier texts, singling out four: the *Iliad*, the *Odyssey*, the *Aeneid*, and the *Divine Comedy*.[76] Tasso is obviously elevating his own poem by setting it alongside those that were generally regarded as models. Yet he also wants to offer one instance from each of those works to illuminate how his own poem follows in a well-established and orthodox tradition; he therefore concentrates on their protagonists as exemplars of "contemplative man," and on their voyages of (self-)

74. "L'Allegoria … rimira le passioni, e le opinioni, & i costumi non solo in quanto essi appaiono, ma principalmente nel loro essere intrinseco, e più oscuramente le significa con note (per così dire) misteriose, e che solo da i conoscitori della natura delle cose possono essere à pieno comprese." Torquato Tasso, "Allegoria della Gerusalemme liberata," in *Tutte le opere*, ed. Amedeo Quondam, n.p. (Rome: Lexis progetti editoriali, 1997), reproduced on the *Biblioteca dei Classici Italiani* website at <http://www.classicitaliani.it/tasso/prosa/Tasso_allegoria_Gerusalemme.htm>.

75. We do not argue here that Marinella was a non-believer and merely adhered superficially to the tenets and practices of the Catholic Church. Rather, through her allegorical reading, she was able to utilize a plot line that would seem antithetical to the culture and belief system of her times, thus simultaneously asserting her abilities as an author. It is interesting that in her earlier *Arcadia felice*, whose tradition also goes back to classical antiquity, mythology is "scarcely present" [scarsamente presente]: Lavocat, "Introduzione," xlvi–vii. This is an argument in favor of allegory as the tool for Marinella to recapture mythology and refashion it to fit her cultural horizon.

76. Tasso, "Allegoria," n.p.

discovery and engagement.[77] From this vantage point, it makes no difference that Dante the pilgrim is traveling through hell, purgatory, and paradise to find "the path that does not stray" in his life,[78] while Achilles and Aeneas are generals prodded to action by pagan deities during and after the Trojan War. They are all allegorically on a quest, one of the crucial elements of the epic mode.[79]

Even as Marinella includes references to and reworkings of Dante and other texts,[80] she injects her distinctly pro-woman stance throughout her poem. Lest we imagine a negative tension between the form and the meaning of her allegory, such strain is always present in this mode. To quote Angus Fletcher's seminal work, "At the heart of any allegory will be found [a] conflict of authorities. One ideal will be pitted against another ... Allegories are far less often the dull systems that they are reputed to be than they are symbolic power struggles."[81] In order to understand this tension, in addition to the literary and moral-religious background, it is necessary to shed some light on the historical and cultural frame to which *Amore innamorato* belongs. Marinella's dedicatee was Caterina Medici Gonzaga, daughter of Ferdinando I Medici and Christine of Lorraine and duchess of Mantua through her marriage to Ferdinando Gonzaga. Her cousin and predecessor, Eleonora Medici Gonzaga (to whom Marinella herself had dedicated *Arcadia felice*), had been the dedicatee of Ercole Udine's poem *Psyche*, printed in Venice in 1599 by Ciotti (Marinella's own printer for *Colomba sacra*, the first two versions of *La nobiltà, et l'eccellenza delle donne*, and *Arcadia felice*). Udine (1544–1608) was a courtier in Mantua and Vincenzo I's ambassador to Venice (which might explain why two of his works were printed there). As Bodo Guthmüller elucidates, the courts in Ferrara and Mantua appreciated Apuleius and read it in translation;[82] Udine therefore exploits "a subject matter considered—just like

77. It is possible that an echo of Tasso's "Allegoria" is also present later on in Marinella's *oeuvre*, specifically in *Enrico*, where she offers an alternative version of Ulysses's fate to those in both the *Odyssey* and the *Divine Comedy*: see Stampino, "A Singular Venetian Epic Poem," 61–62.

78. Dante Alighieri, *The Divine Comedy, Digital Dante* edition (New York: Columbia University Libraries and Department of Italian, 2014), <https://digitaldante.columbia.edu/dante/divine-comedy/inferno/inferno-1/>. The original famously reads "diritta via."

79. On this aspect in Italian early modern epic, see Sergio Zatti, *Il modo epico* (Rome: Laterza, 2000), 59–63.

80. Jo Ann Cavallo points out antecedents for the episode in Ludovico Ariosto's *Orlando furioso* concerning Astolfo's flight to the moon, which includes a version of previous encounters with harpies, and other journeys to hell in the same poem: Jo Ann Cavallo, *The World beyond Europe in the Romance Epics of Boiardo and Ariosto* (Toronto: University of Toronto Press, 2013), 190–92. The so-called katabasis, or trip to the underworld, is a trait of the epic: see Zatti, *Il modo epico*, 19–22.

81. Angus Fletcher, *Allegory: The Theory of a Symbolic Mode* (Ithaca, NY: Cornell University Press, 1964), 22–23.

82. Matteo Maria Boiardo translated Apuleius's *The Golden Ass* in Italian around 1479; Niccolò da Correggio penned a verse retelling of the story of Cupid and Psyche in Latin in 1491 or thereabouts

Virgil's works—as belonging to Mantua's cultural patrimony."[83] Additionally, Udine's poem was enhanced by an allegorical reading of the myth of Psyche by the Genoese Benedictine monk and poet Angelo Grillo, and was the earliest in Italian to use the form and conventions of a "heroic poem" for this subject matter.[84] Pompeo Vizani's own version, *Favola di Psiche e di Cupido* (originally printed in Bologna in 1607), was also accompanied by an allegory of the plot; it, too, was reprinted several times, including in Venice, and including by Domenico Imberti in 1616 and by his heirs in 1621.[85] Marinella could have been aware of the interest in Apuleius at the courts of Ferrara and Mantua,[86] and, given her frequent publications and support by printers such as Ciotti, was likely to appreciate both the allegories appended to these reworkings and the popularity of the topic among book buyers and readers in Venice (and elsewhere). This helps explain her choice of dedicatee, and connects her allegory not only to Tasso's example, but to her chosen topic. All these translations and adaptations follow Apuleius's plot and characterizations. Regardless of what text Marinella had more vividly in mind,[87] there are two original interventions that bear Marinella's mark. On a larger level, she is disrupting the form of allegory, with characters who are supposed to be understood within a specific key being in fact independent and autonomous from it; at the plot level, her take on characters and situations indicates her ideological pro-woman stance.

Summary and Analysis

The plot of *Amore innamorato* is not complex, but it is at times convoluted and somewhat repetitive. Cupid looks upon the world, and identifies Iridio as the only

---

and dedicated it to Isabella d'Este; and Galeotto del Carretto reworked it as a play in Italian in 1499. See Bodo Guthmüller, "Amore e Psiche a Mantova: Sulla *Psiche* di Ercole Udine," *Rassegna europea di letteratura italiana* 14 (1999), 27. Ussia notes that Boiardo's translation had ten printings between 1516 and 1549: Ussia, *Amore innamorato,* 15.

83. "[U]na materia considerata, al pari delle opere di Virgilio, appartenente al patrimonio culturale mantovano." Guthmüller, "Amore e Psiche a Mantova," 28.

84. Ibid., 29. Although in *ottava rima,* the language in Udine's poem is far simpler (or: less Baroque) than in Marinella's. It is possible to read the third edition of this poem on the Biblioteca Digital Hispánica website: Ercole Udine, *Avvenimenti amorosi di Psiche; poema eroico con l'erudita allegoria del molto illustre Reverendiss. P. Abbate Grillo* (Venice: Ciotti, 1617), <http://bdh-rd.bne.es/viewer.vm?id=0000052196&page=1>. Angelo Grillo (1557–1629), who published his poetry under a pseudonym, was a friend of Tasso.

85. Ussia, *Amore innamorato,* 16–17. Ghirardo Imberti printed Marinella's own *Enrico* in 1635.

86. Guthmüller, "Amore e Psiche a Mantova," 27.

87. Ussia underscores that Marinella takes "structural elements" [elementi portanti] from Apuleius, and "what is not secondary, sometimes she does so with Apuleius' very words" [fatto non secondario, a volte lo fa con le stesse parole di Apuleio]: Ussia, *Amore innamorato*, 32.

human who is resisting his powers. Determined to make him fall in love, Cupid sets up an encounter between Iridio and Ersilia, a beautiful young noblewoman and a devotee of Diana. However, Cupid's arrows have no effect on either of them. Upset and disappointed, Cupid returns to Venus's palace, where he falls asleep before his mother's return. Meanwhile, Jupiter gathers the gods to a council and decrees that Cupid will suffer in the same way that he makes others grieve: he will fall in love and pine. Jupiter dispatches Mercury to carry out this task. Having stolen an arrow from Cupid's quiver, Mercury wounds him while Ersilia is hunting nearby. Immediately smitten with Ersilia, Cupid lets fly another arrow and wounds her, except that he mistakenly utilizes one whose point is made of lead rather than gold, thus provoking her aversion for him and prompting her to run away. Cupid chases her and manages to see Ersilia as she bathes in a stream (a rare sensual episode in Marinella's works). Continuing to seek with no luck, Cupid mourns his own plight, dreams of Ersilia, and travels to the netherworld searching for her; there Cupid helps Charon find Eurinia, his beloved.

Venus rescues Cupid, takes him to her palace, and scolds him for traveling to a dangerous place. Cupid concocts a plan to fly up to Jupiter and make him forget everything, including Jupiter's verdict against him. He steals away from Venus's palace to carry out his plan. Having convinced the god of sleep to aid him, they reach Jupiter and, as the ruler of the gods is fast asleep, Cupid steals Jupiter's thunder to blast Iridio and exact his revenge on him. The clamor wakes Jupiter: he punishes Cupid, who is stunned and loses his mind. Cupid looks for Ersilia, finds her, again tries to make her fall in love, fails for a second time, and is left alone and disconsolate. Meanwhile, Venus searches for Cupid, and, after a nymph shares with her his general whereabouts, she finds him. Cupid hides his love for Ersilia and his actions from his mother. Venus takes Cupid back to her palace, but soon notices that he wants to escape, so she tries to confine him.[88] When Venus leaves him alone, he takes advantage of her absence to wreak havoc on her delicately decorated palace and rich gardens before he runs away. In despair, alternating between violence and sorrow, Cupid lays waste to many other places, murders innocent shepherds and shepherdesses, and chases and kills a white doe. When Venus returns and inquires about who was responsible for the destruction, a nymph reveals that it was Cupid. At first, she is astonished and disappointed; then she summons her chariot to look for him again. She finds Cupid languishing among the perennial snows of Mount Caucasus; he is almost dead. She entreats Jupiter to have pity on her son. When Jupiter bestows his forgiveness, nature is

88. Malpezzi Price and Ristaino have underscored that "the imprisonment of Cupid in Venus's garden recalls another illustrious imprisonment of Love in Petrarch's *I trionfi*": *Lucrezia Marinella and the "Querelle des Femmes,"* 56. Venus's role, crucial for Marinella, is altogether missing in Petrarch. It is worthwhile noting that Petrarch's poem is written in *terza rima*, Dante's own invention for the *Divine Comedy*, providing a connection between allegorical and lyrical modes.

restored to its springtime glory, and Venus prepares a celebratory meal for Cupid and Mars.

As Marinella states at the opening of her work, her allegory is based on the tripartite division of man first put forth by Plato.[89] Her subtle undoing of patriarchal stances is evident in her attribution of each part to different characters: it makes sense that Cupid represent the concupiscent component, tied to desire and physical longing; likewise, it is not wholly surprising to imagine Iridio as the irascible component. The wise, restrained, balanced, rational soul is embodied in Ersilia, the virginal devotee of Diana who escapes from Cupid, unharmed and independent, and then disappears from the plot.[90] Going against the traditional criticism of women as irrational, endowed with too much blood in Hippocratic/Galenic terms and therefore humid and lacking dependability and consistency, Marinella bestows the most prestigious allegorical role on the only female human character.

An underlying tension runs through *Amore innamorato*: although the Allegory dwells on human characters, the plot is largely driven by gods and goddesses, chiefly Cupid, Venus, and Jupiter. While Cupid is equated with man (subject to passions and resisting divine help), Venus is nominally akin to nature, and Jupiter to reason. These parallels get easily erased, while the characters gain liveliness rather than continuing as the bidimensional figures found in Prudentius's narrative. The weight accorded to classical divinity also allows us to see the continuities and differences in relation to Apuleius, which make Marinella's creativity and independence surface more distinctly. In more general terms, and in addition to the gender considerations and family structures that we will underscore throughout, Marinella trades positions and features between human and divine characters. While the latter emerge as petty, fallible, or prey to emotions (indeed, as we will see, Cupid comes close to death), the former acquire a moral loftiness

89. See in particular Book 4, 439e–441a, of Plato's *Republic*, ed. and trans. Chris Emlyn-Jones and William Preddy, 2 vols. (Cambridge, MA: Harvard University Press, 2013), 1: 418–425. The Greek word for "soul" is "psyché." Tasso's "Allegory" also utilizes this division. Boccaccio's retelling of the tale of Cupid and Psyche in his *Genealogy of the Pagan Gods* offers a different allegorical reading in which Psyche is "the rational spirit" and her sisters "the vegetative" and the "perceptive" ones, respectively. Giovanni Boccaccio, *Genealogy of the Pagan Gods*, ed. and trans. Jon Solomon, 2 vols. (Cambridge, MA: Harvard University Press, 2011), 1: 695. See also Ussia, *Amore innamorato*, 143–45.

90. It is not accurate to state that Ersilia's "complete disappearance" occurs in "the last canto" (i.e., Canto 10), as Malpezzi Price and Ristaino assert (*Lucrezia Marinella and the "Querelle des Femmes,"* 58), as she last appears in Canto 3. Her fate is not dissimilar from the one that Marinella will devise for the Byzantine warrior and archer Emilia, who at the end of *Enrico* retreats to the woods (27.87–88). "Vanquished" [vinta] but alive and back to hunting in her preferred milieu, she becomes a goddess by the same name, inscribing her power onto immortality. See Stampino, "A Singular Venetian Epic Poem," 55–56, and Maria Galli Stampino, "Poema eroico alla veneziana: il problema retorico ed ideologico della Quarta Crociata e la soluzione marinelliana," in *L'Enrico, ovvero Bisanzio acquistato, poema eroico*, by Lucrezia Marinella, ed. Maria Galli Stampino (Modena: Mucchi, 2011), 27.

and reliability that make them admirable. As we consider all cultural and literary elements at play, we will also include Ovid, important to the tradition of lyrical love poetry and also to this poem. In fact, we could go as far as to say that Marinella's plot operates parallel to that of Ovid with respect to deities: against the Homeric and Virgilian dichotomy pitting pathetic humans against great and admirable gods, Marinella turns the tables and builds a revisionist story.

Apuleius: The Source Text

As noted at the beginning of the Introduction, the narrative kernel of *Amore innamorato et impazzato* is largely based on the famed story of Cupid and Psyche, found in Apuleius's second-century CE work *Metamorphoses* (or *The Golden Ass*). Its significance as the central and most important episode in Apuleius's work cannot be underestimated; as E. J. Kenney points out, the tale of Cupid and Psyche "does not occupy a book or books to itself, but straddles the divisions between Books IV, V and VI in the manner of the complexes of episodes in Ovid's *Metamorphoses*."[91]

Apuleius's story may be summarized as follows: Lucius, the first-person narrator, recounts the sad story of Psyche, third daughter of a wealthy family in an unnamed Greek city, whose beauty prompts fellow citizens to worship her in lieu of Venus herself. The goddess, overcome with wrath, plans her revenge on Psyche: she is to fall in love with a hideous creature. Cupid, sent to carry out his mother's decree, disobeys her, because he is instantly smitten with Psyche. When the latter, in funeral attire, jumps off a cliff, Zephyr, the west wind, carries her off to Cupid's palace; there she lives in solitude, visited by Cupid only at night, and under strict orders to never look at him, now her lover. Soon she is pregnant; she prevails on Cupid to allow her sisters to visit, and when they see her lavish abode, they become envious and convince Psyche to betray her lover's trust. One night, armed with a dagger and a lamp, Psyche takes a look at what she believes to be her monstrous husband; startled by Cupid's beauty, which instantly captivates her, she spills some oil from her lamp, waking him up; although burnt, he rushes away. Psyche, distraught, starts wandering, looking for Cupid; she is subject to two trials, ordered by Venus, through which she learns that she has to serve the goddess of love herself. Her tribulations, however, are not finished: after being tortured by Worry and Sadness, handmaidens to Venus, she undergoes three additional trials before being sent to the underworld to retrieve some of Proserpina's beauty in a pyxis (a covered container). Helped by some figures of the underworld, Psyche carries out her task, but is vanquished by her curiosity and opens her vase, which contains no beauty, but deep sleep; she instantly collapses in slumber. There, she

91. See E. J. Kenney, "Introduction," in *Cupid and Psyche*, by Apuleius, ed. E. J. Kenney (Cambridge: Cambridge University Press, 1990), 5.

is found by Cupid, who has recovered his health and flown away from Venus's palace. He helps Psyche by removing sleep from her face and placing it back in the pyxis; then he lifts her to present the vase to Venus. Lastly, he successfully implores Jupiter to allow his marriage to Psyche. Jupiter calls a council of the gods, in which he enjoins Venus to renounce her hatred for Psyche; he then bestows ambrosia on the girl, so that Cupid will not marry a mortal. The story concludes with a happy wedding banquet, celebrating the couple.

Cupid, now joined to Psyche in wedded bliss, is depicted by Apuleius as lustful and yet capable of positive emotions and actions. He is first presented in keeping with classical tradition, as an unruly and mischievous boy: he is

> that most reckless of creatures, whose wicked behaviour flies in the face of public morals, who armed with torch and arrows roams by night through houses where he has no business, ruining marriages on every hand, committing heinous crimes with impunity, and never doing anything good.[92]

After this brief introduction, he disappears from the narrative, at least explicitly, since Psyche does not know the identity of her nighttime visitor. His actions, although anonymous, are forcefully male. Joel Relihan, in the introduction to his 2009 translation, pulls no punches and writes that the events to which Psyche is subject on her first night in his abode are tantamount to rape,[93] as a careful reading of the relevant passage suggests:

> Night was well advanced when a gentle sound was heard. Then, all alone as she was and fearing for her virginity, Psyche quailed and trembled, dreading, more than any possible harm, the unknown. Now there entered her unknown husband; he had mounted the bed, made her his wife, and departed in haste before sunrise.[94]

The description of the events is concise and matter-of-fact, in keeping with a socio-cultural background in which any woman was "made … his wife" by her husband, and passive demeanor on her part was the only possible acceptable

92. Apuleius, *Cupid and Psyche*, 43. The Latin text appears on the facing page (42): "satis temerarium, qui malis suis moribus contempt disciplina publica flammis et sagittis armatus per alienas domos nocte discurrens et omnium matrimonia corrumpens impune committit tanta flagitia et nihil prorsus boni facit."

93. Apuleius, *The Tale of Cupid and Psyche*, trans. Joel C. Relihan (Indianapolis: Hackett, 2009), 70.

94. Apuleius, *Cupid and Psyche*, 53; "iamque prouecta nocte clemens quidam sonus aures eius accedit. tunc uirginitati suae pro tanta solitudine metuens et pauet et horrescit et quouis malo plus timet quod ignorant. iamque aderat ignobilis maritus et torum inscenderat et uxorem sibi Psychen fecerat et ante lucis exortum propere discesserat" (52).

sexual choice. Psyche is presented as weak, frightened, and concerned above all "for her virginity"; Apuleius leaves no doubt about investing his characters with a traditionally patriarchal worldview.

Physically, Cupid is lovely—so handsome, in fact, that Psyche is "unnerved at the sight" [tanto aspectu deterrita][95] when she holds up a lamp to take a look at him, against his stated commands, and following the urging of her sisters:

> She saw a rich head of golden hair dripping with ambrosia, a milk-white neck, and rosy cheeks over which there strayed coils of hair becomingly arranged ... The rest of the god's body was smooth and shining and such as Venus need not be ashamed of in her son.[96]

Apuleius's narrative structure invites first-time readers to mirror Psyche's discovery, since Cupid's name is not used to refer to him as her lover until she discovers his identity; the first clue is given at the end of the passage just cited, as he is the son of Venus. In addition to his handsome appearance, and in contrast with Apuleius's first description of Cupid, he is endowed with a pleasant nature. Even when he is awakened by scalding oil from Psyche's lamp, he speaks to her in calm and magnanimous terms:

> He spoke to her ... with deep emotion: "Simple-minded Psyche, forgetting the orders of my mother Venus ... I myself flew to you ... as your lover. But this I did, I know, lightly; I, that famous archer, wounded myself with my own weapons and made you my wife."[97]

His gender position is clear and consistent with the passage cited before: it is a man's prerogative to "make" a woman his wife, as Cupid simply states above. His equanimity and pity do not extend to Psyche's sisters, whom he knows to be the instigators behind her actions. As a god, he can dole out punishment on them; he decrees that "those worthy counsellors of yours shall speedily pay the price of their pernicious teaching" [illae quidem consiliatrices egregiae tuae tam perniciosi magisterii actutum mihi poenas].[98] It is up to a (male) god to mete out kindness or retribution in a way that is presented and accepted as fair.

95. Ibid., 75 and 74.

96. Ibid., 75; "uidet capitis aurei genialem caesariem ambrosia temulentan, ceruices lacteas genasque purpureas pererrantes crinium globos decoriter impeditos ... ceterum corpus glabellum atque luculentum et quale peperisse Venerem non paeniteret" (74).

97. Ibid., 77; "Sic eam graviter commotus adfatur: 'ego quidem, simplicissima Psyche, parentis meae Veneris praeceptorum immemor,... ipse potius amator auolabi tibi. sed hoc feci leuiter, scio, et praeclarus ille Sagittarius ipse me telo meo percussi teque coniugem meam feci.'" (76).

98. Ibid., 79 and 78.

One additional noteworthy element in Apuleius's Cupid is found at the end of the plot, and it concerns his actions toward and relationship with Jupiter. Despite being "eaten up with love, looking ill, and dreading his mother's new-found austerity" [amore … peresus et aegra facie matris suae repentinam sobrietatem pertimescens],[99] he takes the initiative and flies to Jupiter to plead his case, manages to receive his forgiveness, and is rewarded with marriage to his beloved. In other words, he is proactive and recognizes that his authority is limited by the (male) ruler of the gods, to whom he addresses his entreaties. In fact, Apuleius's narrator underscores Jupiter's status in several complementary ways. His words are the last ones cited in the story. Furthermore, his actions are decisive: he "order[s]" [iubet][100] that Psyche be brought to him, and by offering her a cup of ambrosia he seals her marriage to Cupid, subsequently celebrated through "a lavish wedding-feast [that] appeared" [cum cena nuptialis affluens exhibetur].[101] Alongside this salute to Jupiter, the conclusion of Apuleius's story displays a celebration of marriage, made central visually and ideologically: "In the place of honour reclined Psyche's husband, with his wife in his arms and likewise Jupiter with his Juno, and then all the other gods in order of precedence" [Accumbebat summum torum maritus Psychen gremio suo complexus, sic et cum sua Iunone Iuppiter ac deinde per ordinem toti dei].[102] Rhetorically, Apuleius underscores the primacy of men, as even goddesses are mentioned as the property of their male counterparts. Furthermore, the hierarchy within the family is repeated outside, through the seating arrangement of the gods at the banquet—something that would have resonated in early modern Venice.[103]

Because the characters of Cupid and Venus are so intertwined in Marinella's poem, let us now move to Apuleius's depiction of the goddess of love. One thing is obvious in the Latin model: she is not a positive character. She is self-absorbed, short-sighted in her perspective, and excessive in her emotions, as manifested in one of her earliest mentions in the text, when she reacts to Psyche's beauty and its effect on mortals:

99. Ibid., 111–13 and 110–12.

100. Ibid., 115 and 114.

101. Ibid.

102. Ibid.

103. The ceremonial aspect of Venetian life has been studied extensively. Iain Fenlon discusses the connection between the heart of the city, St. Mark's Square, and its self-display in *The Ceremonial City: History, Memory and Myth in Renaissance Venice* (New Haven, CT: Yale University Press, 2007), particularly chapter 3. Elisabeth Crouzet-Pavan examines social and political elites and their symbolic interactions within and outside their ranks in *Venice Triumphant: The Horizons of a Myth* (Baltimore: Johns Hopkins University Press, 2002), especially chapter 5. Joanne M. Ferraro concisely presents social contacts and tensions in *Venice: History of the Floating City* (Cambridge: Cambridge University Press, 2012), primarily in chapter 4.

> Unable to contain her indignation, tossing her head and protesting in deep bitterness, she thus soliloquized: "So much for me, the ancient mother of nature, first beginning of the elements, Venus nurturer of the whole world! I must share with a mortal girl the honour due to my godhead, and my name, established in heaven, is profaned in earthly dirt! It seems that my name is to be worshipped in common and that I must put up with the obscurity of being adored by deputy, publicly represented by a girl who is doomed to die! ... she will be very sorry, whoever she is, that she has usurped my honours. I will see to it that she regrets this beauty of hers to which she has no right."[104]

Apuleius describes Venus in vivid terms: from her head shaking to the fact that she is talking to herself, from insisting on her own divinity to her referring to herself in the third person, the goddess of love is oblivious to the fact that her identity is being exalted, not diminished, by Psyche's beauty and people's reactions to it. The narrator's emphasis is on superficiality and emotions, traits that recur in this depiction. In fact, the punishment Venus devises for the unfortunate girl is in keeping with these two elements, as it involves love (and sex) and status:

> "Let this girl be ensnared by a burning love to the lowest of mankind, some creature cursed by Fortune in rank, in estate, in condition, some one so degraded that in all the world he can find no wretchedness to equal his own."[105]

The difference between genders is clear: the peak of distinction is beauty and desirability for women, "rank, estate, [and] condition" for men. Venus is not only aware of it, but subscribes to it through her actions.

Once Venus discovers that Cupid has contravened her orders, going so far as to make Psyche his woman, the goddess's ruthlessness comes fully into focus. It does not matter that he is ailing, because of the oil that has burned him; her scathing rebuke is merciless:

104. Apuleius, *Cupid and Psyche*, 43; "Inpatiens indignationis capite quassanti fremens altius sic secum disserit: 'en rerum naturae prisca parens, en elementorum origo initialis, en orbi totius alma Venus, quae con mortali puella partiario maiestatis honore tractor et nomen meum caelo conditum terrenis sordibus profanataur! Nimirum communi nominis piamento uicariae uenerationis intertum sustinebo et imaginem meam circumferet puella moritura... .sed non adeo gaudens ista, quaecumque est, meos honores usurpauerit: iam faxo eam huius etiam ipsius inlicitae formonsitatis paeniterat.'" (42).

105. Ibid., 45; "'uirgo ista amore fraglantissimo teneatur hominis extremi, quem et dignitatis et patrimonii simul et incolumitatis Fortuna damnauit, tanque infimi et per totum orbem non inueniat miseriae suae comparem.'" (44).

> "I suppose you think, you odious good-for-nothing seducer, that you are the only one fit to breed and that I'm now too old to conceive? Let me tell you, I'll bear another son much better than you—better still, to make you feel the insult more, I'll adopt one of my household slaves and give him those wings and torch, and bow and arrows too, and that gear of mine, which I didn't give you to be used like this."[106]

Venus needs to reassert her primacy in her own domain, starting with her ability to generate new life; as she does this, she demeans Cupid and reiterates the reason for her superiority in a physical, embodied way. Instead of coming across as a loving mother, she is presented as narcissistic, to the point that at the end of her tirade the narrator adds this quip: "With these words she rushed violently out in a fury of anger such as befitted Venus" [sic effata foras sese proripit infesta et stomachata biles Venerias].[107] She embodies the ever-changing, capricious, and undependable traits believed to taint only women, boosted by her divine nature.

Even harsher than Venus's considerable disdain for Cupid's actions is her violence against Psyche. When the bedraggled, lonely young woman arrives at the goddess's palace, her welcome befits Venus's contemptuous mien. The consequences for Psyche are dire:

> As soon as Venus saw her brought in and presented to her, she laughed with wide open mouth, as people do in a rage; and shaking her head and scratching her right ear, "So," she said, "you have finally condescended to pay your respects to your mother-in-law? Or have you come to visit your husband, who lies under threat of death from the wound you have given him? But don't worry, I am going to receive you as befits a good daughter-in-law." Then, "Where are Care and Sorrow, my handmaids?" she asked. They were called in, and Psyche was handed over to them to be tormented. In obedience to their mistress's orders they whipped the wretched girl and afflicted her with every other kind of torture, and then brought her back to face the goddess. Venus, laughing again, exclaimed: "Look at her, trying to arouse my pity through the allurement of her swollen belly, whose glorious offspring is to make me, if you please, a happy grandmother. Happy indeed, to be called grandmother in the flower

106. Ibid., 85; "'sed utique praesumis nugo et corruptor et inamabilis te solum generosum nec me iam per aetatem posse concipere. uelim ergo scias multo te meliorem filium alium genituram, immo ut contumeliam magis sentias aliquem de meis adoptaturam eurnulis, eique donaturam ista pinnas et flammas et arcum et ipsas sagittas et omnem meam supellectilem, quam tibi non ad hos usus dederam.'" (84).

107. Ibid., 87 and 86.

> of my age and to hear the son of a vile slave styled Venus' grandson! But I'm a fool to speak of a son: the marriage is not between equals, and what is more took place in the country, without witnesses, and without his father's consent, and cannot be held to be legitimate. So it will be born a bastard, if indeed I allow you to bear it at all."[108]

It is difficult to grapple with the vicious and misogynistic nature of Venus's remarks: against the understated, unemotional rendition of Psyche's first night in Cupid's abode, here Apuleius's narrator insists upon the goddess's vitriol. Venus mocks Psyche's status in her agnatic family, orders torture to be inflicted on her, then makes fun of her pregnancy and condemns her offspring. The narrator underscores several elements of physicality in this passage: from Venus's laughter, deforming her mouth, to Psyche's pregnant belly, subject here to mockery and torments, rather than a mark of honor and respect. Women are primarily physical and bodily; their emotions are faulty, to boot.

In sum, Apuleius's Cupid disobeys his mother's command in order to help the helpless Psyche (and, admittedly, to satisfy his lust); moreover, he enjoys his divine perks but is presented as genuinely merciful to those who are deserving. Conversely, Venus is capricious and selfish, putting herself, her position, and her consideration ahead of all others.

Marinella's Amore innamorato et impazzato (Love Enamored and Driven Mad)

In contrast to the approach of Apuleius's narrator, Marinella consistently expresses her appreciation and respect for female characters and her criticism of male ones. Let us start, again, with Cupid. In *Amore innamorato*, it is he who is self-assured to the point of boastfulness, he who wants to exact vengeance on a mortal:

108. Ibid., 97; "quam ubi primum inductam oblatamque sibi conspexit Venus, latissimum cachinnum extollit et qualem solent furenter irati, caputque quatiens et ascalpens aurem dexteram, 'tandem' inquit 'dignata es socrum tuam salutare? an potius maritum, qui tuo uulnere periclitatur, interuisere uenisti? Sed esto secura, iam enim excipiam te ut bonam nurum condecet,' et 'bi sunt' inquit 'Sollicitudo atque Tristities ancillae meae?' quibus intro uocatis torquendam tradidit eam. at illae sequentes erile praeceptum Psychen misellam flagellis afflictam et ceteris tormentis excruciatam iterum dominac conspectui reddunt. tunc rursum sublato risu Venus 'et ecce' inquit 'nobis turgidi uentris sui lenocinio commouet miserationem, unde me praeclara subole auiam beatam scilicet faciat. felix uero ego quae in ipso aetatis meae flore uocabor aiua et uilis ancillae filius nepos Veneris audiet. quanquam inepta ego quae frustra filium dicam: impares enim nuptiae et praeterea in uilla sine testibus et patre non consentiente factae legitimate non possunt uideri ac per hoc spurius iste nascetur, si tamen partum omnino perferre te patiemur.'" (96).

> Because the son of the Cytherean saw himself dear to the heavens and to the world, he did not yield to the highest god, who ruled the heavens, in praises and esteem. Cupid wanted man to glorify him first, and he daringly wanted to put his foot on Jupiter's head. He wanted every line and rhyme to praise him. One day, as Cupid fixed his eyes on a plain painted with flowers, jeering at the heavens, he said:
> "I am god, I am god to myself, and there is nothing in the heavens that can conquer or match my deity. Not even you, great god, who fling your three-pronged weapon and govern everything and rule the world. Nor you, who hold the great trident with a green veil and have a comfy seat among soft seaweed. Nor you, who sublimely sit with eternal command between dead souls in the Kingdom of Avernus.
> "I reign over the heavens, the earth, the air, the sea, the woods, the hills, the valleys, the fields, the meadows, the rivers, the springs, and the lakes. There, I have already taken and bound even the proudest beasts with my weapons. There is only one disloyal, useless, and superficial young man who is armed with more insanity than sense. This one battles against me and with his boastings shows my lost honor to all." (1.7–9)[109]

The impact of this extended utterance is amplified by its position, soon after the opening of the poem. In parallel to Venus's anger at Psyche, in this case, too, Iridio is not aware of any fault or slight of his against this godhead. This passage is notable for the words that underscore Cupid's arrogance: the repetition of "Vuol" [wanted] at the beginning of two consecutive lines; "audace" [daringly] attributed to his foot; the fact that he addresses the heavens "schernendo" [jeering them]; and the conceit expressed by his professed superiority to Jupiter, Neptune, and Pluto. Notable as well is its sharpening of Cupid's focus on one young man, and its closing on the mention of the slight to Cupid's honor.[110] In this, Marinella's

109. We will note canto and octave(s) parenthetically throughout. "Perche'l figliuol di Citerea si vede / Caro al Ciel, caro al mondo, in laude, e'n stima, / Al maggior Dio, che regga il Ciel, non cede, / Vuol, ch'à lui porga l'huom la gloria prima; / Vuol por su'l capo à Giove audace il piede; / Che se lodi ogni verso, alzi ogni rima. / Poiche in un pian di fior dipinto fisse / Le luci un giorno, il Ciel schernendo disse. // 'Dio sono, a me son Dio, ne c'è nel Cielo / Chi la mia Dietà vinca, o pareggi; / Ne tu gran Dio, che' l triplicato Telo / Vibri, e'l tutto governi, e'l mondo reggi; / Ne tu, che'l gran Tridente in verde velo / Tieni, e fra le lievi alghe hai dolci seggi; / Ne tù, che frà mort'alme à i Regni Averni / Sublime siedi con imperi eterni. // In Cielo, in terra, in aria, in mare ho impero, / In selva, in Monte, in Valle, in campo, in Prato, / In fiume, in Fonte, in Lago il cor più altero / Hò già co' l'armi mie preso, e legato. / Sol c'è un giovin sleal, vano, e leggiero, / Ch'è di pazzia più, che di senno armato, / Questi contra me pugna, e scopre fuore / Coi propri vanti il mio perduto honore.'"

110. It is noteworthy that Marinella's Cupid is not blind at the beginning of the plot (1.5), or when he has fallen to the depths of madness and despair. In this, too, she follows the classical tradition closely,

text closely follows Apuleius's use of the divine: a god pitted and bent on revenge against a human. Her intervention consists in the gender switch (a god and a young man instead of a goddess and a young woman). Marinella goes beyond Apuleius in that her Cupid asserts his power over all human and divine beings, since he can make gods and goddesses fall in love just as easily as men and women. The match between the two texts is notable, but what is crucial (if subtler) is the fact that in Marinella's narrative gender roles are reversed. It is a male (Cupid) who is envious and spiteful, a male (Iridio) who resists the god's sway, and a male (Jupiter) who decides to punish a subordinate (Cupid) for asserting his power over his superior. The power structure is therefore more complex than in Apuleius: this is not solely a family struggle (Venus vs. Cupid) over the free choice of a mate, and there is a clear hierarchy (Jupiter, Cupid, Iridio) that cannot be subverted without the risk of undermining the basic building block of community: family.

It is in connection with the latter that Marinella brings Venus into her narrative, specifically as a distraught mother looking for her missing son. Her depiction of the goddess of love could not be further from that of Apuleius: she is affectionate, loving, and caring toward her son.[111] Here she is, in Canto 8, as she tries to nurture Cupid back to a happy disposition, after he has been snubbed by his would-be beloved:

> She said: "Alas, my son, why do you derive happiness and pleasure from staying away from me, in darkness and gloom, through harsh dangers, all splendor drained from your eyes? Why do I see your handsome innate color disappear from the pretty whiteness of your white lilies? Yes, you used to be handsome, just like a laughing rose when the sun appears.

---

as well as the Platonic idea that "the noblest of emotions [i.e., love] enters the human soul by the noblest of the senses [i.e., sight]": Erwin Panofsky, "Blind Cupid," in *Studies in Iconology: Humanistic Themes in the Art of the Renaissance* (New York: Oxford University Press, 1939; rpt. New York: Harper and Row, 1972), 103. In fact, it is Cupid himself who wonders why he is not blind, when he is in love and unrequited (4.9). Only at the end of the poem, as we will see, does Venus decide to cover his eyes (10.51–52 and 89–90, with its allegorical reading in the Allegory to Canto 10).

111. In one of the earlier retellings of Apuleius's story, Antonio Minturno's *L'amore innamorato* (*Cupid in Love*), printed in Venice by Rampazetto in 1559, Venus is presented as maternally worried for Cupid's absence, but more enraged with his beloved (here named Eroina, rather than Psyche): Ussia, *Amore innamorato*, 22 and 28–29. It is safe to assert that the complete lack of hatred in Venus is Marinella's contribution, already noticed by Malpezzi Price and Ristaino: *Lucrezia Marinella and the "Querelle des Femmes,"* 57. Marinella utilizes prose and verse in *Arcadia felice*, and it might be worthwhile exploring if she borrows any structural element from Minturno's poem, which also alternates prose passages and poetry, with a preponderance of the former. See Antonio Minturno, *Amore innamorato*, ed. Gennaro Tallini (Rome: Aracne, 2008).

> "Now I see you sad, languishing, and in tears! Do you fear, perhaps, that the graces and the beauty that used to dwell in your noble loving face may never return? Don't you know that even if the sun is hidden by clouds, the day will still come back, happy and blazing? In the same way ultimate beauty comes back, although lost from where it belongs.
> "Chase away from your brow and your eyes the ice and fear that surround your soul! What do you fear? You are in your mother's arms now, and your mother's pity embraces and holds you." The wretched boy, whose breast burned and froze, was afraid to uncover himself, held his sighs, and showed his cloudy face all clear, with a smile.
> She laughed when he did so, as does a mother who mirrors her son's wish: she cries if he does, she grieves if he does, and she mingles her wails with his; if he unveils and shows joy in his heart with very sweet words, she is satisfied. Love always makes one heart out of two, and one soul out of two. (8.2–5)[112]

Cupid's handsome features are, in his mother's recollection, part of his carefree past rather than the source of admiration for a young woman; Venus utilizes images from his childhood to encourage Cupid to look positively to the future, because he is no longer alone, but with his mother, a nurturer and a healer. Additionally, Marinella underscores her presentation of Venus with the extended simile in octave 5: the goddess is humanized as a mother whose mood and behavior correspond to those of her offspring.

Cupid, however, is still a wayward adolescent: hiding his feelings of love from his mother, he "showed his cloudy face all clear" [Mostra sereno il nubiloso viso]. The weather-related metaphor that Marinella utilizes is noteworthy: it underscores the natural (as opposed to educated or refined) state that Cupid displays; while this might not provoke a modern reader's reaction, it would have contrasted with the reader's expectation implicit in Marinella's text, as a "natural" state was

112. "'Deh; perche Figlio gioia, e piacer pigli / Star da me lungi in tenebroso horrore? / (Ella dicea) per tanti aspri perigli / E da gli occhi fuggito il suo splendore: / E nel vago candor de' bianchi gigli / Sparito veggio il bel natìo colore; / Bello eri dianzi sì, com'esser suole / Ridente rosa à l'apparir del Sole. // Et hor mesto, languente, e lagrimoso / Ti veggio? Temi forse, che ritorno / Non faccian nel tuo viso almo, amoroso / Le gratie e'l bel, che'n lui facean soggiorno? / Non sai, che ancor, che il Sol fia in nubi ascoso, / Lieto anco torna, e fiammeggiante il giorno? / Cosi; benche smarrita in propria sede / Quella estrema bellezza anco poi riede. // Da la fronte, e da gli occhi hormai discaccia / Quel ghiaccio, e quel horror, che l'alma cinge, / Che temi? Hor sei ne le materne braccia, / E materna pietà ti abbraccia, e stringe." / Il misero, il cui seno arde, et agghiaccia, / Teme scoprirsi, e'l pianto entro ristringe, / E'l sospirar raffrena, e con un riso / Mostra sereno il nubiloso viso. // Ride ella al riso suo, qual Madre suole, / Che del figlio al voler col suo risponde, / Se piange, piange, se si duol, si duole, / A sue querele il lamentar confonde; / Ma s'egli con dolcissime parole / La gioia del suo cor svela, e diffonde; / God'ella, e sempre di duo cori un core, / E di duo spirti un sol ne forma Amore."

typically connected to women rather than to men. Put otherwise, Marinella indicates indirectly that she shapes her characters in ways that do not follow accepted norms. Cupid is presented as profoundly human: he still has to feel despair and lose his sense to understand his utter dependence upon his mother, whose mission is to find him, rescue him, and bring him back to health. Marinella conveys Venus's reaction when she chances upon him, having fainted and close to death, among the snows of Mount Caucasus:

> She stood like a woman whose dear son has taken off to enjoy himself, who then sees him struck by a mortal wound, her noble pawn having reached his bitter end. She felt her soul bewildered and her life getting weaker; agony so struck her senses that she did not feel pain, stunned and confused as she was. She could not move or utter words.
> Although she knew that a god could not taste the poisonous arrow of death, still she feared that her unhappy son had experienced that ultimate evil. So she poured copious tears from her eyes, feeling a harsh, indeed mortal, pain. Never did Dawn cry over the extinguished stars with such beautiful tears. (10.4–5)[113]

Gendered expressions figure prominently in these two octaves. From the mention of "colei" ("a woman") to the use of "ella" (which is redundant in Italian, as verb endings express their subject) in the first line of each stanza, to the multiple adjectives used in the feminine, to the selection of Dawn as the goddess to whom Venus's beauty is compared, everything signals emotions and behaviors that are specific to a woman, indeed to a mother. Here, Venus is not a goddess who wants to be all-powerful and forever young, but principally and fundamentally a mother. Her surfeit of feelings is not presented as a negative feature, but as the only possible response; instead of the violence and vindictiveness depicted by Apuleius, we have motionlessness and silence. This is particularly striking in the context of a poem in which the narrative thrust is dominated by Cupid's madness, presented as his loss of self-control and rationality and resulting in violent actions.

Marinella's Venus, in contrast, acts because she is concerned with her son's health; after crying over him along with the Graces (who are consistently presented as kind, caring, and attentive helpers: see in particular 8.9–11 and 10.16–20), she rises to Mount Olympus in a last-ditch attempt to help him:

113. "Restò, come colei, da cui partita / Fatt'hà per gire à scherzi il figlio caro, / E'l vegga colto di mortal ferita, / E giunto il nobil pegno al fine amaro. / Sbigottir l'alma, indebolir la vita / Sente, e i martir sì il senso à lei legaro, / Che stupida, e confusa non si duole, / Andar non può, ne sà fermar parole. // Bench'ella sappia, ch'ad un Dio non lice / Sentir di morte il venenoso strale; Pur teme, che di morte lo'nfelice / Habbia provato in se l'ultimo male; / Onde fuor de begli occhi in copia elice / Lagrime, e sente duol crudo, e mortale. / L'Aurora mai con lagrime sì belle / Pianse piena di duol l'estinse stelle."

> She appeared in heaven with lugubrious clothes, plentiful tears, and scattered and disheveled hair. Similarly we see a pale star appear with a dark cloak in the night veil. Play, Laughter, and Song did not accompany her, roses plucked from their native stem did not adorn her; alone, untidy, shabby, and neglected, she stood devoid of daring and closed up on herself.
> A whisper, a muffled murmur rose among the blessed gods out of immense Aethra, when they saw her with sick shabby brow, pale face, and dewy eyes. With deep and frequent sighs she showed the sorrow and grief that anguished and consumed her. She was quiet and did not look, and even if she looked, her humble, languid, slow eyes shed dew.
> They said: "She is the one who used to be Cupid's beautiful mother, when celebrating and laughing; with her pretty actions and beautiful face she used to wound all chests and burn all souls. She used to have paradise in her countenance, was the queen and goddess of hearts, and with angel-like words stole Mars's sword and the sun's rays." (10.26–28)[114]

Marinella depicts Venus in ways quite removed from classical and early modern representations; she is not erotically charged, lavishly appointed, or otherwise enticing. When read against Apuleius's narrative, these lines are even more striking: in both appearance and demeanor, Venus is not the cocky, egotistical goddess that takes her revenge on Psyche, physically and emotionally, but a grieving mother who does not know how to help her son. Marinella emphasizes this, perhaps for the benefit of readers who may not have been familiar with traditional depictions, through the gods' "muffled murmur" [mormorar sommesso] of octave 28, which recapitulates Venus's amorous conquests, among others.

What happens to Apuleius's affectionate, mother-defying Cupid in Marinella's poem? He is the source of the entire plot, and not in a positive way.

114. "E con vesti ligubri [*sic*], e largo pianto, / Sparso incomposto il crin comparve in Cielo; / Così apparir veggiam con foscho manto / Pallida stella nel notturno velo; / Non l'accompagna il Gioco, il Riso, e'l Canto; / Non l'ornan rose tolte al natìo stelo; / Ma sola, inculta, squallida, e negletta / Sta priva di baldanza, in se ristretta. // Nacque un bisbiglio, un mormorar sommesso / De l'Etra immenso tra i beati Numi, / Veggendo lei col ciglio egro, e dimesso, / Pallida il volto, e rugiadosa i lumi. / Mostrar col sospirar profondo, e spesso, / Che duol, che pena il cor l'anga, e consumi, / Tace, e non mira, e se pur mira il guardo / Stilla rugiade, humil, languido, e tardo. // Dicean, quest'è Colei, che'n festa, e'n riso / Bella Madre d'Amore esser solea; / Che co' gli atti leggiadri, e col bel viso / Ogni petto impiagava, ogn'alma ardea; / Che portava nel volto il Paradiso; / Ch'era de' cor de' Dei Regina, e Dea; / Che potè co'l'angeliche parole / Tor à Marte la spada, i raggi al Sole." In the physical description of Venus in the first two octaves, Marinella echoes Apuleius's description of Psyche at the time of her wedding/funeral procession.

As we saw in the citation from Canto 1 above, he is haughty, full of himself, and spiteful, indeed the counterpart of the Roman writer's Venus. He is sneaky and violent, and his negative behavior is consistently directed toward his mother or her belongings. In other words, while Apuleius depicts Venus as eliciting her revenge on Psyche, here the violence works across genders: a man wants to chastise a woman—and not just any woman, but his own mother. Yet the violence is indirect: Marinella devotes several octaves of Canto 8 to describing Cupid's destruction of Venus's palace and gardens (8.41–52), tellingly starting with Venus's own bed (8.43). In the following canto, Cupid's destruction moves geographically further, from Arabia to Hyrcania, a remote wooded Asian region:

> That evil boy uprooted wild ash trees and strong firs from the tangled ground, like tender nettles and weak dills; he knocked out tall beech trees with a single hit. The woods on wide Erymanthos did not remain happy, either; he unleashed his strength there, breaking ancient pines. His right hand, accustomed to wounding hearts, snapped each tree. He knocked down bears and killed fierce strong lions. Who vouches for this? That such a refined body harbored such terrible strength? He made it patently clear: he ran, crazy lunatic, through those huge fields, winning over agile and swift deer. Like a wounded bull, he happened to carry in his heart the arrow that would kill him. (9.3–4)[115]

The destructive power of Cupid, alongside his qualification as a "crazy lunatic" [forsennato], suggests the comparison with the bacchantes, women followers of Bacchus, whose wild actions and music culminated with an animal sacrifice.[116] The original term, which comes from the Old French *forsené* (from *fors*, out; and *sens*, reason), has notable literary antecedents: the most illustrious one is very possibly Dante, who described Hecuba crazed by Polyxena's death in the following manner: "she barked, out of her senses, like a dog" [forsennata latrò sì come cane] (*Inferno* 30.20).[117] In juxtaposition to traditional negative female depiction, Marinella leverages characters that are typically minor and bestows recurrent positive roles on

115. "Come tenere Ortiche, e frali Aneti / Svelle il villan da l'intricata terra; / Cosi Frasin selvaggi, e duri Abeti, / E gli alti faggi à un crollo solo atterra; / Ne de l'ampio Erimanto i boschi lieti / Restare; quivi le forze sue disserra; / Frange gli antichi Pini; ogn'arbor spezza / Quella sua destra, à ferir cori avezza. // Atterra l'Orso, e morto il Leon rende / Feroce, e forte; e chi da fede à questo? / Che un corpo si gentil forze si horrende/ Havesse, e pur ciò mostra manifesto; / Pe'i campi immensi forsenato stende / Il corso, e vince il Cervo agile, e desto; / E qual Tauro ferito avien, che porte / Nel cor lo stral, che lo conduce à morte."

116. Thanks to Frank Palmieri for the insight regarding the bacchantes.

117. Dante Alighieri, *The Divine Comedy*, <https://digitaldante.columbia.edu/dante/divine-comedy/inferno/inferno-30/>. On this site, the Italian is Petrocchi's definitive edition, and this translation is Mandelbaum's (Longfellow's is also available).

them. For example, nymphs are observers who provide Venus with crucial information about Cupid (7.52–53 and 9.40–46). As the goddess searches everywhere for her son unsuccessfully, it is nymphs who have to tell her where he is and what he has been up to: although they are lesser deities (indeed, one of them says candidly: "I'm not allowed to bring comfort to the great pain of the highest gods, because I'm lowly" 9.45),[118] but as with the Graces, Marinella portrays them as more than just beautiful maidens spending their days near the water.

Ersilia, like the nymphs, is more than just the stock character of the chaste young woman pursued by a god. Furthermore, in contrast to the Furies, she is rationality personified. In Marinella's hands, a woman rises to become the model of virtue and humanity, while a male god is irrational, even more violent than the Furies in his murderous rampage. Likewise, the connection with a woman and with an animal[119] underscores Marinella's transformation of Cupid in ways that make his actions differ from traditional depictions: her question in octave 4 is not rhetorical, as she includes an explicit answer later on in the same stanza. Cupid's behavior "made … patently clear" [mostra manifesto] that he was a strong man, not the gentle child found in classical and early modern images. This is further emphasized by the accumulation of species of trees and wild animals in these stanzas.

Canto 9 marks the peak of Cupid's fury and his miraculous, and completely unexplained, recovery:

> At last the thick cloud of insane fury lifted through the rays of his mind. He saw his state and was saddened by it; harsh and strong pain clutched his heart. Repentant and aching that he had wanted to offend the immeasurable father of the great gods, he now wanted to ask his forgiveness for his past mistakes, with the sorrowful sounds of his humble voice.
>
> Full of deep humility, he stretched his arms, bent his knees, and unleashed vast tears; he said: "Great father, turn your eyes to me with mercy, be so merciful that I might dry off my cheeks, wet with tears, and reduce my pain a bit! Forgive my mistakes! Ruler of the world, eternal Jupiter, may your goodness benefit me!"
>
> He was silent, because he could not say anything else. He found himself on Mount Caucasus, which separates India from Scythia; on it winter generates ice, and deep snow rests. It was good to observe its top: it shone and smiled like a star in the sky, almost similar to a man who learns by himself the nature, path, light, and movement of the stars.

118. "A me, che vile son, de'sommi Dei / Porger conforto à gran dolor non lece" (9.45.5–6).

119. The phrase "wounded bull" [Tauro ferito] is paradoxical, given that bulls embody physical strength and masculinity—in this case, however, sapped by an injury.

> The wretched boy fell in its perennial snow and cold ice, which the sun never melts in water as it circles; he fell where fierce and biting winds blew all the time and thick fog hid the clear air. Cruel Jupiter did not yield to his moans, his love, or his harsh and deep pain; if Cupid had given him love wounds, he had also bestowed sweet mercy on him. (9.55–58)[120]

In Marinella's allegorical explanation (found at the beginning of Canto 10), she presents Cupid as man who is led astray by temptations and then sees his ways and asks for god's forgiveness:

> Tired, weary Cupid reaching Mount Caucasus, guided by his own fury, then returned mostly to his senses there and asking Jupiter for forgiveness, will be understood to be man: after he is tossed and roiled by the stormy waves of the crazy furies of the senses, in the end he is lifted by the wings of reason to the mountain of rightful thinking and he recognizes that he is tainted and made ugly by a thousand iniquities and perversity, so that repentance is born and he asks the eternal maker for forgiveness. (10 Allegory)[121]

The tension between the divine character, "guided" by irrationality and craziness, and his allegorical meaning ("man" in general, in an abstract, philosophical sense), underscores the hubris inherent to any construal of gender imbalance: both men and women are created by and subordinate to divine action; furthermore, the would-be pinnacle of divine creation, man, is potentially victim to folly.

120. "Ai rai de la cui mente pur si tolse / De' suoi pazzi furori il nuvol denso; / Onde vide il suo stato, e si se'n dolse, / Che'l cor li strinse aspro dolore intenso. / E pentito, e dolente, che già volse / Offender de'gran Divi il Padre immenso, / A cui di voce humil con mesto suono / Vuol chiedere de' passati error perdono. // Pieno d'alta humiltà le braccia aperse / Le ginocchia piegò, slegò un gran pianto, / Sien di pietà tue luci in me converse / Disse, ò gran Padre, e ancor pietoso tanto, / Ch'asciugar possi queste guancie asperse / Di lagrime, e scemar mio duolo alquanto, / L'error perdona, e tua bontà mi giove / Rettor del mondo, ò sempiterno Giove. // Tace, che non può oltre, hor si ritrova /Su'l Monte Caucaso, che divide / L'India da Schitia, sopra cui rinova / Il verno il ghiaccio, e neve alta s'asside, / A la cui sommità di mirar giova, / Com'aurea stella in Ciel scintilla, e ride, / Quasi vicina à l'huom, ch'à se fa noti / Le lor nature, i corsi, i lumi, e i moti. // Fra sue perpetue nevi, e ghiacci algenti, / Che mai rotando il Sol non scioglie in onde; / Ove ogn'hor soffian fieri, horridi venti, / E vapor denso à l'aere il puro asconde, / Il misero caddè, ne a' suoi lamenti, / Né al suo amor, nè à sue doglie aspre, e profonde / Piegossi Giove (ah crudo) à cui se diede / Piaghe d'amor, die ancor dolce mercede."

121. "Cupido, che stanco, e lasso giunge (guidato da' suoi propri furori) sopra il monte Caucaso, e quivi ritornato alquanto in se, chiede perdono à Giove, s'intenderà per l'huomo dopo che fù gittato, e aggittato dalle tempestose onde de gli insani furori del senso, che finalmente innalzato dall'ali della ragione sopra il Monte delle giuste cogitationi, conosce se stesso ammacchiato, e brutto di mille iniquità, e perversità; onde nascendo il pentimento dimanda perdono all'etterno Fattore."

In keeping with the prevailing ethos and beliefs of her time, Marinella's Allegory to Canto 10 shines the light of salvation on the conclusion of the plot, underscoring the will of the "eternal maker" and the actions of male or female saints interceding for humans, represented by Venus in the plot. One could conclude that the latter allegorical element undermines the presence and power of the main female character; on the contrary, it is also possible to view the role of Venus (and of the Virgin Mary) as specific to a woman, indeed to a mother, excluding the possibility that a man might ever carry it out.

Virginia Cox has rightly defined Marinella's works as "programmatically ascetic," setting them apart from the experimentation that other women writers carried out in genres other than the love lyric.[122] In part, however, *Amore innamorato* bucks this trend, as erotic love is ever present and always implied, if never achieved. Certainly familial love and maternal affection triumph in the end; indeed, Jupiter's forgiveness restores Cupid to his sanity and to his role, rather than sanctioning marriage as in Apuleius. Still, restoring Cupid's role means recognizing that it is critical: an absence of physical love would condemn humanity to death. There is a break in the narrative frame at the very end of the poem that seems to indicate Marinella's awareness of this possible conclusion:

> His mother now prepared him a new bow, new arrows, and new torches, then hid his eyes with a white veil, so that he would not turn them to golden stars and poke fun at heaven. Thus thereafter he always mixed and confused beautiful flames with the ice of love, and he seemed to wound old and young and pretty chests, without any difference.
> Everything was convivial; pretty flowers smiled with their purple and white in his face, and joy and laughter took up his heart, where wrath and fury had finally quieted. Sometimes, sitting by a river and joking, he would temper the hot flames of his arrows in its waters and repair broken nets; at times he prepared ties, at others he made ice, and yet at others he stirred his flames.
> Now, satisfied with that, he enjoyed it as a pretty sight, removed from dark and sad pain; he knew how humility conquered heavenly grace through harsh torments. Let man rejoice, then, when he enjoys little peace mixed with long and harmful pains: humility and travails make him worthy of eternal glory and of the heavenly kingdom. (10.89–91)[123]

122. Cox, *Women's Writing*, 152.

123. "Nov'arco, novi strai, nove Facelle / Li prepara la Madre, e'n bianco velo / Li occhi li asconde; perche à l'auree stelle / Non li rivolga, e beffeggiarne il Cielo / Cosi poi sempre à le sue fiamme belle / Mesce, e confonde l'amoroso gelo, / E senza differenza par, ch'impiaghi / Antichi petti, e giovinetti, e vaghi. // Tutto è festoso, ridon nel bel viso / D'ostro, e di latte i vezzosetti fiori, / S'asside nel

As Marinella approaches the conclusion of her work, she adds another notable revisionist intervention to tell the back story of Petrarchism: Cupid is tamed and included in a family, rather than being presented as the all-powerful, pain-bestowing god of love. Marinella then devotes the last four lines of the poem to a reminder of the allegorical connotation of the character of Cupid, lest the distance from the explanation at the beginning of the canto and the vividness of the happy ending impress the implied reader with a pagan and erotic meaning of the entire poem. Otherwise stated, Marinella's parting words address the allegorical significance to complete the frame she has placed around her plot, and in so doing they reconfirm it and expunge any possible connotation of physically charged attraction.

Petrarchan Beauty in a New Context

One of the interesting facets of *Amore innamorato* is the application and extension of the Petrarchan topoi of physical beauty to a longer narrative form, and to both male and female characters. It is not surprising that Marinella presents Ersilia as appealing: after all, she is, first, Cupid's vehicle for his intended revenge on Iridio, and later the object of his unrequited affection. She enters as a vision:

> an angelic countenance appeared to him: golden hair, scattered and flowing in the air, a face where it is eternally spring, a sun that burned and shone as it laughed, a nymph who, like a goddess, awakened roses and violets as she moved her feet. (1.15.3–8)[124]

Twice in six lines Marinella emphasizes her otherworldly nature ("angelic" and "goddess"), yet she embodies the traits of stylized Petrarchan beauty: golden hair, white skin, and youthful appearance.[125] Furthermore, she is of noble lineage, the

---

suo cor la gioia, e'l riso, / In cui pur s'acchetaro ire, e furori: / Talhor scherzando appresso un fiume assiso / Tempra de strai co'l'onda i caldi ardori; / Rotte reti rintegra, hor lacci appresta, / Hor ghiaccio indura, hor le sue fiamme desta. // Hor di ciò satio, in gratiosa vista / Gode, lungi da doglie oscure, e meste; / E sà pur hor, come humiltade acquista / Per via d'aspro martir gratia celeste. / Per questo l'huom s'allegri, quando mista / Ha poca pace à lunghe pene infeste, / C'humiltade, e travagli lo fan degno / Di gloria eterna, e di celeste regno."

124. "Ecco apparirli angelica maniera: / Ecco un crin d'or, che sparso à l'aura ondeggia: / Ecco un volto, ove eterna è primavera; / Ecco un Sol, che ridendo arde, e lampeggia, / Ecco una Ninfa, che qual Diva suole, / Desta al moto del piè rose, e viole." The anaphora in lines 3–7 insists on engaging the reader, with its repetition of the epideictic adverb that attracts attention toward the object described. It is possible, if not likely, that Marinella's use of the adjective *angelica* [angelic] would evoke a reference to Ariosto's female love object in the *Orlando furioso*, Angelica.

125. Such physical attributes are reiterated and more fully explained a few octaves later, specifically in 1.19.

only daughter of King Emireno (1.17). She is so arresting that even Iridio, impervious to erotic longing, is swayed by her: "He looked and was in awe of her golden hair, her sweet face, and her beautiful ways, and of her white skin that shone like splendid stars" (1.21.1–4).[126] Her devotion to Diana introduces wisdom and athleticism to her attributes: she has "serious mind, celestial gait, and pretty brow" (2.47.5–6);[127] nevertheless, struck by his own arrow, Cupid cannot recognize that she will deny herself to his longing, and his dogged pursuit brings about a voyeuristic moment, quite exceptional in Marinella's works, in Canto 3. There, he spies Ersilia bathing herself in a clear brook,[128] and this episode allows Marinella to reiterate the catalogue of her physical attributes (3.25–33), adding a key one: her "white foot" [bianco piede] (3.37.4), which allows her to flee from him.[129] After this arguably inappropriate appearance, Ersilia is present in the poem only in Cupid's words and songs (notably in 4.16–18 and 7.19), as his "noble goddess" [alma … diva] (6.22.2).

It goes without saying that Marinella describes Venus as physically attractive. The pull of classical tradition as well as her gender are undeniable. When she first appears, her "immaculate body" is "softer than swan plumes and whiter than milk" [corpo … candido, e molle / Più, che piuma di cigno, o bianco latte] (1.63.1–2), and her chest "looked as if immaculate ivory was richly adorned all around with gold" [sembra tal, come se d'oro intorno / Candido avorio è riccamente adorno] (1.64.7–8). Physical attributes are rare, however; toward the end of the poem, Marinella calls her "the noble goddess with serene eyes, who deserves the first place as far as beauty" [l'alma Dea da le luci serene / Che merta di bellezza il primo honore] (10.87.3–4), but details are scant. What is striking is the frequency with which Marinella refers to her (or has characters do so) as "mother," increasingly towards the end of the poem: from the first occurrence in Canto 4, we have six in Canto 5, one in Canto 6, four in Canto 7, eleven in Canto

126. "Mira, e loda del crin l'aureo splendore, / Il dolce viso, e le maniere belle, / E del seno di latte il gran candor, / E'l folgorar de le splendenti stelle."

127. "[D]'Ersilia il senno grave; / L'andar celeste: e'l gratioso ciglio."

128. The Ovidian connection is to the tragic story of Actaeon recounted in Book 3 of *Metamorphoses*: having chanced upon Diana bathing in a spring, he was transformed into a stag and devoured by his own hunting dogs. Ersilia is a devotee of Diana, but this ending is not nearly as bloody, reiterating that for Marinella female characters are more restrained and composed than in classical antecedents.

129. Malpezzi Price and Ristaino have underscored the significant parallelism between Ersilia's flight in *Amore innamorato* and that of Angelica in Ludovico Ariosto's *Orlando furioso*, along with a crucial difference: "Angelica becomes prey to the same passions that affect her male counterparts. Marinella's Ersilia, on the other hand, does in no way participate in Cupid's desire." In this way, she "closely resembles Risamante, [Moderata] Fonte's main character in *Tredici Canti* [*sic*] *del Floridoro*." *Lucrezia Marinella and the "Querelle des Femmes,"* 50. Nevertheless, we do not agree with their assessment that Marinella "quietly develops Ersilia as the central figure of [her] poem" (ibid.), as she disappears from the plot early on.

8, five in Canto 9, and nine in Canto 10.[130] The cumulative effect is to underscore Venus's loving role with respect to her wayward son much more emphatically than her physical appearance. In other words, Marinella desexualizes Venus even as she depicts Cupid in more erotically charged terms.

Two male characters are notable for their beauty: Iridio and Cupid. The former is described only in passing, since his role is to be the foil to Cupid's arrow, as his introduction makes clear: "Iridio, the most beautiful, wise, and prim young man to ever adorn the world, and the coldest of hearts in our or in ancient times. He was a despiser of Cupid" [Iridio: è un giovinetto / Il più bello, il più accorto, il più pudico. / Ch'adorni il mondo, il più agghiacciato petto, / Che sia nel nostro, o fosse al tempo antico: / Sprezzator di Cupido] (1.13.1–5). More physical details emerge when Marinella describes his death and metamorphosis into an iris [iride], in Canto 6: nymphs

> discovered that a flower had been born from him, pretty to behold and endowed with a beautiful color. Its shape resembled the lily's, because its petals gathered around its stamens. As far as color, I liken it to the pallor that death spreads on a dead face or to the loving pallor found in a pretty violet. It didn't fear love's cruel clutches, and kept the beautiful name that it had when a mortal body weighed it. (6.39.7–40)[131]

His importance transcends the plot, because through this character Marinella underscores her own authorial intervention: not only does she create a metamorphosis, following in the footsteps of Ovid and Apuleius (and recalling the title of Apuleius's novel, on which she modelled her plot), she emphasizes her agency through a first-person verb that describes her involvement in poetic terms ("liken" [rassomigliare] is directly related to a crucial poetic trope, the simile). Their paucity (there are only sixteen such utterances in the whole poem) underscores its strength and import.[132]

Lastly, as the namesake of the poem, Cupid is a more frequent presence and more precisely described: Marinella mentions "his white and gold wings" [le

130. Specifically: 4.8.8; 5.Allegory; 5.21.2; 5.21.7; 5.58.1; 5.60.4; 5.60.5; 6.29.6; 7.36.3; 7.59.2; 7.62.2; 7.63.1; 8.Argument; 8.Allegory (twice); 8.5.1; 8.18.4; 8.19.1; 8.22.3; 8.24.7; 8.30.3; 8.68.6; 8.71.3; 9.13.5; 9.25.7; 9.29.1; 9.31.3; 9.53.2; 10.10.7; 10.10.8; 10.13.8; 10.15.8; 10.19.2; 10.28.2; 10.67.7; 10.72.8; and 10.89.2.

131. "[T]rovar, che di lui nato era un fiore, / Grato di vista, e vago di colore. // Che fra i coltelli di sue foglie accolto / Simil la forma sua dimostra al giglio, /A quel pallor, che morte in morto volto / Distende, nel color lo rassomiglio, / O qual vaga viola ha in se raccolto / Pallidezza amorosa. Il crudo artiglio / Più non teme d'amor, serba il bel nome, / C'hebbe mentre il gravar le mortai some."

132. The other first-person verbs are found in the following lines: 2.16.3; 3.24.1; 4.50.1; 6.43.5; 6.45.7; 8.73.1; 9.60.7; 9.66.7; 10.15.7; 10.30.3; 10.62.7 (twice); 10.67.1; 10.69.1; and 10.69.5.

bianche, e le dorate piume] (2.9.3), "his blond hair" [chiome bionde] (2.43.4), "his lively eyes" [occhi vivaci] (2.46.2) similar to the sun,[133] and "his swift soles" [veloci piante] (2.46.2). His physical beauty is potentially dangerous, as the few octaves in Canto 3 reveal, when he observes himself reflected in water:

> After he cleaned, washed, and rinsed his shining mane and pretty chest in those pure waves, he took counsel with the river; his pained heart admired itself and was filled with happiness and hope upon seeing the purple, milk, and burning gold of his breast, face, and blond hair. If he hadn't been filled by another love, he would have fallen for his face and become another Narcissus. (3.11)[134]

Marinella develops Cupid's rich physical details, adding the well-worn metaphor of milk to describe whiteness, as well as a reference to purple to indicate the rose of his cheeks. It is bodily attributes that push Cupid almost to the brink of falling in love with himself. Marinella utilizes this octave to indicate that erotic longing for oneself is to be avoided; loving another is acceptable, at the very least because it spares humans from making a serious mistake (one that, in the allegorical frame of this work, would be a serious sin). Cupid retreats from the brink, literally and figuratively. The fact that physical beauty is dangerous could be seen as a reference to Apuleius, in which good looks attract Venus's rage against Psyche and provoke the latter's clumsiness and hurting of Cupid when she first observes him by the light of her lamp.

Comeliness is a fundamental trait of Cupid's in *Amore innamorato,* and as such it endures even when he is hurt both bodily and emotionally. An excellent example is in Canto 4, when Marinella first presents his fury:

> He struck his white breast, he dyed and colored the whiteness that stole the prize from snow. His ivory was such that if a virgin hand adorned it with roses, its honor would rise to the sky. Like an apple becomes redder in the sun, hour after hour in a pretty meadow or on a happy hill, similarly his handsome white chest became flushed to the exceedingly hot emotion of insane wrath.

133. "[H]is sun-like eyes" [occhi quai soli] (2.61.1). Elsewhere, Marinella dubs them as the place "where the wondrous light of the sovereign beauty of heaven is kept" [in cui del Ciel si serba / Di sovrana beltà mirabil luce] (3.4.1–2).

134. "Poiche la chioma, e'l sen vago, e lucente / Purgò, terse, e lavò ne la pur'onda, / Si consigliò col fonte, il cor dolente / Mirandosi di gioia, e speme abbonda; / Che vede l'ostro, il latte, e l'oro ardente / Del sen, del volto, e de la testa bionda; / S'altro amor no'l tenesse, del suo viso / Amator diverria novo Narciso."

> Who could say how he complained, how he wounded the sky with his pained notes, how he broke and tore his rippled golden tresses, how he scratched his chest and red cheeks? Say it, you who have tamed earth, sea, and the heavenly wheels with your strength! Now say it, you who feel the cruel flames of your own fire that sets you ablaze and gives you no rest! (4.12–13)[135]

In the first of these two octaves, Marinella juxtaposes cliché language derived from Petrarchan poetry (breast as white as snow and ivory, roses adorning it) to a nature-based simile in the latter half. In addition to striking the implied reader as unusual, this trope assimilates the work of the sun ripening red apples to that of Cupid's madness provoking harm to his body; in other words, the author conjoins two elements that seem antithetical. The reader is left with the impression that madness is a natural occurrence, akin to the sun's rising and falling according to a specific cycle. This intriguing figure of speech is then followed by an indirect reference to Marinella's authorial role and by a direct address to Cupid himself. The first literary device is a rhetorical question concerning the very possibility of describing Cupid's laments and violent self-destructive acts; given that previous octave was dedicated to them, it is clear that the implied answer refers to Marinella herself. Piling rhetorical strategies onto each other, Marinella then moves to an apostrophe to Cupid, here identified as a powerful god and capable of expressing the pains of love that he is experiencing. Octave 13 suggests an assimilation of Marinella the author with Cupid himself, at least as far as his artistic abilities are concerned.

Marinella's Poetics

Marinella's knowledge of canonical classical and Italian vernacular literature, and her rhetorical abilities, are on display at the beginning of Canto 3. After a single octave advancing the plot, Marinella describes Cupid's cries in two stanzas that include as many references to lyrical achievements to be emulated:

> Like Procne, removed from the joy of her children, fled her home lamenting, her heart already turned to cold ice, going among branches and dry twigs, opening up the sad feelings of her afflicted soul to

135. "Si batte il bianco sen, tinge, e colora / Il candor, ch'à le nevi il pregio tolle, / L'avorio è tal, se lui di rose infiora / Verginea man, ch'al Ciel d'honor s'estolle: / O tal e'l Pomo al Sol, che d'hora, in hora / S'invermiglia in bel prato, o in lieto colle, / Qual s'impurpurea il bel candido petto / De l'ira insana al troppo caldo affetto. // Chi potria dir, come si lagni, e come / Ferisca il Ciel co'sue dolenti note, / Si frangia, e straccia l'auree crespe chiome, / Si graffia il seno, e le purpuree gote: / Ma dillo tu, c'hai co tue forze dome / La terra, il mare, e le superne rote, / Hor dillo tu, che provi del tuo foco / Lo'ncendio crudo, ond'ardi, e non hai loco."

> heaven in pitiable song, such that it seemed that the wood itself cried with her and accompanied her sadness with its own, so the most hidden nooks of those thick woods resonated with handsome Cupid's mourning and cries, and valleys and beaches responded to his laments and deep pains. Wild animals and birds left their caves and nests; myrtles, alders, and laurels became pale. Compassionate Echo felt pain for his pain, and she seemed to shed her tears with his tears. (3.2–3)[136]

Marinella devotes the entire octave 2 to a simile, whose term of comparison only emerges in the following stanza. Cupid's pained shouts are likened to Procne's, whose wrenching story is narrated in Book 6 of Ovid's *Metamorphoses*. For anybody familiar with her tale, such a simile would be surprising on two accounts. First, in Ovid's tale, Procne is an ambiguous character: much wronged by her husband, Tereus, who rapes and then maims her sister Philomela, she exacts her revenge by killing, cooking, and feeding their son to him. That narrative does not mince words in describing Tereus's lust after Philomela, his sexual and physical violence against her, and Procne's resolve to kill her own son. Marinella reshapes Ovid's character in a much more positive manner: she is a mother crying over her lost children. Additionally, rather than as a human deprived of the ability to speak, then changed into a swallow, Marinella praises her for her "pitiable song." This indirectly calls into question the standard reference to Procne in Italian poetry, Francesco Petrarca's sonnet 310, "Zephiro torna, e 'l bel tempo rimena" [Zephyr returns and brings fine weather back], in which she is depicted as "warbling" [garrir].[137] Marinella uses a verb ("querelarsi" [lament]) that can be attributed to humans, while Petrarch's term only designates the cry of a bird. Through a single simile, Marinella refashions Ovid's story and Petrarch's language, going deeper than the superficial figurative connection based on irrational (one could even say unnatural) behavior: Procne abandons maternal instincts, and Cupid forsakes the instinct for self-preservation.

Elsewhere, Marinella reveals an affinity for the verbal and syntactical features that mark Baroque texts in both Italian and other European traditions. In

136. "Qual Progne, à cui sia tolto il suo diletto / De' cari figli, il cor già freddo gelo, / Querelandosi fugge il suo ricetto, / E fra i rami ne và di un secco stelo: / E'n miserabil canto il mesto affetto / Scioglie de l'alma afflitta verso il Cielo, / Par che la Selva del suo pianto piagni, / E mesta il suo doloro mesto accompagni. // Così del bel Cupido à i pianti, à i gridi / De' folti boschi i più riposti horrori / Rimbonbano altamente, e valli, e lidi / Ai suoi lamenti, à i gravi suoi dolori: / Lascian fere, ed augelli, ed Antri, e nidi, / Impallidiscon Mirti, Alni, & Allori; / Eco pietosa à la sua intensa doglia / S'addoglia, al pianto par, che pianto scioglia.

137. Francesco Petrarca, *Petrarch's* Songbook = *Rerum Vulgarium Fragmenta*, trans. James Wyatt Cook (Binghamton, NY: Medieval and Renaissance Texts and Studies, 1996), 349 and 348.

the course of a few octaves in Canto 4, for example, she insists on the use of polyptoton[138] in order to underscore the power of love in every setting (including the netherworld) and therefore Cupid's now sapped sway:

> So spoke the one who bound, burned, and tied souls with fire, nets, and knots—now wounded, burned, and bound. Since he had grasped others, it was right that he was tied with his own ties! Charon heard him, and his heart was filled with hope, as his face was full of joy: "Now listen and be quiet," he said; "I want to lead you where you want to go, as long as you pull me out of this sorrow." (4.44)[139]

Repetitions and redoubling of terms serve to identify Cupid, and to express the narrator's agreement with Jupiter's penance. As Cupid is willing to help Charon find his beloved, the act of falling in love is described as follows:

> She [Eurinia] kindled in such a way that pitch and sulfur placed in the middle of fire kindle and blaze less; already her heart, predisposed to burning, was consumed by the flames of love. She would have passed out little by little, because of this fire, if she had not relinquished all fears and decided to leave all of a sudden where her beloved was, himself ablaze with love. (4.57)[140]

Marinella utilizes the extensive metaphorical vocabulary of love as fire to impress on her readers her verbal abilities, as well as her knowledge of past poetic examples and her willingness to expand on them.

The prevailing rhetoric of Marinella's text is also enriched through her references to Venus as a distraught mother. One example among many comes from Canto 10, in one of her pleas to her long-lost son:

> "Where are the lilies and beautiful roses of your face, heaven's song and my gift? Where are the pretty loving flames of your eyes, my glory? Where did they go? Where are the rays of your shining hair,

138. A stylistic device in which words derived from the same root are repeated in close proximity. Marinella uses polyptoton in several instances throughout the poem.

139. "Così disse colui, che l'alme avinse, / Arse, e legò con foco, reti, e lacci, / Ferito, arso, & avinto, e s'altrui strinse, / Giust'è ben, che co'lacci suoi s'allacci, / L'udì Caron, di speme il cor si cinse, / Empio di gioia il volto, hor odi, e tacci, / Dice, e dove tu vuoi, condur ti voglio, / Pur che me ancor tu traggi di cordoglio."

140. "S'accende sì, che men s'accende, e 'nfiamma / La pece, e'l solfo in mezzo al foco posto; / E già'l suo cor da l'amorosa fiamma / Ne vien consunto, ad arder già disposto; / E per cotal incendio à dramma; à dramma / Meno verìa; s'ogni timor deposto, / Non havesse conchiuso andar repente: / Ov'è l'Amante suo d'amor ardente."

> which I took from heaven's most sublime throne? I once was a happy mother; now I am an unhappy mother because of this pain and because of unhappy Cupid." (10.10)[141]

Here, in addition to the reiteration of the physical attributes denoting beauty, attributed to Cupid (and to him as her son, not as a beloved), Marinella employs anaphora. "Where" [ove] recurs three times, with the first iteration in Italian being that of the shortened form [u'], and the juxtaposition of "happy" and "unhappy mother" occurs in connection with "unhappy Cupid," which in Italian is set in chiastic format ["madre infelice"—"infelice Amore"]. The fact that Marinella often utilizes "Amore" to refer to the god of love, instead of his name,[142] renders many of her comments more general and more paradoxical at the same time: it is clear that Cupid is unhappy, within the context of Canto 10, and this octave serves to acknowledge that being in love can be the source of despondency.[143]

In sum, then, while Marinella builds on classical antiquity and the vernacular tradition of lyrical poetry in Italian, she also enriches both ideologically and rhetorically, even as she transforms them by injecting them with gender. *Amore innamorato* reiterates that analyzing women's texts does not merely "add" another facet to an established pattern, as it compels us to modifying and enriching it in unexpected ways.

Marinella as an Observer of Her World and Society

Lastly, we want to spend a few words drawing attention to Marinella's abilities as an observer, both of everyday life and of an amazing range of details that she obviously collected in her own readings—demonstrating her remarkable erudition. In *Amore innamorato* she packs a great deal about a wide variety of subjects: flora and fauna (the turkey oak and plane tree, the snake that "shakes three tongues" as it regenerates, and a startling reference to the orca);[144] a virtual atlas of geographic regions and features (from Arabia Petraea to the island of "Thile," or Thule);[145] food both divine (ambrosia: 8.9) and familiar (marzipan: 10.84); the comets that were studied by famous astronomers and feared by common folk. Her world is

141. "U' sono i gigli, ove le belle rose / Del volto tuo, pompe del Ciel, mio dono? / Ove le fiamme vaghe, et amorose / De gli occhi tuoi, mie gloria, ov'ite sono? / Ove i rai de le chiome luminose, / Che nel Ciel tolsi al più sublime trono? / Gia fui Madre felice, hor di dolore / Madre infelice, e d'infelice Amore."

142. In this, too, Marinella follows classical antecedents: see Manuel Baumbach, "Cupid," in *The Classical Tradition*, ed. Anthony Grafton, Glenn W. Most, and Salvatore Settis (Cambridge, MA, and London: The Belknap Press of Harvard University Press, 2010), 244.

143. On Marinella's utilization of *repetitio* and *amplificatio* see Maggi, "Introduzione," 20–21.

144. Found respectively at 7.33; 1.12; 5.32; and 2.28.

145. Mentioned at 8.68 and 2.61 respectively.

one that has seen the horrors of the plague (9.60), but also celebrates the agricultural cycle with its "singing" wheat fields (1.34).

Her biblical references run the gamut from the feeding of the Israelites in the desert to the "tongues of fire" that hover over the apostles at Pentecost. She also incorporates into her poem references to cult deities (Diana of Ephesus, Cybele, and Jupiter Ammon) whose worship and influence were pervasive throughout the territories of the Roman empire. The presence of Cybele, in particular, underscores Cupid's madness; she causes the madness, self-mutilation, and death of the young shepherd Attis, who becomes a cult deity in his own right, and her worship includes rituals that evoke the mad frenzy of the Furies.

All of these details, then, whether well known or arcane, contribute to the rich panorama of society and culture against which Marinella sets her tale.

Afterlife

It is difficult to ascertain the popularity of *Amore innamorato*, as of most texts printed in this span of time, since precursors of gazettes or newspapers did not yet circulate that would give us a sense of how Marinella's contemporaries reacted to it. Judging by the lack of reprints, we have to conclude that it was not very successful. It is nevertheless the case that the story of Cupid and Psyche continued to be recounted even after Marinella's poem appeared. In particular, Canto 4 of Giovan Battista Marino's *L'Adone* (originally published in Paris in 1623) includes an extensive retelling of Apuleius's story (293 *ottave*), to which he attaches an allegorical reading based almost literally on Fulgentius (rather than on Plato).[146] Marino was particularly attentive to his antecedents, in literary and linguistic terms, and many scholars have researched his numerous sources.[147] Nowhere does Marinella appear among them, which is not surprising, given the non-canonical status of her works. As Antonio Franceschetti has pointed out, Marino builds his poem in mosaic-like fashion, evoking works by others, "avoiding texts accessible and exploited by everybody, turning instead to those that are almost unknown or utterly forgotten."[148] It is therefore possible that Marino knew *Amore innamorato*, especially when we consider that he lived in Venice in the first decade of the seventeenth century and that his two-volume collection of *Rime* was printed in 1602

146. Ussia, *Amore innamorato*, 156–57. On Fulgentius's interpretation, see ibid., 142–43.

147. Giovanni Pozzi's apparatus, which accompanies his critical edition, includes a section devoted to them: Giovanni Pozzi, "Le fonti," in *L'Adone*, by Giovan Battista Marino, ed. Giovanni Pozzi, 2 vols. (Milan: Mondadori, 1976), 2: 89–102.

148. "[M]eglio evitare i testi accessibili e sfruttati da chiunque, e ricorrere invece piuttosto a quelli che sono pressoché sconosciuti o affatto dimenticati." Antonio Franceschetti, "Ancora su Amore e Psiche: la molteplicità delle fonti," in *The* Sense *of Marino*, ed. Francesco Guardiani (New York: Legas, 1994), 39.

by Ciotti (who published Marinella's *Colomba sacra* in 1595, *La nobiltà* in 1600 and 1601, and *Arcadia felice* in 1605).[149]

It is clear, as Giovanni Pozzi has pointed out, that Marino utilized both Apuleius and Udine's adaptation as his primary sources.[150] Pozzi uncovered four discrepancies between *L'Adone* and its antecedents, two of which could indicate that its author was aware of Marinella's poem.[151] The first one is an explicit omission of the fourth and final task that Venus imposes on Psyche, requiring her to go to the underworld to fetch Proserpina's makeup (4.277–78). Marinella does not include any chore in her poem, but she does include a trip to the underworld. This does not conclusively prove that Marino avoided this particular element because Marinella had exploited it, but it is worth noting.

Pozzi's second difference is "the presence in Marino of narrative segments absent from his models, or only sketched in them: such is the case with octaves 69–79, 84–87, and 136–43."[152] This is a more substantive possible instance of Marinella's impact on Marino's poem: stanzas 69–79 describe "the abandoned young woman" [giovinetta abbandonata] (4.69.1) utterly lonely and dispirited, in tears and addressing nature to express her feelings, as Cupid does in Canto 8 of *Amore innamorato* (see 8.15–18). In particular, octaves 4.79 of *L'Adone* and 9.12 of *Amore innamorato* present the response of mythical dwellers of the waters (nymphs and tritons in Marino, nymphs only in Marinella) to the dejected protagonist's cries.[153] With the redundancy that characterizes her poem, she does not confine Cupid's complaints to a few octaves (Marino has Psyche soliloquize in 4.72–77), but continues beyond, with more stanzas of Cupid's own words after the comments offered by those lesser deities (9.17–20). Here, too, we do not have any irrefutable proof of direct influence, but the possibility that Marinella's *Amore*

149. A thorough introduction to Marino's life and works is Alessandro Martini's entry dedicated to him in the online *Dizionario biografico degli Italiani:* <www.treccani.it/enciclopedia/giovan-battista-marino_(Dizionario-Biografico)/>. Claudia Micocci has underscored how Marino's Venus has bourgeois traits, making her closer to Marinella's than to many earlier depictions: Claudia Micocci, *Sondaggi sull'*Adone *di Marino* (Rome: Aracne, 2009), 44–46.

150. Pozzi, "Le fonti," 263.

151. Giovanni Pozzi, "Commento. Canto quarto," in *L'Adone*, by Giovan Battista Marino, ed. Giovanni Pozzi, 2 vols. (Milan: Mondadori, 1976), 2: 263–64.

152. "Presenza nel M. di segmenti narrativi assenti nei modelli, o in essi abbozzati: è il caso delle ott. 69–79, 84–87; 136–43." Ibid., 2: 264.

153. "Many nymphs and tritons lifted their heads to see who was consuming himself in such painful and sad notes; they broke the foam with dense circles. Surrounded by the sun that lights up the water, their cold chests touched by heavenly heat, they hurriedly fled and scattered pearls and corals all over the beautiful crystals" (4:79). [Per risguardar chi sia che si consuma / in note pur sì dolorose e meste, / rompendo in spessi circoli la spuma / molte ninfe e tritoni alzar le teste, / ma, cinti da quel sol che l'acque alluma / e tocchi il freddo sen d'ardor celeste, / per fuggir frettolosi, i bei cristalli / seminaro di perle e di coralli.] Giovan Battista Marino, *L'Adone*, ed. Pozzi, 1: 208.

innamorato influenced the longest narrative poem in the Italian literary tradition should be accepted and explored further.

Note on the Translation

Establishing the text of *Amore innamorato* is not difficult, as no manuscript has surfaced and there exists only one printing (by Combi in 1618), which is not particularly rare.[154] We have based our translation on the digitized version from the Università degli studi of Turin.[155]

In our translation, we have striven to render Marinella's poetry accessible to a twenty-first-century reader, in prose, while maintaining a sense of the complexity and richness of her language. As Laura Benedetti has pointed out about *Exhortations to Women and to Others*, Marinella "is a tough writer, displaying the characters of the Baroque prose of her time, full of convoluted sentences, repetitions, magnificent and redundant adjective usage, etc."[156] The same is true of her poetry in *Amore innamorato*: Marinella often repeats adjectives, phrases, sentences, and even short episodes. To twenty-first-century readers, most of it comes across as rhetorically clever; some of it, however, has the feel of lax or hurried writing. While not as polished as the heroic language of *Enrico*, Marinella's register is entirely appropriate to the topic and in keeping with prevailing taste and practice. Our translation of the whole text perforce reflects it in its entirety, with its brilliance and unevenness. We have not embellished it, since our goal is a faithful translation.

While Marinella writes in *presente storico*, a common stylistic choice in Italian, we have used the past tense throughout, as the use of the present to talk about the past is much less customary and could come across as contrived in English.

Lastly, as we mentioned above, Marinella often utilizes "Amore" (or even the term in lower case; capitalization was rather haphazard in early seventeenth-century printing) to refer to Cupid; in this, she mirrors the practice of classical authors such as Apuleius and Virgil. For the sake of clarity, we have differentiated references to the god of love (by using "Cupid") from mentions of love as a feeling

154. WorldCat shows eight copies in as many libraries in the US, and two in Germany. The Catalogo del servizio bibliotecario nazionale in Italy lists twelve libraries holding this volume, including the Biblioteca nazionale Marciana in Venice, which has two copies. The copy at Padua's Biblioteca civica is annotated in an anonymous hand. There exists a digitized copy from the Bilioteca nazionale centrale in Rome and another one from the Biblioteca storica di ateneo "Arturo Graf" at the Università degli studi in Turin.

155. It is found at < https://archive.org/details/imageGIX398NarrativaOpal>.

156. "[U]na scrittrice ostica, che presenta le caratteristiche della prosa barocca dei suoi tempi, ricca di frasi convolute, ripetizioni, aggettivazione magnifica e ridondante, ecc." Benedetti, "Tradurre Marinella," 216. Needless to say, our task as translators of poetry was even more challenging.

or emotion (translated as "love" as verb or noun). We are well aware that this clarification also compromises some of Marinella's "deep, perhaps irreconcilable, difference."[157] The lack of grammatical and syntactical markers in English would have made some instances incomprehensible to an English-language reader, so we opted for consistency.

Our goal in presenting this translation is to illuminate another facet of Marinella's extensive and wide-ranging literary work, avoiding the pitfall of privileging only a limited and ideologically skewed portion of this corpus and thereby enriching our appreciation for it in its entirety.

157. "[P]rofonda e forse irriducibile, differenza." Benedetti, "Tradurre Marinella," 219.

LOVE ENAMORED AND DRIVEN MAD
A POEM BY LUCREZIA MARINELLA

With arguments and allegories to each canto

To the Most Serene Lady
Caterina Medici Gonzaga
Duchess of Mantua and of Montferrat

Printed with permission of the authorities, and privileges, in Venice 1618
by Giovanni Battista Combi

Dedicatory Letter

To the Most Serene Lady
Lady Caterina Medici Gonzaga
Duchess of Mantua
and of Montferrat

There are many, indeed infinite, obligations that I have to the most serene House of Gonzaga, and in particular to the Most Serene Lady Leonora, now unhappily deceased.[1] She honored and praised me, not many years ago, both with titles and with magnificent gifts: So that I determined that all those fruits that might come from the garden of my hardly fertile mind belong to her, as if consecrated and offered to a temple of virtue. Hence, as I now send to the press my poem entitled Love Enamored and Driven Mad, I dedicate and address it to Your Serene Highness. My poem seeks only to represent the glorious victory that our divine half obtains over the senses—a small token of the many things I owe you, but accompanied by a great desire that it may in some way please and be enjoyed by you. And if it is accepted by you, who have in yourself the summit and perfection of every excellence, with the calmness of Your Most Serene brow, it will not discharge my obligations, but will increase them and render them greater.

Here I end, bowing humbly to Your Most Serene Highness.

Venice, May 6, 1618

The most devoted and humblest servant of Your Most Serene Highness,
Lucrezia Marinella

1. A reference to Eleonora Medici Gonzaga, who died in 1611. Her cousin, Caterina, became duchess of Mantua and Montferrat in 1617.

Allegory of the Poem

It seems to me (and I am not in doubt about this), Most Serene Lady, that the plot of my poem forms a unity (as everyone can see), and it is such that we can easily retain it in our memory. Its parts are united in such a way that it resembles an animal, a perfect animal, such as man. Since according to Plato there are three powers or rather faculties of the soul in man, which are called the rational, the irascible, and the concupiscent, we will say that Cupid is a symbol of the concupiscent, whose desire is to continue to take pleasure at the apex of all vain delights, and to be contrary to reason, just as Aristotle says in Book 7 of the *Ethics* in these words: "Concupiscence opposes reason";[2] Plato, too, in speaking of this, says in the *Phaedrus*: "We say that concupiscence is aberrant, departing from reason, and inclining toward baseness."[3]

Ersilia, pursued by Cupid so that she may yield and give in to his desires, will be understood as the rational part, of which Plato says in his book of virtue: "Reason is the power of the mind whose action is the search for truth."[4] Philosophers sometimes call this "intellect" and "mind," according to their various functions; holding the highest part of our nature, it is contrary to love, being of a noble and royal essence, and its desires lofty and venerable.

Iridio represents the power of irascibility, whose function is to contrast that of concupiscence, as Plato shows us in chapter 31 of the *Phaedo* in these words:

2. Throughout her Allegory, Marinella includes Latin quotations for which she does not always provide sources. In this case, she refers to Aristotle's *Nicomachean Ethics*, although her direct source is unknown; she may have chosen to use the canonical medieval Latin translation by Robert Grosseteste, with William of Moerbeke's revisions, or a humanistic Latin one, such as that of Leonardo Bruni. For a comprehensive study on the Latin translations of Aristotle's *Ethics* in the Renaissance, see David A. Lines, *Aristotle's* Ethics *in the Italian Renaissance (1300–1600): The Universities and the Problem of Moral Education* (Leiden: Brill, 2002). Unfortunately, no documents exist concerning the books that Marinella read and owned. It is also probable that unidentified Latin quotations were found in collections of citations, also known as *centoni*, which were often organized by topic rather than by author.

3. Plato's *Phaedrus*, composed ca. 370 BCE, was written as a dialogue between Socrates and the Athenian aristocrat Phaedrus, a member of the philosopher's inner circle. See also the note to the Allegory of Canto 10.

4. The "book of virtue" was *De virtute*, a text that was considered spurious in antiquity but in early modernity reputed to be authentic; as such, it was translated and published in Marsilio Ficino's Latin translation of Plato's texts, *Platonis Opera Omnia*, first printed in 1484. See Paul Oskar Kristeller, "Marsilio Ficino as a Beginning Student of Plato," *Scriptorium* 20, no. 1 (1966), 43–44. Although *De virtute* had been translated into Latin before Ficino, his *Platonis Opera Omnia* was the most widely circulated Latin translation of Plato's works in the early modern period. See James Hankins, *Plato in the Italian Renaissance* (Leiden: Brill, 1990): 1: 84 and 307. While we cannot be certain, it is highly possible that Marinella's source text for both *De virtute* and *Phaedrus* was a printing of Ficino's *Platonis Opera Omnia*.

"The irascible power of the soul opposes concupiscence."[5] As we have said, Cupid begs, invites, and persecutes Ersilia with promptness and diligence so that she might bow to his desires; however, she (who, as I said, is the image of reason) does not give in to his amorous prayers, but rather lives in solitary and secret woods. Indeed, reason values little or not at all the vain sensuality of the world; it is content with itself and confines itself to the woods of its noble thoughts.[6] There she adopts beasts, which should be understood as virtuous habits, because they are acquired only with difficulty and over a long period. Nor does she look at Cupid, who represents the senses; like an importunate lover he entreats and begs her not to disdain but to give in to his desires. He leaves nothing untried in order to delight in the pleasantness of pleasure, but his efforts are all in vain because a mind well grounded in goodness and in the excellence of good deeds does not hear false reasons that the deceitful senses offer but, taking pleasure in real delight, shuns and flees their bitter sweetness, withdrawing forever to the peak of its highest thinking.

The son of Venus, who would like to gratify himself, hates the chaste Iridio with bitter anger, who, as mentioned above, stands for the faculty of irascibility, which fights for rationality, as Plato in the *Phaedo* says in these words, speaking of such power: "It fights for reason." Indeed, the former battles for the latter, and battles ferociously, knocking down flattering blows and soft words, so that the sense of her venerable nature lives happily by acting well. But Cupid, although chased off and scorned by Iridio, does not hesitate to raise his daring brow, and moves his troublesome forces against him; like the horrid beast of Lerna, if deprived of a head it feels countless heads replace the one cut off, he is drunk and driven by the flames of the desire to satisfy all his foolish appetites.[7]

Cupid, stealing a lightning bolt from the hand of sleeping Jupiter, shows us that sensual desires of pleasure sometimes rob the intellect of its command, as Aristotle wisely wrote in Book 3, chapter 9 of the *Ethics*: "Pleasures, if they are overpowering, remove the mind from its realm."[8] Cupid, when he strikes Iridio

5. Not to be confused with *Phaedrus*; for a possible source, see the previous note. While *Phaedo* is divided into chapters, chapter 31 does not include the sentence cited, but refers to the persistence of desires as souls reincarnate successively.

6. In the original, "ragione" (reason) is grammatically feminine; it coincides with Ersilia, who embodies it, rendering the two indistinguishable in this passage and supporting Marinella's choice of a female character to embody a trait that—as we note in the Introduction—was traditionally associated with men. Likewise, later on in this paragraph, "mente" (mind) is feminine in Italian, leading Marinella to underscore the difference between Cupid (the senses) as masculine and Ersilia (reason, the mind) as feminine.

7. The "horrid beast of Lerna" is the hydra, a nine-headed snake with a miraculous ability to regenerate each one of them when they were cut off. Hercules succeeded in killing the hydra as the second of his twelve labors.

8. Book 3, chapter 9 of the *Ethics* deals with bravery. The section dealing with pleasures appears to be Book 7, chapter 14.

with the stolen lightning bolt, makes clear to us that concupiscence sometimes conquers and subdues irascibility, too. But see, he is now struck by Jupiter, which represents just judgment, that is, the intellect functioning with free will. Then Cupid, though struck by lightning, does not remain lascivious but becomes a weak warrior. Like a new Briareus, son of the earth,[9] he gathers his false appetites to assault reason, which, having already adorned itself with the armor of virtuous actions, like a tower, not only resists but topples the impregnable war-machines that the enemy continuously invents against it. In the end, he is vanquished and defeated by it and he throws away the alluring weapons of fleeting pleasures, and obediently surrenders to the empire of the intellect, which, answering Venus's prayers, ceases to torment him. Venus represents nature, as Lucretius intended in Book 1 of *De rerum natura*, where he says:

> Mother of Aeneas and of his Rome, and of gods
> and men the joy, dear Venus, who underneath the gliding
> heavenly signals busies the seas with ships and makes
> earth fruitful (for only through you are living things conceived
> and because of you they rise up to bask in the light of the sun).[10]

But Jupiter, understood as the intellect, knows that by removing the actions of Cupid he would cause the human race to dwindle, and so he stops afflicting him, as I already said. Cupid, as if laying his own nature aside, takes pleasure in the orders from rational Jupiter, who wants Cupid to be blindfolded as a penance for his past errors, so that in the future he may be contained and confined by justice and the reason of his rule, rather than be moved by a pleasing object. Jupiter does not want Cupid to get upset at what is a just and honest wish and, as if blind to the enticing beauties of the world, desires that Cupid let himself be guided by Jupiter's righteous will and no longer turn a defiant face against him. Therefore, the plot of my poem will resemble that glorious victory that our supreme part obtains against concupiscence.

Then, paintings, flowers, springs, gardens, waters, gold, palaces, gems, and other charms will be understood as objects of pleasure and lust that will invite the senses to enjoyment and transitory delights.

The Council of Jupiter[11] is intended to mean the union that the intellect summons among the virtues in order to oppose the senses. The arrow that Cupid

9. In Greek mythology, Briareus is one of three monstrous giants endowed with fifty heads and one hundred arms. Dante places him in the ninth circle of Hell to guard Cocytus, the frozen river inhabited by the souls of those who have betrayed their guests, family members, and citizens (*Inferno* 31).

10. Translation from Lucretius, *De Rerum Natura = The Nature of Things: A Poetic Translation*, trans. David R. Slavitt (Berkeley: University of California Press, 2008), 1.

11. A reference to the council called by Jupiter in 2.15.

constructed of various materials to wound Iridio and was stolen from him by Mercury, god of science and cunning, will signify the sharpness of those rebuttals that a wise and just man utters to a vicious and ignorant one.[12]

Iridio transformed into a flower[13] will signify virtuous men, who, like a flower full of inestimable sweetness, radiate precious spirits from their perfect actions.

The wedding of Cerberus and Megaera[14] symbolizes the company of vicious and evil people.

The muddy springs, dry fields, dark air, troubled sky, sad and dying animals, and the entire world reduced to its ultimate misery, will be understood as a soul deprived of divine grace, without whose aid, as the theologians say, it cannot live "or continue to exist."[15]

The return of Cupid to the beauty of soul and body, by which the world (about to fall into its original confusion) becomes beautiful, indeed perfect, will show us the coming of the celestial grace in the dry soul deprived of every good; clear fountains of divine nectar grow in it by the salutary and sweet countenance of celestial nectar, and the Heavens of the glory of God open and each virtue laughs with him.

Cupid having returned to the palace happy, healthy, and full of tranquility will be an example of a man who has lived according to the senses, but, having been touched by the pious hand of supreme mercy and having seen his errors, spends hours, nay, days, in the softness of a pleasant and holy rest.

The sad images of war and ruins that left the depths of hell to perturb and torment the world will show us that the evil hordes of Avernus[16] flee from any man who has put himself under the powerful hand of God.

Mars, Venus, and Love, who enjoy a lavish banquet together, will show that the rational disdain of a noble soul at the arrival of pleasantness and harmony, as symbolized by Venus and by Cupid having gotten rid of anger and ferocity, allows peace to return. In this way I desire that Mars, who inflames and ignites the unconquered hearts and the generous breasts of great and magnanimous princes, may accompany Venus and Cupid, who represent, as we have said, pleasantness,

12. Mercury steals the arrow from Cupid in 2.54.

13. Iridio is transformed into an iris in 6.39–41.

14. This occurs in 5.9–11.

15. In Chapter 3 of *De gratiarum sanctificatione*, Saint Albertus Magnus states that "Primo generaliter, et sic gratia est adjutorium divinum creaturae gratis impensum, et indifferenter ad quemcumque actum, quia sine hujusmodi adjutorio gratiae nihil possumus facere, imo nec in esse durare" [first, in general, grace is a divine help bestowed to any human for free, regardless of any action, such that we cannot do anything since the help of grace, much less continue to exist]. Albertus Magnus, *Compendium theologicae Veritatis* (Venice: Ioannes Antonius Rampazettum, 1588), 443.

16. The underworld. See the note to 2.24.

harmony, and friendship. In this meeting, may Mars lay aside the cruelty of his anger and his wrath in slaughtering, killing, and reducing everything to a miserable end, so that in our afflicted and miserable days peace may arise, at whose gracious return Heaven may laugh, sprinkled with shining white lights. The earth will surround itself with a cloak of joyousness and everything will rejoice in the breast of happy merriment, so that we can say with a happy brow: "fields laugh, houses rejoice, the temples of the immortal gods are happy, and in all things you will find beauty."[17]

17. This quotation, which can be identified thanks to a telling typographical mistake (*agri* instead of *agra*), is taken from Antonio Ricciardo, *Commentaria symbolica in duos tomos distributa* (Venice: Francesco de' Franceschi senese, 1591), 265.

Permission

I, Friar Giovanni Lodovico of Ravenna, reader in Holy Theology of the Order of Preachers and Commissioner of the Holy Office of the Inquisition of Venice,[18] have diligently read the book entitled "Love Enamored and Driven Mad," a poem by Lucrezia Marinella, and I did not find anything in it against our Catholic Faith and any other laws.

In Venice, on this day, 29 December 1617

18. Giovanni Lodovico Sechiario, a Dominican friar and "native of Ravenna or nearby," who was serving as a *commissario* or assistant to the chief Inquisitor of Venice, Giovanni Domenico Vignuzio, at the time this was written (the Dominicans were known as the "Order of Preachers," or *Ordo Praedicatorum*, abbreviated O.P.). On Vignuzio's death in 1622, Sechiario was appointed to succeed him. In supporting Sechiario's appointment, the papal nuncio noted "that he was over forty years of age and a Doctor of Theology," thereby satisfying the directives of the Inquisition as published in Rome in 1578. See Brian Pullan, *The Jews of Europe and the Inquisition of Venice: 1550–1620* (London and New York: I. B. Tauris, 1983), 31.

To the Reader

I was forced by the nature and condition of my poem, in which I write about Cupid, which the ancient poets placed in the realm of the gods, to use words such as God, Deity, Angelic, Divine, Heaven, Holy, Heavenly, and other similar words such as Chance, Destiny, and Fatal. It is not my presumption to bias in any way imaginable against the most certain truth of our faith or our most Holy Roman Church; to which I professed to be the most obedient and humblest daughter, as you very well know from my devout and sacred texts written by me and put into print.[19]

19. In her words to the implied reader, Marinella alludes to her previously printed works on religious or devout topics to establish her *bona fides* as a faithful follower of the Catholic Church. For an overview of Marinella's volumes published before *Amore innamorato* in 1618, see the Introduction. Throughout the poem, however, her use of biblical phrases—beginning with the reference to "tongues of fire" in the Allegory to Canto 1—clearly demonstrates her scriptural knowledge and devotion to the Church.

Canto 1

Argument of Canto 1

Cupid[1] becomes proud, mocks and scorns not just Iridio, a wise man with a firm soul, but he also disdains and does not care for the sublime excellence of the great Jupiter. He observes the pomp and beauty of images and flowers and manages to wound his enemy. Then he falls asleep in a bed of flowers in the breeze. The goddess, Cupid's mother,[2] arrives in Cyprus.[3]

Allegory

Cupid, mocking and vilifying Jupiter, will be understood as man who takes pleasure in the awfulness of evil deeds: led astray by the hand of the devil and having placed aside any obligation to reverence and any fear of blasphemy, he curses the name, the works, and the power of the heavens. Hurt Iridio, hounded by Cupid, will signify the just man who leaves behind the vanities of the wretched world and entrusts everything to God: he despises bittersweet things and baits hidden by manna[4] that the senses, his enemy, and the world with its thousand perils, its thousand tricks, and its thousand deceits place in front of him, so that he is attracted by the falseness of their flattery, may abandon heaven, and fall in the lap of eternal damnation. The images of the gods, the beauty of the royal palace, and of the garden of love will show us those grandeurs, honors, and riches.

Consequently, an ambitious man enters into a sea of pride, driven by the overblown winds of grandiosity, and raises himself with a mind full of boastfulness such that he not only mocks others, but does not care for heaven, on which he should train the eyes of his soul not at times, but I dare say always.

Cupid sleeps in the softness of the grass and of the flowers; our soul, drunk with sensual sweetness, sleeps among the flowers of lasciviousness, love, and pomp, without hearing heaven calling it to eternal beatitude with a thousand tongues of fire.[5]

1. Cupid was the Roman counterpart of the Greek Eros, the god of sensual, physical love and desire.

2. A reference to Venus, the Roman goddess of beauty, who was Cupid's mother by Mars (the Greek Ares), god of war.

3. Venus is sometimes called Cypris because the island of Cyprus was one of her most important cult sites, claimed by its residents as her birthplace.

4. As told in the Bible (Exodus 16), the Israelites were fed manna during their peregrinations in the desert, sustenance sent from God when they had nothing else to eat.

5. This is undoubtedly a reference to the events of Pentecost (Acts of the Apostles 2:1–11), in which the Holy Spirit descends on the place where Christ's Apostles and other followers have gathered. Tongues of fire appear above their heads, giving them the ability to speak in, and understand, all languages.

1. I sing of the way in which the great Thunderer, overcome by wrath, wounded Cupid with too bitter a love. I sing of the tears, the sighs, the sorrows, and the weeping of the one who became lover, and once was love. Like a sumptuous new giant governing the gods, he boasted of ruling and of reigning over them. I sing of how he became mad for love, and how he pulled out his hair and tore his golden plumage.

2. You, who steal other people's great merits away from consuming time with the hand of immortal glory, Muse, narrate the power, the magnificence, and the embellishments of him, whom the envy of ancient times conceals.[6] Tell how he was hurt, how he scorned the famous acts of the gods, and how he wandered foolishly on a lovely slope: The heavens laughed at his pain and at last lifted him back to his honors.

3. Cupid was enjoying himself by tempering simple beautiful souls with small flames and arrows; and although he gave the gods mortal punishments in the form of cruel fire and large wounds, they welcomed him and their souls were happy and content while in pain and sickness. He, satisfied, lived amid celebrations, at ease, enjoying games and laughter in splendid palaces.

4. Where the beautiful goddess, who appreciates leisure and wantonness, uncovered the utmost peaks of her beauty and pearls and roses, there he set his kingdom and took residence. Here was his diligence and grace to awaken amorous flames in others' breasts, inflict hoped-for wounds, and set strings and nets for unattached hearts and happy spirits.[7]

5. Not even a white blindfold covered the lively brightness of his beautiful eyes.[8] No daring tongue turned yet to mock his deity in joke or jest, but rather a group

6. The nine Muses, daughters of Zeus/Jupiter and Mnemosyne (Memory), embodied and inspired artistic endeavors such as music, comedy and tragedy, different poetic genres, and dance. It is unclear which one of the nine Marinella invokes to support her endeavor; Clio, the muse of history, is often represented as holding a scroll or a tablet on which she had recorded great deeds and accomplishments. It is noteworthy that she includes this requisite aspect of the epic in the second stanza of her poem, in the same position as that of Torquato Tasso's *Gerusalemme liberata*, one of her models, which also (like *Amore innamorato*) devotes the first octave to the subject matter of the work.

7. This is a reference to Venus and her palace, which was also Cupid's dwelling. Marinella foregrounds a location that will be important later on in the plot (Canto 8). It is described in some detail in stanzas 29–37 below.

8. In Canto 10, Marinella creates the story of Jupiter ordering Cupid to be blindfolded as part of his punishment, an event to which she alludes in the following stanza.

of lovers turned to sweet games and peaceful dances, revering him with fond affections and flowers, and sang high praises.

6. The height and proud contempt of his prideful heart, and the praises for himself, gave the heavens such shame and enmity that that unworthy one fell with punishments and cries.[9] The thought that he alone could surpass the gods through his glories and many triumphs was the reason why he was blinded, became mad, and had no shame.

7. Because the son of the Cytherean[10] saw himself dear to the heavens and to the world, he did not yield to the highest god, who ruled the heavens, in praises and esteem. Cupid wanted man to glorify him first, and he daringly wanted to put his foot on Jupiter's head.[11] He wanted every line and rhyme to praise him. One day, as Cupid fixed his eyes on a plain painted with flowers, jeering at the heavens, he said:

8. "I am god, I am god to myself, and there is nothing in the heavens that can conquer or match my deity. Not even you, great god, who fling your three-pronged weapon and govern everything and rule the world.[12] Nor you, who hold the great trident with a green veil and have a comfy seat among soft seaweed.[13] Nor you, who sublimely sit with eternal command between dead souls in the Kingdom of Avernus.[14]

9. Here Marinella offers her readers a reminder of Cupid's fall into madness and the reason for it, with echoes of Lucifer's pride, rebellion, and fall from grace. See for example Dante's concise definition of Lucifer as the one who "contra 'l suo fattore alzò le ciglia" [raised his eyebrows to his own maker]: *Inferno* 34.35.

10. Cythera, one of the Ionian islands of Greece, was dedicated to Venus, who therefore was also known as "the Cytherean." The island came under Venetian control in 1238, some three decades after the end of the Fourth Crusade, until the dissolution of the Republic at Napoleon's hand in 1797.

11. Marinella's phrase recalls a number of scriptural references. Psalm 110 begins: "The LORD said unto my Lord, Sit thou at my right hand, until I make thine enemies thy footstool." More significantly, God punishes the serpent in the Garden of Eden by prophesying that Jesus will "bruise [its] head" (Genesis 3:15) by redeeming man through his death and resurrection. The serpent represents Satan, whose story is also told in Revelation. In his pride, he rebels against God, leading to war in Heaven; he and his followers are ultimately defeated by an angelic army led by Michael, then cast out (Revelation 12:7–10). Lastly, Saint Michael is traditionally depicted in armor, holding a sword, with one foot on Satan's head; and the Virgin, as the new Eve, often is represented as standing on a snake.

12. A reference to Jupiter, ruler of the world, whose presence was felt on earth through his thunder (hence, the phrase "great thunderer" that Marinella uses in 1.1 above), believed to have three prongs.

13. The ruler of the sea, Neptune, was traditionally depicted with a trident in his right hand.

14. The last kingdom that Cupid mentions as beholden to him is Avernus, the underworld, ruled by Hades.

9. "I reign over the heavens, the earth, the air, the sea, the woods, the hills, the valleys, the fields, the meadows, the rivers, the springs, and the lakes. There, I have already taken and bound even the proudest beasts with my weapons. There is only one disloyal, useless, and superficial young man who is armed with more insanity than sense. This one battles against me and with his boastings shows my lost honor to all.

10. "I hit his heart with thousands of golden arrows, and thousands upon thousands of burning flames. He made these weapons dull and extinguished the flames with his bitter repulsion, rebellious to my wishes. Now that he leisurely sits with quiet desire in soft sprouting grass, I want to try again to inflict a cruel wound in his chest so that he may burn and faint.

11. "I will put in front of him the most graceful face that the sun ever saw, the most beautiful eyes that anybody would admire in a goddess in the heavens, a beautiful gait, a sweet smile, and golden hair. I will have my bow in hand, and I will be waiting, arrow ready on the bow, and that arrow will be such that makes tigers fall in love and gives burning affection with a thousand atrocious arrowheads to the chest."

12. He became silent and left happily, as if he had already hurt and captured the chaste and wise young man; in order to find a beautiful face, he chose to look through soft fields and bitter and wild places. Meanwhile, his enemy sang about the chaste goddess, the beautiful pastimes of the woods, and the fleeting beasts, at times in the thick shadows of a tall plane tree, and at times in that of a beech.[15]

13. His name was Iridio, the most beautiful, wise, and prim young man to ever adorn the world, and the coldest of hearts in our or ancient times. He was a despiser of Cupid, finding his delights in the forests, the woods, in the meadow, and in open fields with arrows, darts, nets, and strings, and dogs, to make this fury of bears and tigers useless.

14. Cupid burned with disdain against him because he proudly did not yield to his power. Now, in order to wound Iridio, he was looking for a worthy face that would attest down here to the beauty of the heavens. After he had searched his own realm at great length, he moved his feet, angry and spiteful that he could have not found in all the world as pretty and graceful a face as he desired.

15. The "chaste goddess" is Diana, associated with the moon, hunting, and nature. Devoted to her pursuits, she refused marriage, and her devotees were likewise chaste. The plane tree (*Platanus*), renowned for its shade, provides a leafy setting for conversation in Plato's *Phaedrus*, as well as Cicero's *De Oratore* (On the Orator); a species of this tree, *Platanus orientalis*, is said to have been the tree under which Hippocrates taught his students on the island of Kos.

15. When he least expected or hoped for it, as he returned, upset, to his ancient palace, an angelic countenance appeared to him: golden hair, scattered and flowing in the air, a face where it was eternally spring, a nymph who, like a goddess, awakened roses and violets as she moved her feet.

16. Vulcan's son[16] observed intently that celestial being and her noble face; overcome by amazement, he slowed his steps as if vanquished and conquered by such beauty. He wanted her to be the flame that would fully burn cruel Iridio, who sat in chaste joy. He wanted her to be the fire by which he would be consumed, igniting and drawing out his blood and his bones.

17. She was the only hope of King Emireno, his dear and beloved daughter. He held himself in higher esteem because of her great and supreme gifts than for the beauty that held her all the way up to the sublime heavens. She was adorned with so much virtue and extreme beauty that the sun had never seen before or after, but she was an enemy to love and lovers: her bosom drew great delight from woods and beasts.[17]

18. She was an illustrious follower of the one who shows her white face to us below from the high spheres,[18] nor was she inferior to her in her graces; these appeared in her eyes like a goddess. Her golden hair shone, partly loose in the air, partly to be admired in beautiful twists. Yet tied or loose, her hair made hearts prisoners with thousands of ropes. Indeed, all the light that we admire in a goddess seemed gathered in her.

19. Her eyes were not only eyes, but ardent flames in which her modest honor lived and hid, more lively, clearer and brighter than the sun when it shines its rays in the middle of the sky. Purple and milk extolled her face by mingling their beautiful colors, and on her mouth a happy ruby gleamed red, or the color of roses burned and shone.

20. So that Iridio might look at her and burn for her and be stricken by the light of her beautiful divine eyes, he made a dog that was dear to her pass by and then run away toward Iridio's dogs. She followed it so that he might return to her; she loved it so much that she disregarded twigs or thorns. Once she had gotten closer to the young man, she called her dog. He looked at it, praised it, but did not love it.

16. In one of the many versions of the myth of Venus, Vulcan was one of her lovers. Cupid was typically not presented as born of Venus and Vulcan; throughout the poem Marinella either misremembers her ancient mythology, or (more likely) she purposely adds a facet to the already complex pantheon of gods she utilizes in her poem.

17. In introducing Ersilia, Marinella echoes some of the terms she will use to present the character of Erina in her epic *Enrico*; see Stampino, "A Singular Venetian Epic Poem," 57–59.

18. Another reference to Diana, here through her identification with the moon.

21. He looked and was in awe of her golden hair, her sweet face, and her beautiful ways, and of her white skin that shone like splendid stars. Aware of all this, Cupid struck their hearts with arrows, nets, ropes and lightning, and flames. In time, Iridio dulled the arrows, iced the flames, tore the nets, and undid the rope.

22. As if hurling a weapon against hard marble, or as if throwing fire into icy waters, they were blunted and extinguished: the torments of love could not find a place in his chaste bosom. Ice cannot continue to exist by ardent flames, or flames by ice: in a short time, opposite qualities consume each other and together they battle all the time and there is no hope for peace.[19]

23. Similarly, the intense burning and the hard freeze of chastity and of love battle every time, or rather, they don't battle, I conceal the truth: ice won over the fire that enamors. Cupid filled earth, air, and the heavens with laments and amorous cries. The cruel one was in anguish and pain, and he was upset that human will could have such influence over divine power.[20]

24. Like a common farmer who sees the needed fodder scattered on the ground by the rage of the heavens that fells pines, scatters and hurts his dear flock, and brings war to everything, he sat, stunned, by himself.[21] Pale and sighing, he stared at the ground and groaned; he did not hear anyone else, since his mind was fully concentrated on his many injuries.

25. Thus was Cupid. The young maiden returned with her loyal companion to her usual place.[22] The chaste young boy stood and unleashed a yell as he called his dogs, Olympus and Atus, to the hunt. Cupid remained alone, harboring, indeed nurturing, disdain and hatred. Sad and inconsolable that he could not hurt Iridio, he could find no peace, torn apart and undone by shame and pain.

26. He was engrossed in thoughts, holding on to an idea that he would immediately let go, only to grab on to another that emerged, but not for long, going back

19. Here, Marinella incorporates in her epic poem the rhetoric of Petrarchan love, expanded and intensified by her Baroque contemporaries; the paradoxical juxtaposition of fire and ice is used to describe the alternating and bewildering emotional states of a human in love.

20. Marinella underscores her own rhetorical abilities both implicitly (see the chiasm at the opening of the stanza: burning is to love as freezing is to chastity) and explicitly, via the first-person verb (*'l vero io celo* "I conceal the truth")—including even the first-person pronoun, which is redundant in Italian since the verb ending includes it.

21. Through this simile, Marinella uses agriculture as a way to depict the expected cycle of nature and life, and the destruction and destabilization that its breach generates. Another one is in Canto 9 (specifically, 9.53).

22. It is clear that Ersilia's "loyal companion" is her dog; this also serves to reinforce Cupid's failure to turn Iridio into her human companion and partner.

to the first one again only to discard it, picking up another one that floated up. At last, becoming bitter, he realized that the young man was made of jasper,[23] and thus by himself he took the decision to make an arrow so strangely hardened that he would cry and sigh forever.[24]

27. This thought immediately chased the thick clouds of discontent from his troubled brow, and sweet light winds of hope cleared his face by changing the atmosphere. His many beauties laughed happily, like the sun when it pushes the clouds away from itself, and the free leader of the army of love shone with a sweeter light. What sun surrounds itself with rain clouds? The courageous leader struck the crowd of lovers with a very soft light.

28. He happily returned to his palace to rest his dear and divine limbs. It stood in a flowered countryside and among fresh rivers, and it was richly appointed. Here were happy events free from sadness, laughter, parties, and play all together. All comfort and pomp were admirable gifts of his father, Vulcan.

29. That sublime mansion burned and shone like a diamond in which the sun reflected itself. Its tall spire almost brought the huge building, wonderfully adorned, up to the sky. Above its golden top an image of Cupid shone and emitted light. That statue, adorned by excellent art, pushed its foot on the ground, demonstrating its tremendous force.

30. This showed his power and indicated that he was lord and master on earth and in the heavens, wherever Phoebus spread its golden rays and led the day and drove out sleep.[25] You could never see such dear and precious labor, nor could one ever see such elsewhere. Here the desired worth and the delicate gold yield to the fine work of illustrious hands.[26]

23. Jasper, a form of quartz prized in ancient times, is mentioned both near the beginning and at the end of the Bible, in corresponding Old and New Testament references. In Exodus 28:20, it is the last of the twelve stones in the breastplates of the high priests, each stone representing one of the tribes of Israel; in Revelation 21:19, it is the first of the twelve stones making up the foundation of the city walls in the New Jerusalem. Jasper's protective qualities, then, appear to prevent Iridio from being hurt by Cupid, and have the same effect on Ersilia in 3.8.

24. Marinella's description of Cupid's confused and bewildered thoughts offers an early example of how he feels once he loses his senses due to Jupiter's punishment.

25. Phoebus (meaning "bright") was the most common epithet for Apollo, Diana's twin brother; he was at times identified with Helios, the Greek god of the sun, and it is in this sense that Marinella refers to him here.

26. Rhetorically, Marinella attempts to involve her implied reader in her description with a reference to "you" and the deictic adverb "here," indicating proximity. On "the fine work of illustrious hands," see also 8.46 and 9.52.

31. The doors shone with the finest silver, resounding hinges and leaves were made of gold; the floors were made of rubies and emerald, and the columns of bright diamonds. Here in a hundred places were effigies of gods, of divine men who were captured in the battles of love, different in their faces and features and made of gold and enamel.

32. While looking through the gold-adorned doors at a beautiful garden, one saw a tall alder and a greening laurel tree, a vine soaring to the sky from its twisted trunk, shadowy woods, high hills, and above them bright palms and the sacred myrtle,[27] cool rivers, magnificent springs, calm lakes, low valleys, dark caves, and joyful meadows.

33. Here the harsh breaths of cruel Boreas did not disturb the serene sky with dark horror; neither did trembling crystals transform into chilly ice or pluck flowers from blooming fields. Not a damp Auster hidden in a veil could beat the flowers down, destroy the pastures, and flood the meadows, or by squeezing the clouds add the crash of thunder and the flash of lightning to this place.[28]

34. Instead, the calm sky was dressed in pure white and in sweet joy lighted by blazes. Not even the evil poison of a menacing comet could mar and perturb the lighted fields.[29] Under such a dear lovely sky, without a plough moving or marking it, the earth brought out all that it could give: blond spikes wavered in the open fields, singing.[30]

35. Lovely flowers and fronds preserved an eternal smile with perpetual beauty. Beautiful Narcissus, desirous of his own beauty, gazed at himself in the water from

27. Palm branches were awarded to winning athletes in ancient Greece, and in Roman times the goddess Victory was often represented as holding a palm frond. The myrtle is a flowering shrub common in the Mediterranean area; in mythology it was considered as sacred to Venus (hence Marinella's adjectival choice above), and in Roman times it was a symbol of victory.

28. In Greek mythology, Boreas was the god of the northern wind, which would bring winter; Auster was the southern wind, carrying humidity and rain with it.

29. In Marinella's time comets were considered bad omens. She was a child when the Great Comet of 1577 passed close to Earth and was viewed by people across Europe and Asia Minor (including the Danish astronomer Tycho Brahe and the Ottoman scholar Taqī al-Dīn), but it is possible that family members and older friends would have spoken of it. Coincidentally, in 1618 (the year of the publication of *Amore innamorato*), Marinella and her fellow Europeans would experience another "Great Comet" passing over Earth. Cf. the reference to "an unholy comet" in the "high fields" of the sky in 2.5.

30. A standard poetic reference to wheat.

a high bank.[31] Clytia turned her pale face to the yellow and ardent hair of her beloved. Live roses covered in celestial dew glistened happily.[32]

36. The air was the reason why happy trees preserved everlasting honors and remained invincible, and a loving spirit the reason why grass and flowers were awakened with sweet murmuring. With perpetual style you made way for fecund plants in those places and in this one, without anybody's work, flowers, fronds, and fruits: some were born, others got old, and others matured.[33]

37. Charming little birds sang happy songs in intricate paths made up of branches. Their loving notes and endearing dances drove their flights, early or late, but fast. Moving crystals sweetly echoed their song and pleasant caroling.[34] The air dancing among leaves and waves responded to their joy with their whispers.

38. Pastures, caverns, valleys, hills, woods, mountains, fronds, flowers, leaves, fruits, herbs, air, leafy shades, warm sky, clear lakes, fresh springs, sweet songs, pleasing odors, lofty palaces were the resorts of love, whether the sun set or rose. No poverty or discomfort was seen here; among such beauty was a pleasing meadow, and laughter and song dwelt in the grass.

39. Among them, Hebe was the goddess who always maintains the honor of youth in her pleasant appearance: age did not change her magnificent and serene eyes, the lively purple on her cheeks or the lilies on her breast. She was crowned with roses, her blond hair was undone, and each word she said was sweet; she wore a green skirt, and among red, purple, and yellow flowers, she enjoyed beautiful dances.[35]

40. Having arrived at his palace, Cupid stopped his wandering feet in a lovely room, in which he admired the excellence of sublime painting: the worth of gold

31. The story of Narcissus is narrated in Book 3 of Ovid's *Metamorphoses*: having rebuffed the nymph Echo, he was subjected to the revenge of Nemesis, fell in love with his own reflection in a pool of water, committed suicide, and became a flower (the daffodil) that grows by the water.

32. Clytia was a water nymph who fell in love, unrequited, with Helios, the sun god, to whom Marinella alludes through his "yellow and ardent hair." She turned into the flowering plant heliotrope, whose name invokes the action of turning toward the sun, as octave 41 explains. Her story is briefly narrated in Book 4 of Ovid's *Metamorphoses*.

33. It is difficult to understand who Marinella addresses directly in these lines. The most logical possibility is an apostrophe to Venus as the giver and source of life, following classical authors like Lucretius.

34. The phrase "moving crystals" [mobili Christalli] has a notable antecedent in Tasso's *Gerusalemme liberata* 16.9.3, in the description of Armida's garden, which later (octave 12) also includes references to singing birds.

35. As the stanza makes clear, Hebe was the Greek goddess of youth, who also served as cupbearer for gods and goddesses on Mount Olympus.

yields to the art that he himself admired. He saw himself in every image in such a way that you would say that he loved and breathed without breath,[36] had senses, life, and motion; if you turned your eyes to it, you would not deny that it talked.

41. Let the eyes and spirit be the judges: life was not lacking from those celestial images. You could say that one laughed, the other talked, yet another was lost and fled, and the other cried. One saw Clytia turn her pale face to her beloved sun with loving amorous gestures. Over there was Mercury, burning up and taking great pleasure as he looked at Herse.[37]

42.[38] Not far, the exquisite and highly admirable work of an illustrious artist depicted the beautiful Aegina, burning up and becoming red in such a way that it seemed that Jupiter had manifested himself to her as fire, elsewhere as a shepherd and a satyr, and now in the form of a serpent.[39] These are all effects of love. Great, indeed supreme, heights and indolent desires go together poorly.

43. One could see how he descends as golden light, surrounding beautiful Io in a thick cloud. Elsewhere his glance was chaste, his hair golden, his heart lewd, turning toward Callisto. The honorable load of bow and quiver dangle from his back in an elegant, refined way; he looked like the night sun, the goddess of the stars, by his face, actions, and features.[40]

44. In order to extinguish a recent burning fire, he wore the silver feathers of a white swan. Here he accepted the hiding of his celestial light under the guise of an

36. An example of polyptoton, where different forms of the same verbal root are repeated in close proximity.

37. On Clytia, see the note to stanza 35, above. Mercury, Roman god of commerce, messages, trickery, and eloquence, fell in love with Herse, but her sister Aglauros barred his path to her and was transformed into a statue; the story is narrated in Ovid's *Metamorphoses*, Book 2. In the following canto, Mercury will carry out Jupiter's punishment of Cupid for his pride by making him "unhappy by his own arrows" (2.36).

38. In the original, there is no octave 42, but two octaves are numbered 45. We have therefore corrected the numbering of these stanzas.

39. In Book 6 of the *Metamorphoses*, Ovid tells the story of the "illustrious artist," Arachne, who weaves a tapestry depicting the many guises assumed by Jupiter in his amorous pursuits. Jupiter appears to Aegina "as fire," to Mnemosyne as a shepherd, to Antiope as a satyr, and to Proserpina as a serpent. And just as Cupid will be punished by Jupiter for daring to set himself above "the highest god," the mortal Arachne is punished for daring to challenge and defeat the goddess Athena in a weaving competition; enraged, Athena transforms her into a spider.

40. Marinella alludes here to two further episodes in which Jupiter seduced women. Io was transformed into a heifer in order to hide Jupiter's lust for her from his wife, Juno; there are several versions and literary sources for this story. Callisto, a devotee of Diana, was seduced by Jupiter, who had taken on Diana's appearance; she became pregnant, was banished by Diana, and was transformed into a bear, later becoming the constellation Ursa major (Ovid, *Metamorphoses*, Book 2).

ox, for love; its skin was like snow, its horns appeared like shining jewels, its brow was happy like a human one and its graceful face was handsome, not an unworthy spoil for such a lover.[41]

45. You saw among royal virgins and pleasant flowers the noble daughter of famous Agenor, who spread such beauties and splendor from her hair and glittering eyelashes that it was not, and did not look like, great wonder that she enamored the heavens with her graces; indeed, it was greatly surprising that the one who put everything ablaze through love did not burn himself.

46. There one saw how beautiful Europa, unwise and joyous, sat on the back of a bull. Who did not recognize it to be Jupiter? It carried its hope to the waves and moved with a misleading gait. She had her hair scattered and she sighed and groaned in vain, as her predator did not return her to the herd; she seized one horn and held her beautiful eyes on the receding banks, deprived of hope.

47. Then you saw Phoebus shining with his golden hair, the source of eternal golden light, whose illustrious and venerable brow was not yet encircled by glorious laurel. He ran there without rules or decorum, nor did he care for ditch, valley, hill, or mountain. He seemed to change his gait and to breathe, as though one could hear the sound of his voice and his sighs.[42]

48. He ran, tired, a prey of Cupid. Before, he had despised the power of his bow and arrows. Now he followed, loved, and desired one who hated and fled from him; he foresaw another's evils, but not his own. Here was Daphne turning green; still, he did not forget the passions that were almost fatal to him, kissed those lukewarm branches, and surrounded new fronds with his blond hair.

49. Then one saw the great lord of Dis, burning up, kidnap beautiful Proserpina, his hands rich with jewels. He took her, pensive and alone, from a meadow.[43] There was the most important god of the occean holding Amphitrite's beautiful

41. Stanzas 44 to 46 recount Jupiter's physical transformations to seduce mortal women after whom he lusted. After briefly mentioning how he accosted the Spartan queen Leda in the guise of a swan (Ovid, *Metamorphoses*, Book 6), Marinella describes in detail how he became a white bull to abduct Europa—daughter of Agenor, king of Tyre in Phoenicia—from the seashore and possess her on the island of Crete. Ovid tells Europa's story in *Metamorphoses*, Books 2 and 3, as well as in Book 6, in which she is one of the women depicted by Arachne.

42. On Phoebus (Apollo), see the note to octave 30, above. Here and in the following stanza, Marinella refers to his unrequited love for Daphne, who in order to escape from him was transformed into a laurel tree (Ovid, *Metamorphoses*, Book 1). The laurel was forever after sacred to Apollo.

43. Proserpina was kidnapped by Pluto, or Hades, king of the underworld; because she was the daughter of Ceres, or Demeter, the goddess of grains and agriculture, her yearly absences to return to her husband meant that the growing season was curtailed (Ovid, *Metamorphoses*, Book 5). "Dis," or Dīs Pater, was a Roman god of the underworld whose identity became subsumed under those of Hades

breast and kissing her ivory throat. He showed the power of love, and how it hid ice in fire and fire under the waves.[44]

50. You saw Atalanta, who kindled a thousand souls with her milk-white innocence and ignited fresh roses; her skirt moved as she ran, as tiredness and sweat made her capable limbs even more adorned. Her beautiful hair, much more shimmering than gold, wandered on top of the untouched snow of her white neck. She loved and hated lovers, although she was beloved; love towered over those who harbored mortal fear in their breasts.[45]

51. There was fetching Hippomenes, who conquered the maiden with his beautiful face and golden apples, rather than with a swift run; he received a crown and glory in joy and laughter. Not far from one or the other, sitting with a wild look and a short blonde mane, was the great mother, who changed them into ferocious lions around her ornate cart.

52. There were thousands and thousands of images painted of eternal deities and of mortal men dominated and conquered by Cupid with lightning arrows in horrendous battles. Cupid looked on and reflected about the quantity and identities of the gods that he had already taken and bound; he thought about his high triumphs, his glory, and the palms and victories he had obtained from them.

53. As he looked and thought, a sea of supreme exhilaration spread in his heart and breast; he took pleasure and laughed, full of rich magnificence, that the greatest god was so loaded with crazy madness.[46] He loosened the ties of his biting tongue, which

---

and Pluto, although Dante immortalized him in the City of Dis (*Inferno*, Canto 9). As god of wealth, his hands are "rich with jewels" that originate as minerals found underground.

44. Amphitrite was the wife of the sea god Poseidon (the Roman Neptune), and according to Hesiod was a daughter of the primordial sea deity Nereus, who addresses Cupid in Canto 4. On Nereus and Amphitrite, see the notes to 1.62 and 1.66 below.

45. Atalanta is the exception in this catalogue of women after whom Jupiter and his fellow gods lusted; a princess and daughter to a king who wanted a son, she was brought up to enjoy hunting, and eventually took an oath of virginity to the goddess Artemis (the Roman Diana). Note how Marinella subtly reminds her readers about the choice by underscoring "the untouched snow of her white neck." As octave 51 recounts, Hippomenes won a foot race against Atalanta by distracting her and slowing her down with three golden apples, and was able to marry her. Ovid, in Book 10 of the *Metamorphoses*, narrates how the goddess Cybele ("the great mother") punished them for making love in her temple by transforming them into lions, who ever after drew her chariot (see 9.29).

46. This is a turning point in the narrative: the sheer number of episodes concerning Jupiter's lust that Cupid observes in Venus's palace convinces him of his superiority. His speech, taking up four stanzas (54 to 57), is the first indication of his hubris, and it results in his eventual comeuppance—to wit, in the rest of the poem. This list of Jupiter's conquests echoes the inventory of lovers in Petrarch's *Triumphus Cupidinis* (*The Triumph of Love*), particularly those in Part 2, lines 136ff, which are drawn from Ovid's *Metamorphoses*.

earlier had been accustomed to happy and gay notes; now he eliminated the honors due to the gods and, as he was wont, he boasted his arrows with these words:

54. "Oh, my pomp, my glories, my delights, oh my favorite arrows, you bestow dear affections on the Tagus and the Ganges,[47] but more so on the heavens, and if anyone cries, he cries sweetly! You make clouded intellects clear, you make those who are hurt and in anguish satisfied and happy; you happily sweeten and calm breasts from Jupiter's poisons and Mars's anger.

55. "I tame, I conquer, I exceed the greatest and the most powerful gods that sit in the heavens. As much as the flowers in the meadow yield to the pines or the high oak tree exceeds the low grass, to the same degree their honors yield to my magnificence and their power to mine. If I am the greatest of all gods, why do I have to yield to man? Is there a reason, I ask?

56. "But I will make it so that in the end my enemy will be so battered by me and conquered by cruel and inevitable ruin! He will be a wreck pushed to tears and groaning. Then he'll see that my power is high and divine, once he's tied up in my rope. It won't be that his begging will make me turn or bend until his bones are joined to one another.

57. "I will never be able to accept that a young, inexperienced, and unwise man may mock, despise, and disgrace me, singing to my humiliation among ash and beech trees. I can stand it only so much: will I be compelled to surrender to an alpine heart[48] and to a bitter and savage spirit? Will I remain idle and be offended every hour and upset every hour, without taking my revenge?"

58. As he said this, he moved to go to his garden with his snow-white foot. It was not hard for him to leave the rich gates of his house to delight in cool breeze. Once he arrived where sounds make every bitter care light thanks to air, water, birds, fronds, and leaves, he stopped his lovely step in the grass and he sat, rested, and slept.

59. He seemed made of purple and ivory, in the arms of the flowers, a celestial picture of high beauty, if you did not see the air softly move the crinkly tie in his

47. The Tagus is a river on the Iberian peninsula, which has its source in Spain and its mouth in Portugal. The Ganges is a river born in India and flowing into the Bay of Bengal. Here Marinella utilizes them to indicate all known land, from west to east, over which Cupid believes his power to extend.

48. The Alps are the highest mountain range in Western Europe. Cupid's expression seems to mean that Iridio is a wild, uncivilized man, and therefore his resistance to love is all the more unacceptable to Cupid. The Alps, moreover, comprised such a formidable natural barrier in ancient times that Hannibal's crossing of the mountain range with his army in 218 BCE would be considered one of the greatest feats in the annals of warfare. Cupid could also be saying that Iridio's heart was as hard as mountain rock; cf. his anguish over the "rocky heart" of Ersilia in 3.9.

blond hair. The earth laughed, and the joyful heaven and the luminous day turned around him laughing, the one who made it so that harmful flames would remain alongside ice in one single breast, harboring not insincere a faith to both.

60. It seemed as though every angel sang about that noble son, about his greatness, honors, weapons, bow, nets, ropes, fire, and ferocious claw full of sweetness and free of every trouble. The charming rose and the lily opened up here, and over there a source cleared a way; it seemed that twigs, rivers, and the wavy ocean brought deep rest to him with silent sounds.[49]

61. Here a marine shell came sailing the trembling waves of the calm and sweetness-laden sea, which blowing breezes pushed to the pleasant shore of the famous Cyprus.[50] In it you saw a goddess endowed with angelic features: beautiful rosy face, milk bosom, and golden curly hair, to which the most clear and luminous rays of the sun yielded.

62. The beautiful Cytherean was then happily returning from sweet diversions by way of her native sea. She had been with the silver-footed Thetis, and with Ino, Melicertes, and Panopaea.[51] A gentle appearance sat on her beautiful face, and although her heart did not laugh, she laughed. With her graceful and charming laugh, she made her loving face more beautiful.[52]

63. All of her immaculate body was softer than swan plumes and whiter than milk: gentle frost or pure untouched snow do not come down from mountains or a wandering hill. The bright bosom that extolled her breast seemed to have been made by the very hands of Cupid, endowed with the same whiteness that covers the face of the goddess of Delos in the sky.[53]

49. We have an example of Marinella's complex and somewhat paradoxical word choices: in this case, "twigs" are associated with "rivers" and the "ocean" to help Cupid's rest with "silent sounds."

50. See the note to the Argument of Canto 1, above.

51. Thetis, Ino, Melicertes, and Panopaea were all deities living in waters; here they accompany Venus in her marine voyage back to her palace. Thetis, the mother of Achilles, was referred to as "silver-footed" by Homer in Book 18 of *The Iliad*; she, Panopaea, and Amphitrite (stanza 49) were daughters of the sea god Nereus. Ino was originally a mortal queen of Thebes, and Melicertes her son; they were changed into sea deities and their names changed to Leucothea (the "white goddess") and Palaemon (see also the note to stanza 66, below).

52. Venus's appearance on a shell and accompanied by water goddesses could have reminded Marinella's contemporaries of stage entrances during mythological performances. The incidental remark that "although her heart did not laugh, she laughed" is both a reference to her feelings and to acting out a role in a specific and pointed way.

53. The goddess of Delos, or Delia (see octave 66), is Diana. According to a version of her myth, she was born on the island of Delos, along with her brother Apollo; their mother, Leto, wanted to hide

64. Her blonde hair, free from any ribbon and far shinier than gold, was prey to the air; parts fell, adorning her face with lively purple and beautiful privet,[54] and parts waved downward, undone, bestowing more grace on the snow of her bosom; it looked as if immaculate ivory was richly adorned all around with gold.

65. Thousands of loves sat around her, mocking, charming, and festive young boys. One held her; another spread her shiny golden hair to the errant breeze; yet another offered her white flowers, with enjoyment, sweet smiles, and peaceful features; one presented a mirror, in which you could look with beautiful eyes and delight and be satisfied by her beauty.

66. Through the salty countryside[55] the slim daughters of Nereus sang and danced in sweet turns; likewise, the burning stars honored Delia by dancing in the eternal spheres. The liquid sapphires of the sea splashed on their pretty and charming faces. Good Triton sounded his great horn, and Proteus followed the goddess and Palemon.[56]

67. Only a sweet breeze wrinkled those beautiful waves: winds and sky stopped in front of such a goddess. The god of Delos spread his tempered rays, seized by a loving fire.[57] Zephyrus moved her blonde golden hair instead of sail; it did not long for a nobler veil.[58] Softly and lightly, it led that beautiful ruler from the large sea to her kingdom.

68. She found her son in the grass and among flowers, softly asleep and resting. The air brought him sweet scents: lilies and jasmine opened up and roses laughed. As she admired the conqueror of hearts, her mind became happy and joyful, and she kissed and praised him, since she took him to be the only pledge of her beauty.

---

while giving birth to children conceived with Jupiter, to avoid the wrath of Hera, the Roman Juno, his wife.

54. The privet is a shrub that blossoms with abundant white flowers; classical authors such as Ovid mentioned it as a paragon of perfect whiteness, alongside other flowers such as lilies.

55. A phrase to mean "the sea."

56. Nereus, the "Old Man of the Sea," appears in 4.19–21 as he rises out of the water to address Cupid; his daughters—including Thetis and Panopaea (referred to in stanza 62 above), and Amphitrite (referred to in stanza 49)—were known as the Nereids. Triton, the herald of the sea god Poseidon (the Roman Neptune), was the son of Poseidon and Amphitrite. Proteus was another primordial water deity, known in particular for his ability to change shapes. Palaemon, originally named Melicertes, was one of two sons of Ino (stanza 62, above); he and his mother were changed into sea deities after leaping to their deaths to escape Ino's husband, Athamas, who in madness had killed his other son, Learchus.

57. A reference to Apollo as god of the sun, born with his sister Diana on the island of Delos.

58. Zephyrus is the embodiment of the westerly wind in Greek mythology.

Canto 2

Argument of Canto 2

With his own hands, Vulcan's son tempered a terrible arrow in Etna's great fire.[1] Upset, Jupiter called the eternal gods to a great council in his royal hall. Mercury descended to earth[2] and inflicted a mortal wound[3] to the chest of Cupid, who was attempting to wound the chaste and beautiful Ersilia in her sad brow; instead, he sent cold arrows into her heart.

Allegory[4]

Cupid, crafting an arrow to wound Iridio, presents us with our common enemy: inflamed by fiery anger, he sends against the goodness of a perfect soul a thousand thunderbolts of pride and arrogance and a thousand additional worldly trifles. These vehicles are quite often sent away by the perfection of our righteous mind, and end up striking their own maker in the middle of his heart. Jupiter, calling up a council to rebuke Cupid, will be the reasonable part [of the soul] that calls all virtues, strenuously acquired, to tame and subjugate the senses, as a prudent captain calling his armed troops. Mercury, stealing the arrow from Cupid (who has crafted it himself), will represent to us prudence, who foresees and predicts things and wins over them, crushing the forces of opposing enemies. Cupid, wounded and overcome by Ersilia's beauty, will show us the senses subjugated and squashed by the effective reasons of our better soul. Cupid carelessly wounding Ersilia with a leaden arrow will manifest for us an imprudent man, who carries out his acts without care or reflection; as these mostly turn out to be negative, he most wrongly calls his destiny thankless, believing it to be the author of those errors that he himself imprudently committed.

1. Mount Etna is an active volcano in the eastern part of Sicily. According to Roman mythology, the workshop of the god Vulcan, blacksmith of the gods, was located underneath it. Vulcan was married to Venus, the goddess of love; throughout the poem Marinella calls Cupid "Vulcan's son," though in classical mythology Cupid was Venus's son by Mars.

2. The Italian original reads *al pian*, literally, "to the plain"; this underscores the difference between the lofty, mountainous abode of the gods and the locale where humans live.

3. Since Cupid is a god, and therefore immortal, he cannot sustain a "mortal" wound. Marinella's word choice underscores the radical departure from accepted behavior that she depicts for us, and it anticipates Jupiter's remark in his speech in 2.27 below.

4. On Cupid and Jupiter, see the note to the Argument of Canto 1. On Mercury, see the note to 1.41.

1. After he restored his afflicted soul and his sick senses in the sweet forgetfulness of a welcome sleep, he woke up and opened his eyes. He sat up in a beautiful meadow, going through immense seas of thoughts; then quickly he ran to the thankless chest of Iridio, whose spirits were alight with chaste and noble inclinations. Full of wrath, he wanted to take revenge over his scorn with a vengeful arrow.[5]

2. In order to craft it such that it would wound and injure a heart made of ice, as he wished to do, in such a way that the knowledge and superhuman valor of doctors and magicians would be unable to heal it, he intended to go to Etna to carry out his desires at the crude fire of its sulfurous flames; he wanted to temper his arrow so that it would be better than the arrow of death.[6]

3. He stood up and left the garden and his lofty and illustrious kingdom, admirable in its beauty. He went where that big giant, fierce to behold, strikes disdainful fire from his heart up to heaven.[7] The divine archer[8] wanted to carry out his cruel plan where it was hottest; he boiled, mixed, and blended such things that his arrow might provoke deep wounds.

4. Mad desires, harsh disdain, fiery rage, empty error, sad worries, tenacious hatred, copious tears, great troubles, and sorrowful thoughts all mixed with the unbridled fire of a blind flame, insane fury, noxious fear, false and disillusioned hope, false peace, uncertain happiness, and certain troubles: he added extreme damage to those damaging acquisitions.[9]

5. As he removed it from the fire and unveiled it to the sun, it seemed that it burned and blazed with a mortal fire; similarly, an unholy comet is accustomed to show lethal fire from the high fields.[10] Happy are those who adore and worship

5. Interestingly, the subject of all these verbs is understood in the original; Cupid is present, indeed pervasively so at the beginning of this canto, but his name is absent.

6. The "arrow of death" is Jupiter's thunderbolt, believed to kill whoever was struck by it.

7. Etna is personified as a man, following mythology and the gender of the noun *vulcano* (volcano) in Italian.

8. Cupid was identified as an archer because his most prominent symbols were his bow and arrows, with which he struck the hearts of mortals and gods to make them fall in love, or reject someone else's love.

9. In the last line, Marinella utilizes polyptoton—here, the repetition of the root *danno* (damage) in close proximity—to conclude a difficult stanza and to underscore the negative consequences of Cupid's actions.

10. The sky is often referred to as the "high fields" due to its position as well as to the scattered nature of the stars, which might remind those living in a rural society and agricultural economy of seeds. On

love! Who will it be that might survive his arrows unvanquished? The simple act of looking at it seemed to make its maker turn to fire and ice, threatening him, as he was looking cruelly at it.[11]

6. Cupid made that arrow to hit someone else; he wished to try it, and enjoyed and took pleasure from it. Wretched one! You will feel if it wounds and sets fire in your own chest and heart. Alas, dark fog clouds and removes the shining radiance of your mind! You believe you will wound, but, foolish one, you will be wounded by your own weapons, by a noble face![12]

7. More satisfied than he had ever been, he turned and moved it; he tried to see if it flew fast and wounded cruelly. He extolled its power, he looked over and over at its light that seemed to exceed all others. He believed that it alone would placate all his wrath, that it would make easy prey of Iridio, and that through it he would have an easy victory over his enemy as well as praise, fame, and glory.

8. A man who lives in a humble abode, in great trouble and vast poverty, who spends his tough days in toil and sweat, with poor food and rough clothes, is not as happy when he finds a treasure; then he dwells in delights and comforts, makes grand gestures and acts of kindness, so that heaven shares his happiness and the shores quickly echo his shouts of glee.

9. Cupid left Etna and the gloomy light of its fire, which rises to the sky to show contempt to it. He unfolded his white and gold wings and went back to the kingdom and to his royal abode. Because the comely god was tired, he went to his bed, dressed entirely in gold, but before, he nourished himself with ambrosia,[13] disdaining water, and took pleasure in sweet laziness.

10. He enjoyed peace and rested only briefly, as his heart was aflame and desirous of glory; his daring mind, full of haughty pride, revived itself, swollen and conceited, as a flame that's hidden and concealed in what feeds it suddenly rises to

---

the ominous sight of a comet in the "lighted fields," see 1.34. As discussed in the note to that stanza, comets were believed to bring bad news.

11. Marinella utilizes a Dantean term to refer to Cupid as arrow maker: on one hand, *fattor[e]* is the noun from "fare" (to make), designating a person engaging in that activity; on the other hand, Dante used it to refer to God, the Divine maker, in several important passages of the *Divine Comedy* (e.g., *Inferno* 3.4, *Paradiso* 33.5).

12. Here, Marinella the narrator addresses Cupid directly, conveying in this case a sense of foreboding for his fate, and therefore heightening and underscoring her narrative role.

13. Ambrosia was the food, or sometimes the drink, of the gods. In some cases, when given to mortals, it conferred immortality or other godlike attributes to them. It is through ambrosia that Jupiter transforms Psyche into a divinity at the end of Apuleius's narrative.

the sky, terrible with a thousand sparks, giving light to everything and generating fear in souls.[14]

11. He thought and thought again about the nature and amount of strength and weapons of his great powers. Prideful, he wanted to overthrow Jupiter from his throne and place himself there, all alone. He said: "It is right for all altars to be built to my power, and offerings and bronze and marble objects. If I triumph over everything, if everything yields to me, why should Jupiter come before me?

12. "Godly Amun,[15] you can pray that I'd rather not wound your heart with this sharp arrow, for then you would throw away those crowns that extol your glory so! It so happens that I won't wound or capture you right now, because I don't care much about you: you are god to the gods, but not to me, for I am god to the greatest gods."[16]

13. His proud lies wafted and flew in the eternal tiers of high heaven, then offered themselves to Jupiter without cover or veils, with their ugly faces and worthy of harsh rebukes. Ablaze with anger, he said:[17] "I want the arrow he made to enter and hide in his own heart. May he burn with love, may he love a mortal face without ever enjoying her, and may he become crazy with love."

14. He burned with such outrage that sulfur or black pitch would set fire less easily to hay; a gnawing pain ailed and labored him, because he had made Cupid so great and honored. He didn't want a man's or a goddess's vow, promise, or beseeching prayer to be worthier than his. He wished for him to be dead to goodness, caught in his own nets, and buried by his own evil.

14. Marinella's wording here echoes the description of Etna's fire in the previous stanza, warning her reader that Cupid's fire, like that of the volcano, can only be destructive when used in a prideful way.

15. It may seem curious that Marinella invokes here the name of one of the most important divinities in the Egyptian pantheon, rather than the Greco-Roman one. Perhaps she was trying to avoid repetition (Jupiter's name recurs toward the end of the previous stanza), or she was attempting to separate the blunt statements at the end of this stanza. However, Amun was not only known in Greece but worshipped there; he was equated with Zeus (i.e., Jupiter) and known as Zeus Ammon. Temples dedicated to Ammon were built in Sparta and Thebes (Pausanias, *Description of Greece*, 3.18.2 and 9.16.1). The Romans called him Jupiter Ammon, and his image appeared not just in ancient public structures but in Renaissance residential architecture. Ammon is also referred to in Plato's *Phaedrus*, which Marinella probably knew through Marsilio Ficino's *Platonis Opera Omnia*; see the note to her "Allegory of the Poem," preceding Canto 1.

16. It is difficult to understate the impact of such an utterance in 1618, and indeed throughout the early modern period, in Italy. Cupid is rejecting Jupiter utilizing sacrilegious language, which was usually applied only to the Christian god, profoundly rattling seventeenth-century religious sensitivities.

17. I.e., Jupiter.

15. Since Cupid hadn't shown a dove's heart, but an ungodly snake's, with a troubled face Jupiter had his heralds call the eternal gods to a great council with their golden trumpets. They blew, and a sound emerged that echoed through the sky, the land, and the sea, even to the perennial exile.[18] All the gods heard this sound, but not men; a mortal ear does not register any immortal sound.

16. The celestial sound of an eternal trumpet doesn't match earthly senses, because it is too excellent, I believe; I think it would trouble our frail senses. If human eyes observe the burning sun and its divine flames, so bothersome at noon, they would be damaged, because our frail senses are so mismatched to this sensation.[19]

17. You didn't hear it either, daughter of the one who's a fierce enemy to your son: the god of gods didn't want you to hear the proud sound of those celestial instruments, so that your face (which gives beatitude to the severe heart of the most ferocious god) would not be troubled. The one who was the target of your great father's anger and spite didn't hear it either.[20]

18. Because the noble goddess didn't know any of this, she was in Idalium among flowers and leaves;[21] she offered her blonde hair, touched with a pleasant fragrance, to a nymph for her to comb. Among white pearls and beautiful rubies, she composed loving, calm, and happy notes: she sang of Mars's love, and Adonis's sweet laughter and beautiful face in love,[22]

19. and how, as she was following his beloved face, an ungodly thorn pierced her milky foot; the blood shed by her lovely body did not scatter on the ground, but on leaves and thickets, and the dense white roses were ablaze, made red by her. They acquired such loveliness that young women and rising Dawn adorn their hair with them.[23]

18. Marinella's phrase for hell is more Christian than pagan; the afterlife in Greco-Roman religion is truly an afterlife, that is, a life after the one on earth and similar to it, rather than a "perennial exile" from the presence of the Christian god as presented, for example, by Dante.

19. This explanation is remarkable in its realistic account of humanity's inability to hear the clarion call to the divine council; it is also uncommonly long (it starts at the end of the previous octave). Furthermore, Marinella the narrator makes uncharacteristic references to herself twice in one line in this stanza, positing her knowledge as the source of this explanation and therefore elevating her authority.

20. The reference to Venus in this octave is extremely convoluted, assuming an attentive reader who knows classical mythology in some detail. This directed address follows close on the one to Cupid in octave 6, above.

21. Idalium was a city in Cyprus, in modern-day Dali (Nicosia district), with an important temple dedicated to Venus.

22. Adonis was the Greek god of beauty and desire, often represented with Venus.

23. Aurora was the goddess of dawn, believed to fly across the sky every morning to announce the arrival of the Sun.

20. The highest cloisters echoed with the roaring sound of those golden trumpets; the world echoed with it, and it made a terrible peal for the savage monsters in the caves of hell. Pluto shook in his royal throne, and both the eternal and our low places shook. Everyone prepared to go where the highest, Jupiter, had called them to a great council.

21. At that very moment the sky discarded its beautiful mantle, dyed with dark horror before, and it uncovered the loving flames of its beauty, alight in a white veil and pretty. Flora didn't display more handsome privets or redder roses after cold and ice than those that it revealed in the East:[24] flowers made of purple and milk and burning light.[25]

22. Then each god arrived at the great council, following a white path scattered with snow and stars, going straight into Jupiter's shining and refined abode. This was where the homes of the greater gods stood, filled with noble joy; here and there the dwellings of divine workers were scattered, under other roofs, less rich of gold and choice crafts.

23. Soon the famous gods sat in comfortable seats, enjoying their beautiful order.[26] Jupiter looked around; his great eyes showed themselves to be burning and shining. The woods shook, the rivers swelled, and the horror-filled caves shook deeply; the alpine surfaces shook of Ossa, Pindos, and of other mountains that rise even more toward the sky.[27]

24. Jupiter sat sublime on a throne of stars, around which stood eternal faces full of glory and honor; he waved his ornate golden scepter, of which heaven and the fields of Avernus are in fear.[28] He moved his head, which gave light up above and whose internal rays shone outwardly. Then he turned his terrible eyes all around and, enraged, he let his tongue loose with these words:

24. On privets, see the note to 1.64.

25. Flora was the goddess of spring, a symbol of the rebirth in nature and thus also related to fertility.

26. This expression echoes the description of the banquet at the end of Apuleius's episode, as we noted in our Introduction.

27. Mount Ossa is near Mount Olympus, residence of the gods. According to Greek mythology, giants tried to climb to Mount Olympus by piling another mountain, Pelion, on top of Mount Ossa. Pindos (or Pindus) is a mountain range in northern Greece and southern Albania.

28. Avernus was a crater near Rome whose toxic fumes were said to cause any birds flying over it to die (the name "Avernus" comes from the Greek ἄορνος, meaning "without birds"). Because of this, the Romans believed it to be the entrance to the underworld. Marinella follows both classical and early modern precedents and uses it as a metaphor for the underworld. In 1.8, Cupid addresses Hades as ruler of "the Kingdom of Avernus." The phrase "fields of Avernus" is probably a reference to the larger volcanic area now known as the Phlegraean Fields, west of Naples.

25. "Such blaze of fury did not enflame my heart when the proud Titans brought harsh strife to heaven, with hundreds of hands and arms, instilling fear and dread in us, as I now burn and smolder because of cruel Cupid, who offended me deeply and gave you pain and torment![29] The fire he kindles in me pushes me to an ungodly and wicked revenge.

26. "He was the reason why I took on unworthy appearances to chase mortal beauty, to my great dishonor and to Juno's shame and discredit: I was already married to her![30] He saw that we offer our chests to his weapons, even though at times we reject them; he has become prideful, he despises you, and he wants to chase me away from heaven, day and night.

27. "It is right that he would feel pain due to his arrogance and crazy audacity! I wanted to make him die by his own arrow; then I realized that death is powerless among gods. I would like to turn him into a lover with the harsh arrow that he made to wound the strong chest of Iridio, the young man; I believe that this is certainly a small penance for his offense.

28. "So that he may no longer boast that he can rise to heaven and wound Jupiter and take gods prisoners, I want Neptune to hold him among his wandering waves, that he might never see the sun's lovely rays again. May he release his nets there, make orcas[31] fall in love, live in the sea, and go around in clear rivers." Here the great father stopped; the good lord and ruler of the waves[32] answered thus to him:

29. "May it never be true that Cupid will come down to my kingdom! It is a kingdom of peace and eternal concord, although at times you might see it upset by the cruel scorn of the winds; the sea is then only moved and troubled in its outward portion by their unjust contempt, but it doesn't reach the bottom, where I enjoy a happy life, in serene tranquility.

30. "Yet will I harbor this one, who tries to take away from you, Jupiter, the supreme powers that are owed to you, and put his own seat in my place? I already discern and see him, proud, damage my vast kingdom. It is not good having such

29. The Titans were the sons of the generation of gods before the Olympians. They attacked Mount Olympus and tried to defeat Jupiter (the Greek Zeus), unsuccessfully.

30. Here, Jupiter confesses his many infidelities to Juno, accusing Cupid of being responsible for them; cf. the ekphrastic descriptions of his amorous pursuits in 1.42–46. This part reads like Jupiter's confession, an acknowledgment of responsibilities, albeit rationalized by temptations offered to him.

31. Although it may be surprising to see orcas referred to here, this term originated in ancient Rome, possibly borrowed from the Greek ὄρυξ. The genus *Orcinus* means "of the kingdom of the dead," or "belonging to Orcus," who was a god of the underworld and later conflated with Hades, Pluto, and Dīs Pater.

32. On Neptune, see the note to 1.8.

a haughty soul along, and unfortunately that's right, I'm not raving: he will try to make trouble and great ruin in my palace, which in the end will fall."

31. The god with the trident was silent; great Saturn's noble and generous son[33] then spoke again. "Gods, I didn't call you to a general council to force you or quarrel with you, but to act against the one who acted against us, to chase the one who wants to exile us from heaven. Since you don't want him with you, let him descend to blind hell and burn among its terrors for all eternity.

32. "May he live each hour of his days among those unhappy souls, where only death and horror are gathered. May he wound hearts there, injure sinful chests, and give pain and suffering to the wicked, as I prohibit him from wishing for pure air and beautiful serene fields."[34] The gods laughed and approved Jupiter's noble sentence with glorious and novel voices.

33. Then the one who gives purpose, orders, and law to the black kingdom of Avernus rose, he who placed the unworthy dog in front of that tremendous gate and who rules and reigns over lost souls.[35] He said: "May it not be true that I discover a sign that I yield to your will, which corrects everybody. I don't want that cruel one to trouble, confuse, and bring scorn or war in my kingdom underground.

34. "If the souls there are tortured and pierced by harmful pains, still I don't want him to bring new damages and new distress to them, as well as wrath and pride to my state. Jupiter, you can accept them in your celestial royal palace without fear or sadness; there blessed souls will temper Cupid's bitterness with sweet and pleasing joys.[36]

35. "Yet in my empire, where there are pains, cries, torments, and death, it isn't right that abuse rather than consolation be subjected to those errant spirits. He would think that he can steal my scepter with his sweet notes and beautiful

33. Saturn was the father of Jupiter. Because of a prophecy saying that he would be defeated by one of his sons, Saturn ate all his newborns. His wife, Ops, tricked him, and gave him a stone instead of his last son, Jupiter or Zeus. The latter grew up and overthrew him, freeing all of his brothers and sisters.

34. This is a common phrase to refer to the sky and heaven in classical antiquity. See an example in octave 5 above.

35. The ruler of Avernus is Pluto, or Hades; see the note to 1.8. The "unworthy dog" is Cerberus, the monstrous three-headed dog that guards the entrance of the underworld, preventing the dead from leaving and the living from entering. He was described as having lion's claws, and poisonous snakes instead of fur on his body.

36. The depiction of hell in these stanzas owes much to Dante and considerably less to classical antiquity. From the definition of hell as "blind" (octave 31) to the presence of Cerberus as a gatekeeper (octave 33) and the inhabitants as "errant spirits" (octave 35), the parallels are significant. They also serve as anticipation of the numerous references to Dante in Canto 5 below, already noted by Malpezzi Price and Ristaino, *Lucrezia Marinella and the "Querelle des Femmes,"* 58.

features and bring annoyance. It is good to avoid danger and escape from strong claws, if possible."

36. Thus spoke the one who, burning with love, stole Ceres's beautiful daughter from a Sicilian field, and then sad, miserable Ceres looked for her with teary lashes.[37] Jupiter was uncertain, his noble mind torn by these prayers; finally he alone decided that Cupid be made unhappy by his own arrows, and turning again to his gods he said:

37. "May he be exiled, chased and pushed away from heaven, may he roam and rove away from the center and the sea. I want this great wounder to fall wounded,[38] hit and vanquished by his own weapons. May his fire, pushed away from us, have a path into his chest. May he not rule on earth and under the sky any longer, but love in hot and icy weather."

38. After the great leader of the divine multitude opened and explained his thoughts against Cupid, he turned his blissful eyes to Maia's son[39] with the proud expression that suited him; he called him over, and the latter turned his feet to him, with kind manner and humble demeanor, waiting with a sweet and reverential expression for what Jupiter wished for and would say.

39. "Son, dearer to me than the others, blissful herald of heaven and happy messenger of humans and of gods, pity and care move me against Cupid, and I'm allowed to be moved: he afflicts gods with fire and ice, and he makes humans unhappy. Proud, he despises the terrible arrows that are in my right hand, damaging himself.

40. "Descend, and steal the piercing arrow that he crafted to wound Iridio's heart and chest with your beautiful ways and hidden arts, bringing my wish to fruition; then push Ersilia's lively roses, serene eyes, and lovely countenance in front of him. At that point, throw the harsh arrow and make a cruel, mortal wound in his chest."

41. He fell silent. Modest Mercury lowered his eyes and golden hair reverently; he left, happy and cheerful, as fast as a swift wind, ready to make deceptions and frauds. He tied the light weight of his talaria to his feet with shining knots and

37. On Ceres and Proserpina, see the note to 1.49.

38. The rhetorical figure of polyptoton, in which words sharing a root are used in close proximity to each other, is common in Baroque poetry in all romance languages. Other examples occur in octaves 4, 48, 57, and 59 of this canto, and elsewhere in the poem.

39. Mercury was the son of Jupiter and Maia; see the note to 1.41. He is usually depicted carrying the caduceus, a short staff entwined by two snakes, and wearing talaria, or winged sandals (mentioned in octave 41, below).

picked up his staff, which brings deep slumber even to alert hearts if it touches them.

42. He left heaven and sliced through the air, leaving in it an almost golden furrow, a shimmering light, such as shooting stars from the sky are accustomed to leaving in the clear night. That careful, revered god put his slim foot on happy land; he observed, praised it, and believed it to be the dignified place where Venus is adored and has her kingdom.[40]

43. After the son of the one who was born among the salty wave of the proud sea lifted his blond hair from his royal bed, rested after lying tired in it, he made ample fun of Jupiter's great and deep powers; then he stopped. He took off, full of pomp and pride, to find Iridio and wound his chest.[41]

44. He left the noble royal palace. His back was loaded with his quiver, a welcome weight to him; he carried the arrow he had crafted and in his hand the bow with which he wanted to wound the one who had set him on fire with anger. The difficult, wild, steep, and precipitous path didn't feel cumbersome to him, as he sought to find his enemy. Because he couldn't find him in the usual spots, in his heart he grumbled, whined, and moaned.

45. As a careful hunter sitting and lying in wait for the steps of a beast on the run, turning his eyes stealthily when he arrives and when he leaves to where it might move its swift paws in the valley or on the slopes, where it might feed or rest; and when it seems to him that he will certainly capture it, he jumps over obstacles and doesn't mind aches;

46. similarly Cupid moved his lively eyes and his swift soles here and there. He looked for and found the young man, but exactly where he would have least liked him to be in order to make him fall madly in love. He observed him, followed him, and utilized false evidence to show him Ersilia's beautiful face. Yet he was not successful; in the end, disappointed and tired, he sought a more propitious opportunity and stopped.

47. Filled with ungodly and wicked wishes, he lay in wait for Iridio on green ground that sweet breezes painted white and red; he wanted to make him his prey with his fierce claw. Ersilia's serious mind, celestial gait, and pretty brow were not far. It seemed that the young man had disappeared! Meanwhile Mercury observed, even admired, that rich kingdom.

40. A reference to the island of Cyprus; see the note to the Argument of Canto 1.

41. The switch from Mercury to Cupid happens without much fanfare, given the phrases that Marinella utilizes to introduce the latter. Again, readers have to pay close attention and be knowledgeable in classical mythology.

48. Mercury had spread his wings and was flying to the place where Cupid was waiting for that young man; he found him among beautiful flowers, resting and enjoying the crisp weather at the coolest moment of the day. At that point he folded the shining dazzle of his wings, which dazzled like the sun without any veil, approached him, and with friendly face he expressed the faithfulness in his heart with his faithful face.

49. He told him: "Tamer of the gods, whom you wound and bind as you wish, I don't place Jupiter ahead of you, as you rule over his heart and tie and untie him as you want. My soul, my life, and my senses readily bow to you and offer you prayers: you eternally sit as lord, leader, and rector of heaven, earth, and hell."

50. Proud Cupid enjoyed, even loved, the honeyed praise coming from a false heart; he let his tongue loose with pretty words, calling Jupiter devoid of honor and fame: "As the leader of the gods I lead them as my prisoners, tied in strong knots; everybody wishes for my prison! I like that you do not put Jupiter ahead of my honor, because it is greater than his.

51. "What is beautiful, what is perfect, and what is good comes from me, and through that the universe continues to exist; because of me the sun sheds its ray with lively light and during the shadows Delia comes to give us light;[42] because of me godly Hesperus shines with love-filled light in beautiful mornings;[43] because of me beautiful Dawn climbs in the sky with her rich hair and pearl-studded veil.

52. "Because of me, who am her god, the fertile new season[44] enjoys showing herself beautiful and stately, her happy and beautiful hair girdled with roses, when a loving breeze blows warmly. Unlearned, unknown young virgins, cherished roses on top of their own stems, open their breasts, filled with dear fragrances and beauty."

53. The clever god, credited with being sly, touched Cupid with his fatal staff that brings about sleep, as if playing; thus the latter shut both eyes and took himself to lay down above the green cover of the dirt, strewn with flowers. Mercury liked that the one who made fun of the gods was deep in slumber.

54. Quietly he removed from Cupid's quiver the fierce arrow made of cruel metal, meant to bring torments and cruel pains to young Iridio's proud chest; quickly he

42. Diana, said to have been born on the island of Delos; see the notes to 1.18 and 1.63. She was associated with the moon, which gave light "during the shadows" of night.

43. The Greek deity Hesperus is, in fact, the evening star, and the son of Eos, goddess of sunrise (the Roman Aurora).

44. A reference to spring, presented as the season of renewal and love, grammatically and metaphorically female.

fled and took flight toward where the great leader Emero's daughter was, pushing her to go where Cupid lay like a noble flower among the grass.[45]

55. He made it so that a spotless doe appeared in front of her eyes, beautiful and with fine features; Ersilia admired her as the untamed animal moved her wandering steps nimbly, trying to remove herself quickly from her angel-like traits and loving stars. She followed, ran to where Cupid was, and the latter woke up at her movement, her running, and her cry.

56. He turned at that noise and in that pleasant meadow he saw her, whose hair was adorned with roses and violets. She laughed, carelessly, and turned the lively sun of her pretty, beautiful eyes toward him, serenely. Her kind look didn't only generate in Cupid's chest unique beauties, but also a thousand arrows, a thousand ties, and a thousand strikes and sparks of a fatal fire.

57. As Cupid admired her, Mercury prepared his bow, accommodated his arrow on it, and wounded him in the middle of his chest; he injured him and cut his heart with such cruelty that Cupid thought himself to be mortal and dead.[46] The arrow lit up his chest with burning desire, and placed so much ice in him that it exceeded that fire; he burned and froze, wounded and pushed to love, at last vanquished and overtaken by his own weapons.

58. His heart trembled and his face paled, as the pretty god was not accustomed to such wounds. His sweet laughter no longer shone in his face because of the pain that he harbored in his sad, troubled breast. Almost beside himself, he admired her hair, her face, and her beloved features, and although looking at her increased the severe fire in his heart, he put that ahead of his blaze.

59. The sly god enjoyed that Cupid was set on fire by a fierce blaze and by an unholy and bothersome light, the great wounder now wounded and bound, the one who takes others prisoner now taken prisoner himself.[47] Mercury moved to leave, since no other loving desire or annoying pain competed for Cupid; he put on his talaria and took off like a flame toward the sky, leaving him now hot, now cold.

45. An uncharacteristic mistake by Marinella: in introducing Ersilia, she calls her "The only hope of King Emireno, his dear and beloved daughter" (1.17). Emero is mentioned only here, and the context makes it clear that Ersilia is involved here. We can be certain that this is not a typographic error, because in both instances (1.17.1, 2.55.6) the number of syllables is correct (eleven).

46. The polyptoton here is impossible to translate, since "deadly" does not have the same meaning of "mortal" and English does not have a synonym for "dead" that shares the same Latin root as "mortal."

47. The two examples of polyptoton are here enriched rhetorically by the paradoxes with which lyrical poetry from Petrarch onward had described the physical manifestations of love.

60. Ersilia saw that purple and milk mixed in his noble and sweet beautiful face, she admired the twinkling of his eyes, his noble gait, the shining of his blond hair, in silence; she trembled and feared, as if she hid a fire of love in her chest. Although devoted to Diana, she enjoyed looking at the handsome youth, and bestowed honors and praises on him.[48]

61. While the young virgin observed his sun-like eyes, his beautiful golden hair, and his face (in which roses blossomed in an eternal April), she felt much solace in that noble and kind countenance. He saw all this and said: "The lofty treasure of my graces, famous even in Bactria and Thile,[49] will certainly inflict mortal wounds in her heart, with the immortal weapons of my love.

62. "Since she is wounded, since she is vanquished by the beauty that my body possesses, she will be pushed by my face and my godliness to follow me, to love me, and to ask for my mercy." Such hope had almost extinguished his pain; his face was again calm and his chest happy. He thought that he would wound her and all at once pierce, burn, and tie his beloved's heart.

63. He carelessly extracted a leaden arrow from his golden quiver and placed it on his bow; the string hissed and the arrow flew and hit the virgin's breast, hiding in the middle of her heart. Immediately she hated him: she showed this as she fled and ran, throwing away the roses that used to adorn her hair and scattering them over the green meadow, her face reddening.

64. Cupid realized that, too, so he tormented himself for having shot cold arrows in her breast. He recognized them from their effects, since the beautiful young woman was running away from his gentle countenance. Like a quivering bear, or a roaring lion, he called heaven his enemy and dubbed each star cruel; noble tears streamed and warm emotions and harsh pain grew in his troubled chest.

65. When he saw her flee, he ran after her like a quick hunter behind a doe. Filled with pain and fire, with a panting voice he uttered toward her these sad words: "Don't flee, my life! Perhaps you don't care for a god: being a god harms me! Either give me back my heart and love me, or hit my chest again and give death to a god.

48. See the notes to 1.43 and 1.50 on Diana's devotees Callisto and Atalanta.

49. That is, "famous throughout the lands." Bactria is the historical name for a region in Central Asia comprising parts of modern-day Afghanistan, Tajikistan, and Uzbekistan. Thile, or Thule, was a region in the farthest northern reaches of Europe. The *Carta marina* (Map of the Sea) of the Swedish archbishop Olaus Magnus, created in Venice in 1539, depicted "Tile" as an island south of Iceland and immediately southwest of the Faroe Islands, and included illustrations of two whales (*Balena* and *Orcha*) swimming nearby.

66. “If you don’t want to give me life, at least don’t deny me death, cruel and beautiful nymph! Wretched me, what is this pain, this strong ache that severs my spirit from my body? An unchangeable decree and fixed destiny will keep this servant soul locked in this pain: soothe my heart, my troubled chest at least with a glance and a sweet word.”

67. Thus the wretched one spoke with modest and self-effacing manner, sighing upward in his flames. Because he was crushed by harsh trouble, he fell silent and stopped, barely able to breathe. As he was the reason of his own pain, he burned with spite, aggravation, and wrath; he made the purple and ivory of his noble face dewy with a great sob.

Canto 3

Argument of Canto 3

Cupid cried and looked for his beloved's footprints; when he found them, he knelt by them. In the end he stealthily admired her divine beauty in the water, bared of all veils. Iris made known to him Jupiter's decision and his future downfall; yet he did not fear Jupiter and despised harsh threats of his scorn and signs of his hatred.

Allegory

Cupid, running through the woods pushed by the strength of his pain for Ersilia's flight, will show the concupiscent part [of the soul]: when it sees that the reasonable one denies it sensual enjoyments and alluring flattery of our untrustworthy world, it curls up, all in pain. Venus's son stealthily observing, admiring, praising, and then introducing himself to his beloved will be understood as one who tempts and misleads, showing himself as having sweet manners, false words, and peaceful looks to a just man, so that the latter may fall into the sea of the vice of conceit. Ersilia, who washes herself in the river, having taken off her clothes and tired after much toil, will signify the Christian soul that casts aside the clothes of worldly pleasures and washes away the blackness of its conscience in the wide, pure river of perfect penance. Erimeno's daughter, chased by Cupid and then hidden by Diana in a white cloud, will show us the perfect Christian being, who has fled sensual joys, is gathered in him/herself, and remains hidden from the devil's power thanks to the veil of divine grace. Iris, sent by Jupiter to Cupid, will indicate to us the holy doctors and perfect preachers who exhort, pray, invite the sinner to penance; like Vulcan's son, sinners do not care for, value, or fear threats, reproaches, and admonitions that through their mouths God sends us from heaven.

1. When that lovely daughter hid from his eyes, suddenly, just as the smiling sun hides its shining lashes in the sea, Cupid's clear face and blond hair stood still; in the end he decided to go by himself around the wild branches of that bleak forest and make the sky, the earth, the sea, and the winds feel pity for him with his cries and laments.[1]

1. Just as at the beginning of Canto 2, the first character to appear here, Ersilia, is identified only indirectly. One of Ersilia's most important elements, as Marinella indicates here and in the Allegory above, is her identity as "daughter."

2. Like Procne, removed from the joy of her children, fled her home lamenting,[2] her heart already turned to cold ice, going among branches and dry twigs, opening up the sad feelings of her afflicted soul to heaven in a pitiable song, such that it seemed that the wood itself cried with her and accompanied her sadness with its own,

3. so the most hidden nooks of those thick woods resonated with handsome Cupid's mourning and cries, and valleys and beaches responded to his laments and deep pains. Wild animals and birds left their caves and nests; myrtles, alders, and laurels became pale. Compassionate Echo felt pain for his pain, and she seemed to shed her tears with his tears.[3]

4. He turned his eyes heavenward, where the wondrous light of the sovereign beauty of heaven is kept, and said: "Who can help me? Who can blunt the pain in my chest that pushes me to pine? So, love brings to the heart such a horrid wound, such bitter imprisonment, and such harsh trouble? I thought my illness sweet, my ties wanted, and my fire and ice welcomed!

5. "Now I feel this for you, my live sun, who shines elsewhere, now that you have fled and disappeared! Thus my heart feels pain among horrors and in the dark, that very heart that you burn and light up although you're far and that you remove and steal with your grace. Why don't you give it back to me, since it's mine, you cruel one? And if you don't want to give that back, give me yourself in a sweet love exchange, making me happy; that is allowed!

6. "Dearest part of my soul, darling wished for by my eyes and heart, who takes me away, who removes me from you, my hope, leaving me in harsh pains? Oh, give me my life, tell me where I ought to look for your serene eyes! I will continue to look for you, leaving the forests where wild beasts and fleeting animals live.

7. "Who knows? Perhaps I'll see that beloved face without which I don't wish or hope to have life! Paradise isn't happy because it is there where cruel tigers and ruthless lions growl. We would see laughter if her breast and her heart, her true

2. Procne was the daughter of an Athenian king. She was married to Tereus, who raped her sister, Philomela, and cut off her tongue. Procne found out about it thanks to a tapestry woven by her sister, and took revenge by killing the son she had had with Tereus, boiling him, and serving him to Tereus. When Tereus found out, he tried to kill Procne and Philomela, but they turned into a swallow and a nightingale, respectively. Their myth is narrated in Book 6 of Ovid's *Metamorphoses*.

3. Echo was a mountain nymph who helped Zeus by distracting Hera while Zeus was being unfaithful to her. When Hera discovered what Echo had done, she took away her voice and condemned her to repeat only the last words she heard. Echo fell in love with Narcissus, but when he rejected her, she starved herself to death, and only her voice remained. The source is Book 3 of Ovid's *Metamorphoses*.

nest, were etched somewhere: 'Here she sits, almost a queen, in a high place, burning with incredible beauty.'

8. "Around her are all my wishes, like servants around their lord. My affection sheds great tears, asking for her mercy with ardent words and prayers; yet she is unmoved, like a rock to a wave or an oak to the winds. Oh beautiful, cruel woman, why don't you move your heart, harder than jasper,[4] to warm prayers?

9. "My soul, I still hope to break that rocky heart[5] with my tears, with sad and low laments, with warm and bated breath, the heart that my frail voice could not break in the past, when your breast proved to me, alas, how much love wounds and burns the soul! Who knows? Perhaps a look into your chest will awaken a burning love for me."

10. He was silent; he stood and started, taking hope with him (she is an unfaithful leader for faithful lovers!). He went where a river flowed among beautiful flowers, shining its pure crystals in the sun; he washed, cleaned, and made his face, his chest, and his flowing blond hair beautiful again, then he dried his mane and adorned his happy limbs in the clear rays of the shining sun.

11. After he cleaned, washed, and rinsed his shining mane and pretty chest in those pure waves, he took counsel with the river; his pained heart admired itself and was filled with happiness and hope upon seeing the purple, milk, and burning gold of his breast, face, and blond hair. If he hadn't been filled by another love, he would have fallen for his face and become another Narcissus.[6]

12. But since his heart was flying toward the splendor of her beautiful eyes, like a moth to a flame, it couldn't be that another arrow could touch his heart or a new affection spread its wings in him. "How can it be that my beauty doesn't shoot darts and laces inside someone else's breast and make a mortal swoon, as rare beauty is wont to do?"

13. As he said this he gathered his hair around his face with clever art, beautifying himself; in the same way Dawn adorns her illustrious brow in the mirror of the sea in the light of day.[7] So that you're at peace, I'll tell you, who makes the world shine with your beautiful rays after the night's veil had cast its shadow: he has a prettier face than you, because he is a more refined lover.[8]

4. On jasper, see the note to 1.26.

5. Cf. Cupid's anger over the "alpine heart" of Iridio in 1.57. He again refers to the "alpine rock" of Ersilia's heart in 5.41.

6. On Narcissus, see the note to 1.35.

7. See the note to 2.19, concerning Dawn (Aurora to the Romans).

8. Here, Marinella addresses Dawn directly to underscore that her beauty yields to Cupid's.

14. After the god of love found himself pleasing, having artfully adorned his lovely features, he left the meadow and the clear river in order to find his woman, whose manners he loved. He spread his luscious wings, and the air became gold at the lively light of his golden feathers; it seemed as though a celestial fragrance awakened wherever he went, like lovely ambrosia.[9]

15. Upon seeing the beauty of his serene face, the nymphs took their blonde manes out of their beautiful springs, their hearts full of joy that a new bird would ply the propitious air. He gathered his wings where his chest felt the deep wounds of a cruel arrow, and looked to find or see a sign or a footprint of her beloved foot in the grass or among the flowers.

16. He kissed the place where he sadly recognized that beautiful woman to have put her haughty feet. He said: "Where should I look? Where did you, my beautiful sun, hide your holy beauty, in which I placed my devout wishes and the thought of a faithful lover?" He looked for her, turned and scoured around, often crying and sighing for her.

17. Meanwhile, Ersilia, burning with proper desire, followed the cruelest and most courageous of wild animals in woods and forests. She was full of the deepest sweetness when she vanquished it. She only enjoyed herself when she ran deep into a forest in order to get the dangerous spoils of a proud, wild beast; she did not believe an honor worthy of esteem that didn't come with danger and sweat.

18. She killed a bear with her arrows and her strength, made mountain animals servant to her will, put a harsh muzzle on a fierce lion, and stopped other ruthless beasts rebellious to man;[10] here she defeated a leopard in a swift race, there a deer, a goat, a hare, and slender deer. Then she hung the skulls of noble animals in Diana's great temple, making herself nobler.

19. Never does a pretty pearl uncover itself as shining and beautiful from the rich sea, or love's star show itself in the quiet of morning in the clear sky,[11] or a young rose become gold and purple with such beauty in the morning sun, as Ersilia revealed and uncovered herself with flashes of honor, tempering her heart with majestic works.

20. Now she followed the steps and footprints of a quick deer and wished for the honor of new spoils. It fled and went round in various ways to flee from her, she

9. On ambrosia, the food of the gods, see the note to 2.9.

10. "Man" is a generic designation for humankind in early modern Italian, although some irony on Marinella's part may be implied.

11. The reference is to Venus as the morning star.

who didn't care for or love Cupid.[12] But her noble chest, in which the generous desire for eternal fame wasn't asleep, shot an arrow and wounded it; therefore she was happy and offered honor and praise to her goddess.

21. Meanwhile the tired sun enjoyed some welcome rest, sweetly burning in the middle of the sky; a happy shepherd sat with his flock at the hard foot of a leafy plane tree;[13] a cicada sang its harsh and sometimes tedious song among green fronds; and chaste Ersilia burned in the warm rays, without shade from an elm or a beech tree.

22. Tired from her run, her beautiful brow was already damp and wet with honorable sweat; she stopped her fleeing steps by a hill where a river ran and a clear spring sat. She removed her quiver from around her white neck, tossed her loaded weapons to the flowers, and she untied her white, chaste, and dainty clothes from her body.[14]

23. She wanted to lessen the heat that had tormented her as she went through untilled and wild land, in the beautiful river that carried trembling waves of lively silver to Thetis's bosom.[15] Cupid, where were you? Why did you move so slowly to admire her beautiful and serene face? Already few clothes hid her beautiful body, which was rather covered by her blonde mane.

24. I hear the clanging quiver and moving feathers of burning Cupid, on his way! Poor Cupid was looking here on earth for his celestial light, with pain and fears. The winged god arrived not by chance, but with the solid hope of admiring her; the noble gods led him so that we could feel that pain a heart harbors when it has been wounded, set on fire, and tormented by him.

25. He stood, stunned, where he saw her eyes shine, like two suns at noon, and her beautiful milky face, in which dwelled all the beauty that resided in heaven. If it were possible, his eternal soul would separate from his beautiful, bedecked body. He stood just like one who sees white snow on which the sun doesn't shine.

12. In the original Italian, Marinella utilizes polyptoton, or repetition between the verb "to love" and "Love" as it refers to Cupid.

13. On the plane tree, see the note to 1.12.

14. After mentioning Ersilia's "proper desire" in octave 17, as opposed to Cupid's sexual desire, Marinella insists on her character's chastity by utilizing terms such as "white" (indicative of purity) and "honorable," to remove any possible sexualized interpretation of her actions in this and the following stanza. Similarly, by stressing her sweating, Marinella underscores Ersilia's strength and athletic prowess.

15. On Thetis, see the note to 1.62.

26. Among old trees that cast their shadow on the green meadow with their tall foliage, stunned and wholly ablaze with love's desire, the frenzied lover observed and observed again her beautiful golden hair and her gentle face, which made him miserable and happy at the same time. Behold, she revealed hidden treasures and admirable works made by nature and heaven.[16]

27. She didn't think that she was being observed; casually she put her noble hip in the liquid crystals and soon the beautiful lilies and red roses of her tired body became more beautiful; the beautiful plum of her purple and the whiteness of her ivory emerged as if from glass, having been hidden. Wretched Cupid trembled, cried, wailed, pined, burned, and sighed as he admired her.

28. He didn't dare to show himself. At times his beautiful face was colored as red as the Dawn that grows in the sky; at times all his strength waned inside him to such a degree that he lay cold and he seemed to pass out and die. Fear dyed his roses with paleness, desire revived, lit, and colored them. He looked and desired her, now ice and now fire,[17] confused and lost to himself.

29. He was afraid that if he showed himself, she would conceal the sun from his eyes and hide their beloved object, so he would grieve all the time and melt his wretched heart and the sweetness within in two rivers. If he lay hidden, he would consume himself in his burning desire and warm love. Happy and pained he burned, feared, denied what he wanted, tying and binding his heart even more.

30. In the same manner at times a hungry lion prowls an enclosed sheepfold, making a daunting noise, but the humble flock is so well locked that it does not fear its fury. His base dread served assuredly as a restraint to the burning desire raging in his heart, so he didn't reveal to her divine face that he was as devastated a lover as any other.

31. After Ersilia removed her sweat and dust and extinguished her heat in the waves, she enveloped and hid her wet alabaster limbs in a thin veil, then in a beautiful mantle; with her spotless hand she untied and unfastened her blonde hair onto her shoulders, till then gathered on her head; her breast was not covered by any other veil than her golden mane, which could make heaven fall in love.

16. The opaque terms by which Marinella describes Ersilia's nakedness are belied by the adverb *ecco* in the original, here translated as "behold," which implies the presence of an observer. This scene also evokes Acteaon's coming upon Diana—the goddess to whom Ersilia is devoted—as she bathes, described by Ovid in Book 3 of his *Metamorphoses*. There is an element of voyeurism that is also unspoken but present in the singular fight between Claudia and Meandra in *Enrico*. See Stampino, "A Singular Venetian Epic Poem," 49–51.

17. See 2.59.

32. As soon as Cupid saw her limbs, which vanquish the snow in their whiteness, being hidden in white cloth, he feared that she would quickly move her feet and remove herself from him, swiftly and lightly. He would not be able to ask for mercy for his pining, sweeten the harsh trouble in his heart, give comfort to his pain, or abate the fire burning in his heart.

33. Urged by the desire that alighted his heart he went to her as an arrow shot from a bow; she shone with the sun's beauty, and he came to her as a mortal spirit does to a goddess. As soon as she turned her chaste eyes to him, such chill and fear attacked her heart that she didn't know where to flee. Ice and fire awoke in him, and he didn't know where he stood.

34. "My heart," he said, "are these the eyes for which I burn in ice and shiver on summer days? Are these the lights whose radiance wounded my heart and turned my eyes into open rivers? Yet now they don't show signs of pity for my tears, alas, they are devoid of pity; these lively stars of love only give out signs of rain and storms ahead."

35. As a shy white dove flees a haughty eagle, quickly and hurriedly, or a light doe escapes from a good hunter who is preparing traps, or a fearful young one from a terrible animal, or a helmsman avoids a terrible storm, similarly she took flight from Cupid's words and noble face, in which love was gathered.[18]

36. She fled and he followed her, his foot made faster by the burning urge of loving desire; so he moved in such a way that his quick going was as fast as a Scythian arrow.[19] Yet before him the royal young woman ran, indeed flew, with her pained heart that awakened a thousand vivacious roses of love in the whiteness that nature had placed in her.

37. Her golden tresses swayed free to the wind against her neck, to which snow yielded; a sweet breeze pushed aside the dear weight of her pretty mantle, uncovering her white foot. Burning Cupid called out her beloved name to make her stop, and yet he saw her run away all the more, and the flashing of her beautiful eyes left behind such a fire that he burned and blazed.

38. He said as he ran: "You're stealing my heart from my chest, my soul from my heart, life from my soul! You flee at leisure, so that a nasty rock might not hurt your bodily being … So, you flee slowly? I'll follow you more slowly, I don't want

18. Ersilia's flight from Cupid evokes Daphne's from Apollo (in Ovid's *Metamorphoses*, Book 1) as well as Cupid's pursuit of a white doe in Canto 8.

19. Scythia is the Greek name of a geographic area spanning from the north of the Black Sea to the Hindu Kush. Greek historians reported it as inhabited by nomadic people whose hunting prowess with bow and arrow is incorporated here by Marinella.

to carry the palm of the victor![20] Turn around, you careless woman, at least look at the one you're escaping from, at which god you're wasting, setting on fire, and melting!

39. "Stop, careless woman! Give back to this breast the soul that you, ruthless woman, are stealing from me as you flee! Open up the serene beautiful light of your smiling suns to my darkness! Alas, already I faint in pain and nobody is here to give me help and solace. You, cruel one, leave me prey of a fierce pain, and then arm yourself with harsh severity!

40. "Look at the one you're fleeing! You're not fleeing a god for base people, coming from unknown woods high up or from a valley or a mountain or a humble river! I don't feed well-known herds as an uncouth shepherd, but I am a god among gods who aims to take the fierce lightning bolt from the king of the highest spheres, the trident from Neptune, the weapons from Mars, the fierceness from the sea and the winds, and the hardness from marble."[21]

41. That afflicted lover thus uprooted and pulled these words from his chest, indeed from his heart, like oaks, pines, and other tall trees are uprooted by the fury of the south wind. While he, in pain, complained and moaned, he saw her angel-like face escape. It seemed as though he quickened her soles with his sad accents, such that she fled as fast as the wind.

42. She didn't leave any mark of her lovely foot stamped in the fine sand; had she gone on spikes, she would have barely bent the bendable wheat. She won over a light breeze and went among the rocks and terrible thick thorns full of fear. He followed her, running, and he seemed to fly, but not in such a way that he would steal the prize in the run.

43. She said: "Goddess, to whose great and holy divinity I consecrated my soul and my heart as a girl, goddess of chastity who enjoys the lonely terror of wild woods so much! You who can, then hide my body from another person's blind desire with your favor!" She was silent. Cupid was so near her that he tousled her mane with his sighs, venting his misery.

20. On palm branches and their symbolism, see the note to 1.32.

21. The likely inspiration for Cupid's address to the fleeing Ersilia is Ovid's telling of the Apollo and Daphne episode, in which, among other details, the god describes himself as the opposite of an uncouth shepherd: "non incola montis, / non ego sum pastor, non hic armenta gregresque / horridus observo" [I am no mountain dweller, no shepherd I, no unkempt guardian here of flocks and herds]: Ovid, *Metamorphoses* 1:512–14.

44. Perhaps he would have reached her, pushed by wings and desire, but Diana enveloped and covered her with a white cloud, dashing his hope.[22] Her disappearance opened the door to his complaints and tears; he called her an inhuman wild animal, without faith or love, rebel to love, and more cruel than a full-blown tempest.

45. The torch that lighted his heart and blinded his eyes was the first reason for the torments in his heart. It was the pomp and splendor of Cupid's kingdom, whose cruelty was equal only to the cruel and ungodly rigor of a Hyrcanian tiger.[23] She was whiter than privets,[24] more beautiful than a rose, and wilder and more disdainful than a harsh sea.

46. "Dearest pawn of my soul, good I love more than any other, come back and revive, desired and worthy sun, these dry flowers to an already dead hope! You are air, you are a sweet support! You alone can lighten harsh punishment, stop tears, quiet sighs, and temper my burning desires!" he said.

47. He fell quiet and stopped his steps, because he saw that his hope had already disappeared and fled. Sadly he sat by the hard base of a tall beech, and he trembled like a wounded lion. His pained heart again believed that he could enjoy the extreme beauty of his woman, and believed that he could see her. So he left, hoping to find her, but not disdainful and wild.

48. As he walked, at times he complained about his sad destiny, at others he blamed his own base fear as well as her harshness, since she didn't want to give him death, although she had wounded his heart. He said: "If she shortens the hours of this life, she is afraid that she'll kill my pain; she keeps my life alive, target of a thousand tortures and troubles, so that pain might live on."[25]

22. Cupid's reaction to Ersilia's disappearance stands in contrast to that of Apollo is Ovid's recounting: he embraces the transformed Daphne and tells her he will honor her forever. Cupid's calling Ersilia "cruel" is an ironic evocation of that story as well: Ovid says was brought about "non / fors ignara dedit, sed saeva Cupidinis ira" [not through chance but because of Cupid's fierce anger]: Ovid, *Metamorphoses*, 1.452–53.

23. Hyrcania was a region (satrapy) corresponding to parts of modern Iran and Turkmenistan, south of the Caspian Sea. Its name may come from the ancient Persian "Verkâna" or "Varkâna," meaning "land of wolves," although it was referred to in classical literature as a land of tigers; see, e.g., Virgil's *Aeneid*, 4.365–367. Shakespeare makes references to Hyrcanian tigers or beasts in *Hamlet*, *Macbeth*, and other plays.

24. On privets, see the note to 1.64.

25. Marinella again utilizes polyptoton to insist on the ideas of life and pain, here in more than one place in the stanza.

49. Meanwhile he reached a wet shade of tall and peaceful plane and beech trees,[26] among beautiful flowers full of beauty and perfumes, to the sounds and waters and leaves at the foot of a hill. There he lay down; a flock of birds lifted their song from their musical beaks to the air to sweeten him, and Zephyrus poured a thick cloud of happy flowers from his gown.

50. With his eyes he kept looking for the beloved light of her beautiful face, by which he was vanquished and captured. He didn't yet know that he had offended the great father in heaven in his honor and merit; so at times laughter tempered his fears and abated the fire that was ablaze in him. Full of still sweet hope, he let his pain loose in precious rhymes.

51. Like a gentle poet, with learned meter and lines he lessened the damages to his chest: how he died for a nymph and poured the waters of his cruel pains from his eyes; that it wasn't useful to complain about her to move her to pity, or to use ruses and tricks to catch her. Feeling grand, he mentioned his strength and his spite for Jupiter's strength, rite, and name.

52. While he sang, blowing airs moved the gold of his mane, enjoying it often, since they gave off fragrances and light much more than ambrosia to wandering souls. While he made his long cries and burning love known with sighs from his heart, Jupiter sent beautiful Iris from heaven to bring him the news of his banishment.[27]

53. Wearing a beautiful mantle of purple and gold decorated all around with white and green, she showed herself to him, who, like a singing bird, was venting his fire and praising his beloved's worth. She opened her mouth, where the treasures of heaven's divine and regal secrets were enclosed, and interrupted his song. With a stern voice she spoke to him stiffly:

54. "The great god of gods, who holds the three-tipped thunderbolt for eternity, chases, removes, and excludes you from heaven, sea, and hell, with tears and pains. He wants you to live on earth, in the heat and in winter. It behooves you to do what he wills; otherwise you'll feel how much the extreme strength of his terrible bolt presses down."

55. There she closed the blazing roses of her mouth, climbed on the rainbow, and returned to heaven. Cupid despised Jupiter and what the noble nymph displayed

26. On the plane tree, see the note to 1.12.

27. In classical mythology, Iris is one of the messengers of the gods and the wife of Zephyrus, often represented as a rainbow (see octave 55, below) or a young woman with wings. She is not, however, Jupiter's messenger; Marinella might be singling her out in preparation for and connection to the metamorphosis that she creates in 6.39–41, below, where she receives her name from Iridio.

without cloud or veil. The flames of love had more power in his heart than the dazzling weapon of the great father; greedy affection awakened in his heart more than any intense desire had yet awakened.

56. It seemed that beautiful Iris had stoked fire and flames as she explained the will of his leader to the son. He, insane one, believed it an easy game and didn't perceive his damage. Now he was really ablaze, to the point that he couldn't find his way: his chest transformed into pure flame, and he turned his handsome face toward heaven, full of disdain, and, full of wrath, he spoke thus to him:

57. "One who was my prisoner, whom I bound with a thousand ties and served as a target to my arrow, a servant of mine whom I forced to say that I was a god worthier than any other; now this one insults and threatens me! I vanquished him already, but now he threatens to vanquish me and he assails me with offensive words, believing that he'll make me fear his weapons more than mine?

58. "As if I lacked burning arrows to wound him and push him down, near death! As if I would lie down and be silent, oppressed by base fear, almost devoid of strength and courage! Does he believe that I complain faintly, so that he might stop doing what he threatens to? He doesn't know that any soul accustomed to great things disdains and despises the threats of others.

59. "My body is small, but my mind is large and my strength exceptional. No bomb, lightning, or thunder has movement and sound that a soul fears as much! Both low Acheron and the high throne tremble at the sound of my arrow![28] Jupiter, your might is great and exceptional; mine is excellent and greater still, as it spreads in every heart."

60. The powerful fire that blazed in him and consumed him was more powerful than wrath; he feared the strong ties and wounds that opened up his breast much more than the strong arm of the thunderer from up high. With each hour, love's hot torch and cold ice seemed to grow more bothersome than ever; so he abandoned his wrath and declared a truce to his scorn, since love wounded and stole his heart.

61. Tired Apollo had already hid his beautiful, colorful face in Thetis's bosom. Then the rising night scattered golden flowers on its beautiful, clear mantle. After the day's toil, animals yielded to the assault of sleep, on beech trees, in dens, in holes, and under roofs, soothing harsh worries and bothersome feelings.[29]

28. In Greek mythology, Acheron was one of the five rivers of the underworld; it is present in Dante's *Inferno* as well.

29. There is a long poetic tradition of describing night falling: from the first quatrain of Petrarch's sonnet 164 ("Or che 'l ciel et la terra e 'l vento tace"), which was set to music by Monteverdi in his

62. As sweet sleep calmed an immense sea of stormy worries in the hearts of others, it also gave respite to the hot flames and peace to the intense pain of that noble son. It scattered his troubled breast with Lethe's waters and mellowed his spirit and his senses,[30] so he closed his beautiful eyes and calmed his heart with grateful sleep on the grass.

---

eighth book of madrigals, to Tasso's description in *Gerusalemme liberata* of the quiet of night before battle (12.1) and of Erminia's observing the enemy camp at night, where her beloved is resting (6.103), Marinella had many examples with which to inspire her stanza. Following Tasso, she underscores the tension between the quiet of night and the emotions raging in her character, but differs from him in using mythological references as well as animals.

30. Lethe, the river of forgetfulness, flowed through the underworld.

Canto 4

Argument of Canto 4

In a dream, Cupid imagined Ersilia as compassionate. Once awake, full of pain and troubles, he asked his protean father Nereus[1] what he had to do to chase tyrant love away from his chest.[2] Looking for her, he descended to Pluto's vast royal palace, where wicked souls dwelt.[3] There he led Eurinia to the wretched guide Charon,[4] so that he could enjoy her renowned beauty.

Allegory

Cupid's dream portrays our lives: embracing shadows of false pleasure, we think we enjoy all the goodness and happiness that one can have, but these disappear like a dream and get lost at the height of their greatest satisfaction. The protean sea god, apt to changing into many shapes, will be an example of luck: it shows itself to the eyes of wretched mortals under a thousand guises; unstable by nature, at times it offers its winged hand full and plentiful of riches and comfort, but at others it turns its back to us and shows us its bald hairless head, that is, with no hope for the smallest possible shelter. This variable god will display a wise man's prudence: with his peaceful and sweet nature he adapts to all events, to all times, and to the many diverse humors of humans, keeping friendships and city concord. This is necessary to a prudent man: to please everybody civilly, one could say, he bends his nature into a thousand shapes.[5] Cupid descending to hell will represent for us the curiosity of our soul, trying to look at the core of the most hidden things. Charon, travelling over the Styx and in love with Eurinia, maid to Proserpina, could be similar to some senile old men: instead of spending their short days in works that would earn them that heavenly glory that is above them, by following their fleeing beloved they acquire little glory to their fame, short span to their quick lives, and in the end death to their soul.

1. "Protean" in the sense that Nereus was a shape-shifting god. On Proteus, see the note to 1.66.

2. Nereus was the son of Pontus (personification of the Sea) and Gaia (personification of the Earth). With his wife Doris, a sea nymph, he was the father of the Nereids.

3. Pluto was the god of the underworld; see the notes to 1.8 and 2.33. Marinella puts a Christian twist on the pagan tradition by adding the notation that "wicked souls dwelt" there; in ancient mythology, the underworld was the place were all souls went after death.

4. In Greek mythology, Charon was the ferryman of the underworld. His task was to carry the newly dead from one bank of the river Styx, separating the land of the living from the underworld, to the other.

5. The adverb "civilly" is notable in this context, as it carries at least two connotations: a prudent man should please everybody with civility, that is, with his manners, and within his *civitas* or community. The latter meaning is particularly relevant in this canto, teeming with references to Dante's *Commedia*.

1. While he enjoyed lofty rest in his chest, he imagined seeing Ersilia's noble face, the very face that had taken his freedom, his soul, and all good from him, pretty and in love. Looking at him, then happy and charming, she seemed to say, all restraint to her shame gone: "Why are you crying for me? Why do you sigh, beloved lover, in pain and suffering?[6]

2. "Perhaps your beautiful face or your clear, shining gold mane is to be despised? Perhaps to be despised are the two stars that you carry on your brow, more dazzling than the sun? Your pretty eyes and your handsome features cause you to wound intelligent minds. It isn't that any mortal woman harbors in her heart hatred for Cupid, if she flees, but the fear of dishonor.

3. "She doesn't flee: if she flees, wretched, she would leave the best of her life behind and with you. Do not fear, I have been yours since swaddling clothes squeezed me and I came into this blind prison.[7] If I am beautiful, I am so for you. Forsake tears and sighs, and enjoy with me right now: air, waves, the sky, and the flowered dawn call and invite us to enjoy and love."

4. That was what he thought he heard; therefore, burning with love and desire, he seemed to say, happily: "You know, my love, it has been a long while since I've been taken by your beautiful face and a secret love has been consuming me. Now that you understand my condition, it's right that you don't enforce the ban against loving with Cupid. It's high time that I enjoyed myself for a long while with your snowy breast, and not in a scant or short way."

5. Thus he replied to her when she invited him, his heart satisfied and his face full of happiness. As she saw him say this, she sweetly opened up in a little smile, blushing with compassion. He was transformed into a daring lover and extended his shapely arms to her, laughing sweetly; he kissed and embraced her, and she seemed to cherish that handsome boy's dear charms.

6. The sun was envious that handsome Cupid would have such peace and fun in his sleep and that he would remain in that flowered and happy plain without sighs or tears. It wounded his eyes with a thunder tossed from the waves into the clear

6. Again, the first character of the canto is left unnamed. This is a recurring convention in the poem.

7. The most notable antecedent of the phrase "blind prison" (*carcer cieco* in the original) is Dante's description of hell uttered in *Inferno* 10.58–59 by the Florentine Farinata degli Uberti (although in the opposite order); it is repeated in *Purgatorio* 22.103, identifying Limbo, the first circle of hell, where virtuous pagan writers live in eternity. Marinella utilizes it to refer to earth, in opposition to heaven (in both the Christian and classical senses). Malpezzi Price and Ristaino also note this Dantean reference: *Lucrezia Marinella and the "Querelle des Femmes,"* 58.

sky where the Graces have their home;[8] but it wounded even more his wretched heart, satisfied that it had inflicted an unsoothable hurt in the middle.

7. Sleep and dream fled, and with them that beautiful lover, an enemy to Cupid, and her gold hair, sweet air, and beautiful face, for which he strained and pined away. Similarly, an annoying shadow that was once dark dissolves with Phoebus's lighting,[9] and dim fog that evens night out vanishes with Boreas's blowing.[10]

8. At the sun's dazzling he remained like a careless man on whom a terrible blow descends; he, wretched, understood that it was a clear sign of death. He opened his beautiful eyes and lifted his golden head, from which Apollo almost stole his light; at the same time he opened to laments the roses that his goddess mother had placed on his lips.

9. "Enemy sun, with your rays you killed my heart and wounded my eyes, envious! This is the reason why a harsh, cruel pain saddens my chest and wounds and consumes my heart! I deem the horror of night prettier than you, although you adorn and lighten night and the sky; the shadows of a hidden mirror are prettier than you. Why am I not blind? Why wasn't I born such?

10. "Why am I not made of marble? But even marble comes to life and acquires breath in her presence![11] Fearless memory wouldn't be safe from the weapons of love or from Cupid himself; magic incantations, prayers, advice, or requests for help have no power against them. I blame myself: I see that if I don't flee from myself, then I won't escape those I have to flee from.

11. "Those pretty eyes and that beautiful loving face took my bitter chest and sweetened it, but then, as a lightning stroke, my heart, my life, and my rest fled and disappeared! Thus a clear sky, still air, and quiet wavy sea last a short time before the fierce anger of a cloud or of wind trouble their clear, vast kingdom."

12. He struck his white breast, he dyed and colored the whiteness that stole the prize from snow. His ivory was such that if a virgin hand adorned it with roses, its honor would rise to the sky. Like an apple becomes redder in the sun, hour after

8. The Graces, or Charites, were minor goddesses representing beauty, splendor, mirth, and good cheer, immortalized in Botticelli's late fifteenth-century painting *Primavera*. They appear in Canto 8, welcoming Venus home as she arrives with Cupid; see the note to 8.9.

9. On Phoebus/Apollo, see the note to 1.30.

10. On Boreas, see the note to 1.33.

11. A reference to Pygmalion, a sculptor who fell in love with a statue he had created; after he prayed to Aphrodite (i.e., Venus) for a bride who would resemble his statue, the goddess granted his wish by bringing the statue to life. The story is told in Ovid's *Metamorphoses*, Book 10.

hour in a pretty meadow or on a happy hill, similarly his handsome white chest became flushed to the exceedingly hot emotion of insane wrath.

13. Who could say how he complained, how he wounded the sky with his pained notes, how he broke and tore his rippled golden tresses, how he scratched his chest and red cheeks? Say it, you who have tamed earth, sea, and the heavenly wheels with your strength! Now say it, you who feel the cruel flames of your own fire that sets you ablaze and gives you no rest!

14. He didn't know what he should do; he ran to the tip of the seashore, thought, trembled, and cried; then, laying down his pride and free from anger, he humbly adored the gods of the vast sea. He scattered wine over the waves, without looking at the sky up above (he hated it); into them he threw warm lamb entrails, beloved flowers, and the sacred odors of smoking incense.

15. Before he spoke he talked to himself and thought; then he raised his voice to heaven with a loud cry: "Father Nereus, you rule over an immense flock and feed it in the wet waves; tell me what I should do, as my soul is lit with an inexhaustible flame, so that it burns and boils for a mortal girl. Tell me, so that my fire might be extinguished in her, whose name my tongue cannot say.

16. "Never has the happiest season[12] laughingly opened such white lilies or such beautiful roses, or dawn scattered such beautiful flowers in the clear air as it blew loving breezes, as nature and heaven have placed in the breast, face, and shiny cheeks of my beautiful woman, fit to be praised, who seems made out of ice and alights a great fire in me.

17. "She is whiter and colder than the newly fallen snow ever was on the Apennines,[13] when oaks and pines are hit and knocked about on the coldest and shortest day. She is also so fiery that Etna[14] never lifted such burning light and flame to the sky. She is such that, whether she goes or stays, she can give senses and a soul to lifeless rocks.

18. "There is so much beauty, grace, discernment, sweet manners, and haughty and beautiful countenance in her that my thoughts are suspended as to whether I should look for her on earth or in the heavenly empire. Great Nereus, please, with a word or a gesture, uncover for me the royal palace, the wood, the shelter, or the path where my woman is now to be found, and how I could remove this harsh and heavy weight from my heart."

12. A reference to spring.

13. A mountain chain that runs roughly in a north-south direction through the Italian peninsula. This line is from Tasso's *Gerusalemme liberata,* 9.82: "Pur hor ne l'Appenin caduta neue."

14. On Etna, see the note to the Argument of Canto 2.

19. At the beginning of these utterances a peaceful, calm, and still appearance covered the sea and the sky; no breeze moved leaves on green stems and no lively stream moved inside clear rivers. Behold, the sea swelled and rose: it seemed as though it wanted to soak the face and chest of the god of Delos;[15] a god emerged from his watery cloister, behold, he rose toward the sky and showed himself.

20. A verdant down covered his arms and back, and his eyes had a blue-green tint; the beard and hair covering the sea-god's tough neck and great chest were greenish. He checked a dolphin as his war-horse[16] and showed himself with orcas and seals,[17] as was his wont; with fierce countenance he turned to him, and unleashed his answer with a hoarse sound:

21. "The one who is the reason for your complaints and tears,[18] why you are wounded, in pain, and bemoaning, the same one will extinguish your burning flames, remove your pains, eliminate your torments. This won't happen until you, full of fury before, ask for forgiveness with sad words. Then this will certainly happen." Having said this, the wet leader was silent and dove back in the water.

22. Sorrowful Cupid, who, hapless, believed he understood the opaque utterance of the great sea shepherd, believed that Ersilia would have pity on him, sad and wretched, after a long pining. Therefore, full of hope, he set on his journey, happily moving his baby feet; in order to find her he left the sea shore, sought her, and called her out loud.

23. The one generated by the noble goddess adored on Paphos,[19] among the Graces and flowers, went over sand in the hottest burning heat that the sun ever produces at noon. There were no cool waters from a spring or birds frolicking and singing in the branches, no sweet breezes moving their breath; eyes could not admire leaves or flowers around them.

24. Then he arrived, and there two nymphs, or rather two goddesses, joyously sat at the foot of a mountain. One was weaving a crown of lilies and purple roses for her hair and clear brow; the other, already adorned by much beauty, lifted loving

15. The god of Delos is Apollo.

16. The image is of the sea god mounted on a mighty dolphin who is described as if he were a medieval knight's horse, a powerful and heavy animal. This appears to be Marinella's invention, as "the Old Man of the Sea" is depicted on earthenware vessels as half-man, half-fish, clothed in a *chiton* (tunic). The figure we see here is closer to traditional representations of Poseidon (Neptune) in his appearance and in his dolphin mount. Poseidon was closely associated with dolphins, and it was a dolphin who sought out the daughter of Nereus, with whom Poseidon had fallen in love.

17. On orcas, see the note to 2.28.

18. I.e., Jupiter.

19. Paphos is a city on the southwest coast of Cyprus, the mythical island birthplace of Venus.

notes to the gentle air, with such grace, motions, and good manners that any heart would be bound with indissoluble ties.

25. She sang: "Happy is he who despises the arrows and small fires of love with his pure desires! Devoted to chaste occupations, he does not want to feel cruel, wayward troubles and pain because of love. Happy, he releases sweet lines to the cool air, and he wishes for no other sky or stars than the ones that appear smiling in the night veil to embroider the sky.

26. "Unhappy the one who carelessly offers his breast to the weapons of a fierce small boy, who believes himself a god; he would acquire death or poison from them, and a cutting blade of pain in his heart. The air would never be clear, the sky never fair to him; waves would never be alive, dances never cheery, rhymes never happy; the beauty and joy of birds and flowers would trouble and distress his afflicted chest."

27. The pretty nymph sang that way. Angry Cupid flashed with anger and thunderbolts of disdain; he showed his hot feelings through his haughty appearance. He didn't know what to do: shoot arrows at her? He thought her chest unworthy of his darts, nor did he want her to be caught by his ties, since she offended his godliness so much.

28. He said: "Not only does every celestial being tease and make fun of me, banishing and mocking me; a mortal woman accustomed to the spindle[20] mocks me, blames me, and laughs at me! How far has my preeminent height fallen! Where does my invincible strength lie now? My arrows are blunt: either I am devoid of discernment and acumen,[21] or I am not alive.

29. "Perhaps my spirit dwells in the breast of the one who stole my heart with her beauty; she keeps me alive without a soul, not Cupid any longer, but Cupid's corpse. Because of that, my chest does not retain any memory of its strength or its honor. I don't care about glory any longer! Alas, I burn and die because of the one whom I adore.

30. "I complain to Jupiter in vain, I protest in vain! He laughs at my harm and enjoys my blame. Already full of ornament and high pride, he wishes and asks for honors and praise for himself alone. I wander, banished from the high seat, as

20. A traditional representation of women, whose household chores included spinning fibers to produce yarn; a spindle was used in combination with a distaff, which held unspun fibers. The term "distaff" came to mean the maternal side of one's family, or was applied to women in general. That even a woman at her spindle could ridicule him, therefore, showed Cupid how low he had fallen.

21. The original reads *ulna*, which is likely to be a typo; the ulna is a bone in the human body, and not proverbially or traditionally utilized in a metaphorical manner.

an ordinary god, so my heart pines; I cannot look for that worthy face among the thousands and thousands of goddesses in the heavenly kingdom.

31. "Whether or not Jupiter wants to, whether he grants or denies this to my great valor (which is already thankless), I will look in hell and under the high and blessed roof, without begging or imploring. This is not such a base action that I won't stoop to it, because all is permitted to a heart in love! I want to find her; were I even to pass on, I will capture her, even if she were in Jupiter's own chest."

32. Handsome, haughty Cupid left, full of disdain; desire for his woman pierced his heart. He went where the Franks and the Germans had their empire, arrived at the Indus, the Persus, and the Garamantus, and saw the Tagus, the Don, the Ebro, and the Iberian.[22] The more he travelled, the more removed and further from her he got.[23] He sought, and at every moment he looked to see the sun who alone could make clear his day.

33. Clouds, twirling eddies, thick fog, furious hail, the terrible appearance of a pitiless wild animal, the fire of Sirius, the dog,[24] frigid winter, seas, springs, deep and loud rivers, quiet ponds, or quick brooks could not succeed in stopping the race of that stubborn heart and at extinguishing its blazing fire.

34. Holy Meros had not shut its famous caves so that he could not enter there and look; the Pyrenees and Pelion had not hidden theirs so that his eager eyes might not explore them, and the high and conspicuous ice did not cover the Caucasus to such an extent that he could not look there more than one time. He passed harsh cliffs and looked in the deepest valleys and the most hidden paths again and again.[25]

22. This long list of rivers (some real, some imaginary) is meant to evoke, for the reader, the farthest reaches of the world. The Indus refers to Asia, the imaginary Persus to the near East, the Tagus, Ebro, and imaginary Iberian to the westernmost reaches of Europe, and the Don to Russia. The Garamantus is an invention by Marinella, from the name of an ancient Berber civilization (the Garamantes) living in the Sahara Desert in what is now southwestern Libya.

23. Like Ulysses in Dante's *Inferno* (Canto 26), Cupid's search leads him farther from his goal.

24. Sirius is the brightest star in the night sky, named after Orion's dog, and part of the Canis Major (greater dog) constellation.

25. This octave includes mountains and ranges from a variety of places, to indicate that Cupid went looking everywhere in the then-known world. Meros was a mountain believed to be in India, where the Hyades (rain nymphs) raised the god Dionysus. The Pyrenees mountain range separates France from Spain. Pelion is a mountain in the Greek region of Thessaly; it was named after Peleus, Achilles's father, whose wedding to Thetis took place there, and was also the dwelling place of the centaur Chiron, who mentored several Greek heroes, including Heracles (Hercules). The Caucasus is the mountain range that divides the European and Asian portions of Russia.

35. Whether the sun showed or hid its illustrious face, whether the air was dark or calm and clear, at every hour he looked for the dear eyes and well-known features of the woman who had tied his heart. At last he reached the large river through which Charon led lost souls to that somber kingdom.[26] He was old, wearing a dirty cloak, with a dreary countenance and a smoky beard covering his chest.

36. There the fleshy Titans threatened death with a hundred hands and arms. There the Harpies and the horrible and strange Centaurs dwelt, fearsome and full of anger. There were harsh fear and cruel fright, surrounded by sphinxes and ferocious dogs, with sickly cares, bitter wars, long cries, pale death, high wrath, and trembling souls.[27]

37. There lived brawls, hatred, tricks, hunger, illnesses, old age, offenses, and disdain, harmful strains, deep damages, treacherous envy, and unworthy games. Bloody bandages uncovered signs of high anxiety inflicted by insane discord. There were voracious scyllas, hydras, and chimaeras armed with flames, and other horrible wild animals.[28]

38. After the proud helmsman saw handsome Cupid, who had quickly started toward him, he gave a raw cry with his horrible voice and said: "Where are you going? Who are you? Who sends you here? Where did you leave from? Why are you here? I carry souls to an unholy nest; they used to have a body. It is for you to discover what you are looking for, for heaven bars me from taking you with me on this dark river."

39. Thus the passenger spoke to Cupid; old age seemed to flourish in him,[29] and his horrid, proud face proclaimed the highest terror and unvanquished pride. His eyes

26. A reference to Acheron; see the note to 3.58.

27. In Greek mythology, the Titans were Uranus's first children, giants who ruled over the world in a disorderly manner before Zeus reined them in. The Harpies were monsters with the heads of women and the bodies of birds; they were often represented as pursuing and attacking evildoers. The Centaurs had the head, chest, and arms of a man, and the body and legs of a horse. Because of their dual nature, Centaurs were at times portrayed as positive characters (such as Chiron, the mentor of Achilles and Heracles), but at others as savage beasts. This octave depicts Cupid encountering the bestial, ferocious inhabitants of hell, and risking his own life in order to find Ersilia.

28. Again, Marinella stresses the unearthly nature of hell's inhabitants, personifying negative behaviors and then listing additional mythological figures. Scylla was a nymph with whom Poseidon (Neptune) fell in love; his wife Amphitrite turned her into a sea monster. Hydras were nine-headed snakes endowed with poisonous breath and blood; see the note to the Allegory of the Poem, above. The Chimaera was a fire-breathing monster with body of a lion, two heads (one of a lion, the other of a goat), and a snake as tail.

29. An interesting paradox, in which a negative feature (old age) attaches to a positive verb (flourish, in the original *verdeggiare*, to become green, like trees in spring).

shone like a bloody comet, harbinger of ills in the highest empire; it spread its tail with terrible appearance and darkest poison, scattering diseases and starting wars.[30]

40. With white pearls and purple roses, the haughty son of the goddess of love let loose airs of love with his sighs; thus he spoke to old Charon: "Who else did enemy heaven or bad fortune place in fire or deep misery? I do not want to be this miserable any longer, or feel the flames of love that burn and torment hearts!

41. "Have pity on a languishing heart that, if heaven allowed me, I would think is near death! Have pity on a heart sad and humble due to pain that wishes for shorter hours to its own life! I am Cupid, wounded by love, oppressed by an inimical heaven and by sly beauties. I burn, and as I burn more flames grow in my torment, for my wishes desire her.

42. "These eyes admire the sweet gait and the celestial image of the woman who dwells in my chest; yet they cannot see the chaste beauty of their wished-for object. In order to see her I looked under all roofs, in all plains, beaches, mountains, woods, caves, forests, ponds, rivers, swamps, seas, and lakes; still I could not make these eyes content with the sight of her.

43. "I have already looked in every part of the world and at both poles; miserable me, I was not able to see the happy air that had already wrung so many tears from my eyes. Guide me to the dark bottom, as you already guided the learned Orpheus looking for his beloved Eurydice![31] Thus I'll see that dear and sweet laughter, I'll see paradise in blind hell."[32]

44. So spoke the one who bound, burned, and tied souls with fire, nets, and knots—now wounded, burned, and bound. Since he had grasped others, it was right that he was tied with his own ties![33] Charon heard him, and his heart was filled with hope, as his face was full of joy: "Now listen and be quiet," he said; "I want to lead you where you want to go, as long as you pull me out of this sorrow.

30. On the perception of comets as predictors of ills, such as wars and plagues, see the notes to 1.34 and 2.5.

31. Orpheus was a legendary poet and musician (and thus dubbed "learned" by Marinella), son of the muse Calliope. He was married to the nymph Eurydice, who died after being bitten by a snake. Orpheus went to the underworld looking for her, and his music so moved Hades and Persephone (Roman Pluto and Proserpina) that they allowed Eurydice to return to earth on the condition that Orpheus not turn back to look at her until they emerged. He turned, and Eurydice was lost forever.

32. Here, in contrast to the "blind desire" and blinding torch of Canto 3 (stanzas 43 and 45), Marinella applies the term "blind" to the underworld: as a paradoxical juxtaposition between the place where Cupid is and his beloved, who is paradise itself. Similarly, Dante refers to the Inferno as "blind world" [cieco mondo]: see *Inferno* 4.13.

33. Marinella underscores the concept through instances of polyptoton in this stanza.

45. "It's been a while, in case you did not know, that the beautiful Eurinia, maid to Proserpina,[34] whose hair she binds and unbinds, bound my heart; that noble maid, that lofty virgin still has not unbound and let it go. I would like you to work with your torches and your arrows, so that she would deign to be my wife, although I am old. Wound, set ablaze, and tie the free heart of my beloved!

46. "If you promise to do so and extend your hand in pledge, I will surely take you to the other bank, so that you can look and search again for your noble goddess in that formidable kingdom. You who can, give me help! Wound and pierce that dignified chest, destroy it with a lively flame! Though she is young and has a beautiful face, make it so that she won't spurn an old lover.

47. "It has been many, many years since I have been harboring in my chest the unmatched fire of an immense love! I would have succumbed to such a blaze if I didn't temper it a little with the sight of her; I certainly would have been the object of the utmost laughter and scorn of the kingdom of Avernus[35] if I had uncovered the mortal wound and the loving emotion in my chest.

48. "As though I were not suitable to feel the arrows, ties, and burning torches of love! As though I would not be able to have the shining hair of a pretty virgin etched in my heart!" Then he stopped. Handsome Cupid expressed sweet words with the rubies that were his lips, pledged his faith, and gave him his right hand as a sign of his trust to old Charon.

49. Cupid boarded the small boat and the old man, laden with his great age, carried him to the other shore; he said: "As was your promise, noble child, so may I see your trust." With charming gait he soon entered into the fearsome door of the horrible center of the earth; at his happy appearance wrath and pain disappeared from the choruses of those unhappy throngs.

50. Here I could hear the large infernal tomb and the dark river, residence and seat of the damned and guilty, echoing with the howling and the barking of the three-faced dog;[36] it opposed its horrid features to the noble god and barked. There were thunders on all sides; the snakes became entangled; it turned its sinister and squinted eyes; and it sent lightning bolts, horror, and death.

34. On Proserpina, see the note to 1.49.

35. On Avernus, see the note to 2.24.

36. As the next octave makes explicit, this is Cerberus; see the note to 2.33. The snakes mentioned in the description of the dog's reaction to Cupid are the poisonous snakes that were said to cover its body in place of fur.

51. Cupid touched Cerberus's proud heads with a new arrow, replete with new virtue.[37] The guard dog soon fell in the bosom of sleep, with its heart and its senses both. Then Cupid looked to see that beautiful, serene face on dark, wide paths; he saw children pour the sweet milk they had received out of their dear eyes as bitter tears.

52. Vulcan's son ran, indeed flew around the infernal cloisters;[38] he looked and observed if he could see the one woman who stole his heart, or any sign of his dear beloved. By chance he arrived where beautiful Eurinia, Charon's beloved, was, alone and thoughtful. Quickly, bit by bit, he awoke a new flame in her heart, which before was love-free.

53. He placed in her thoughts the great faith, long love, and warm affection of that old lover; how he told her many times over that she was his love, his joy, his darling; and how he, satisfied, carried her angel-like features etched in his chest. While she considered all that, Cupid lit and consumed her with a blind torch for the old man,[39]

54.[40] and he shaped in her heart the chest and face of the black son of Erebus,[41] his ferocious actions, proud face, undignified occupation, and grey unkempt hair. Yet he made all that appear more white and pink than a rose, pretty and well kept, his white tresses more flaming than gold, his handsome motions, deportment, and name.

55. Say, what can Cupid not accomplish? It would be little to say that he uncovers ugly to the ugly and beauty to the beautiful; his power, his native virtue were that he could show wonders to rise high. In order to disclose to Charon more than clearly the will and kindness of his own heart, Cupid made it look to her as though black glinted white in him and jaundice burned and blazed more than purple.

37. The repetition of "new" (*novo* and *nova* in the original) underscore the exceptional quality of this weapon utilized by Cupid, and never before encountered.

38. The use of this term, which typically denotes religious buildings, signals the exclusive nature of the underworld—once there, one cannot go back—as well as the magnitude of Cupid's exception to this rule. The "infernal cloisters" of Hades also recall the "watery cloister" of the sea god Nereus earlier in this canto (stanza 19).

39. The paradox of "blind torch" also implies the use of a term important to Cupid (see our Introduction) and to Dante's *Inferno*.

40. In the original, two octaves are numbered 53, and the canto ends with stanza 61. We have corrected the numbering of these stanzas so that the second stanza 53 becomes 54, and so on, to stanza 62 at the end of the canto.

41. Erebus (Darkness) was a primordial deity of Greek mythology, associated with Chaos. Charon was one of several children he was said to have fathered with Nyx (Night); see also the note to 5.55.

56. Cupid, you are Argus, not blind, even though you make lovers blind and dazzle their eyes and hearts.[42] You light up their chests as you like, chill them, afflict them, and pain them. Now you hide the truth from them, now you open and lay out for them the pent-up flames from the most secret caves. At times our eyes see straight, at others they see crooked, as you wish, you who tame gods and monsters.

57. She kindled in such a way that pitch and sulfur placed in the middle of fire kindle and blaze less; already her heart, predisposed to burning, was consumed by the flames of love. She would have passed out little by little, because of this fire, if she had not relinquished all fears and decided to go suddenly to where her beloved was, himself ablaze with love.

58. Cupid so incited and goaded her chest, so lit and pushed and forced her, that a great, unbeatable force pushed her to find her beloved, no matter how far; Cupid added wings to her feet and awoke and strengthened her youthful vigor. Although she went sad and ashamed, still an amorous desire pushed to take off.[43]

59. Cupid led the beautiful young woman, already wounded by love, to wretched Charon; the old man held her and kissed her serene brow and both her eyes. "If once you were quickly and willingly cruel to my pain and a rebel to my love, I want to take revenge on you for your harsh rigor with a thousand kisses from my heart.

60. "I lived a hated lover, now I live a loved lover, and you in love enjoy loving your beloved.[44] Jupiter in his starry abode does not live in merrier, more blissful knots!" Then he turned to Cupid, his demeanor humble and grateful; with pleasing manner he praised and thanked him, who ruled over souls as he wished, giving order and law to them.

61. "What I am capable of, what I am, what I have, is all for you, all yours, great king of the gods; even more, this heart of mine is yours, with which I have to do what you like, because you are its lord. I see the soul of my heart only because

42. Argus Panoptes was a giant with many eyes—as many as one hundred in some versions of this myth—who was servant to Hera (the Roman Juno). The issue of Cupid's blindness is emphasized by its use in a direct address to the titular character of this poem.

43. The repetition of the verb "push" three times in the same octave underscores the powerlessness of humans with respect to the power of love.

44. The polyptota involving the root "love" are too numerous and close to be ignored; while they might make the lines burdensome, they serve the purpose of underscoring the power of Cupid, paradoxically while he is punished in the harshest terms by Jupiter. Indeed, in the following octave, Charon proclaims that the god of love is "great king of the gods;" the irony, of course, is that this is true only in the netherworld, despite Cupid's own pronouncements.

of you; thanks to your goodness I will enjoy her, who stole my freedom and my heart, now free from pain, with her pretty face."

62. The one who saw souls freed from their bodies on the stygian waves said as much;[45] everyone could discern in his mien that his fate was fortunate and equal to his wishes. The son of the one who gave wonder to the gods with her face and blonde tresses[46] left the unkempt old man in the arms of his goddess, now fire, now ice, and departed.

45. The "stygian waves" refer to the river Styx; see the note to the Argument, above.

46. I.e., Venus.

Canto 5

Argument of Canto 5

Unhappy, the lord of love looked in the low kingdom for the woman who stole his heart, but he did not find there the celestial appearance of her worthy face; therefore, he dissolved into great waves of tears.[1] The three-mouthed dog abandoned his wrath and resentment:[2] he loved Megaera,[3] and welcomed love in his chest. Loving spirits took Cupid, and Venus overtook him among green myrtles.[4]

Allegory

Cupid descended to hell and rose to heaven: no labor seemed troublesome to him. Thus a greedy man who desires honors and wealth unfurls his sails to the winds, crosses the swollen back of the proud seas, and puts his own life in the grip of a thousand dangers to bring back gold or fame.[5] Megaera, the three-headed dog, and the other monsters of hell will signify the ugliness of [human] vices. The forest filled with the souls of those women who lost their lives because of love is the cogitative part, and those women are the many thoughts that arise within it. Venus overtaking Cupid refers to the awareness of one's own iniquity and the expectation of the many necessary punishments that pierce the soul's soul with the sharpness of teeth. Indeed, nothing troubles and muddles the quiet of our minds more than the memory of past bad mistakes; nothing maintains the tranquil peace of our souls more than the opinion that we hold of our own innocence. Cupid washing himself with river water and removing hell's gray haze from his face and chest is a man who is remorseful and repentant of past crimes and washes their blackness in the waters of repentance. His mother looking for him is like a man who has fully given himself over to God and is still

1. In her wording here, Marinella reminds her readers of two antecedents to this aspect of her plot: both Orpheus and Dante go looking for their beloved in hell, and both come up empty-handed, for different reasons.

2. Cerberus, whom Cupid encounters at the gates of the underworld and has to lull into sleep (4.50–51).

3. Megaera was one of the Eumenides or Furies, the cause of jealousy and envy; see stanzas 9–10 below. She is not to be confused with Megara, the first wife of Heracles (Hercules).

4. Myrtle was sacred to Venus; see the note to 1.32.

5. A likely reference is to Dante's Ulysses (*Inferno* 26), who spares no rhetorical skill to convince his companions to sail away from home looking for "worth and knowledge" [virtute e canoscenza] (*Inferno* 26.120). Marinella's animosity concerning men's thirst for wealth and fame resonates in different settings in her other works; for example, in *Enrico* 5.73ff., the young noblewoman Clelia scolds her husband Lucillo for putting his wish for military renown ahead of his own safety and their future together.

invited and claimed by a thousand lovely faces, false sirens, and useless comforts, so that he may fall back to mortal miseries.

1. The noble child[6] in vain looked and looked again inside those hell pits and around them,[7] but he did not see that sweet human look, pretty demeanor, and adorned bearing. He was bothered by the great fire and strange smoke that filled the evil residence of the wicked souls. He saw Tityos sprawled on the ground in that terrible cave, tormented by a cruel bird.[8]

2. He was a wretched example for the wicked! He heard a languishing moan, the heavy sound of dragged irons, the cries of those who were in pain and pining away, and blows that almost sounded like peals of thunder. One betrayed his land, another killed a just king with a trick and stole the throne; one extinguished his brother and another his father, and that one dipped his sword in his mother's blood.

3. Some were turned on wheels, others were suspended in the wind; some in fire, some in water, and some more spread out under a firestorm. Some were green in the shape of a tree trunk, leaf, and frond. Some were hit by mud, others were hurt by thirst; yet more were full of leprosy and other ills. Each soul cleansed itself in these and other pains, then rose to heaven, beautiful.[9]

4. The one who creates harsh torments to our souls cared little for their hardships: in his chest he felt a painful scourge, so he walked sadder and more discontent than them. He cried because he could not see the celestial light of that beautiful

6. Here the reference to Cupid (the "noble child") is indirect rather than understood, as in Cantos 2 and 4.

7. The term that Marinella utilizes, *bolge*, is the same as that used by Dante in the *Inferno*, where "Malebolge" is the eighth and second-last circle of Hell. As this word was not commonly used, the connection and reference to that canonical poem are unmistakable.

8. According to Greek mythology, the giant Tityos attempted to rape the goddess Leto, and was killed by her children, Artemis (Diana) and Apollo. In the underworld, Tityos was punished by being stretched out in the dungeon of Tartarus as two vultures ate his liver, which regenerated itself each night for all eternity. Marinella modifies the myth slightly, while still providing a striking example of the consequences of violence (here, specifically, attempted violence against a woman).

9. In this octave, Marinella evokes several of the punishments to which souls are subjected in Dante's *Inferno*. Nevertheless, in the last couplet (which in the original Italian is underscored by its rhyme: *terge* [cleansed] / *emerge* [rose]), she introduces the possibility of redemption, more akin to purgatory than to hell. These are the purifying fires of love, rather than the punishing fires willed by the monotheistic god. An example of purifying fires can be found in the last terrace of Dante's *Purgatorio* 26, where the lustful purge their sins by walking through fire.

face in which he was absorbed; he called himself more wretched than anybody else, because he could not find her, whom he wanted to find.

5. He deemed his own fire and pains graver than those suffered in hell; he believed it certain that his afflicted heart felt greater pain and suffering. As hell did not have any serene hours, he did not harbor any sweet peace in his breast. Hell had the same torments and burning fire as him; if it harbored ice, he had piercing ice.

6. Such appeared the serene face of the noble son among hell's horrors, as the beautiful splendor that comes down from our high, starry roof[10] in the dark of night or among black cloud and dark terror of horrid thunder and resounding hail, if the sun turns its shining eyes to the weight of the earth to admire such fury.

7. Those souls stood dazzled in the clear light that his blond hair shone all around in a circle; the sun, peeking from among painted feathers, awakened day among those eternal shadows. Tantalus abandoned his apples and clear river, and Ixion's wheels did not turn around him,[11] so that they could see the beauty of that noble face, which seemed a paradise in blind hell.[12]

8. Eumenides stopped combing her hair made of wicked snakes; Sisyphus stopped his rocks; the pitiable Belides ceased their useless work and rested their tired sides; all to admire him, who already had instilled his divine strength in those hearts deprived of all good, and who had placed sweet thoughts and loving affection in those pitiless hearts.[13]

10. A metaphor for the night sky.

11. Tantalus was a human welcomed by the gods on Mount Olympus, where he offered them a banquet: he served his own son, Pelops, after having boiled him and cut him up. He then stole nectar and ambrosia from the gods. For these reasons, Zeus (Jupiter) sent him to the underworld, where he was punished by having to spend eternity in a pool of water under a fruit tree, unable to reach the water and fruit that were very close to him. Ixion falsely promised his father-in-law a gift in order to marry his daughter, then invited him to a feast and pushed him into burning coals, killing him. Zeus took pity on him and brought him to Olympus, where Ixion tried to seduce Hera. Zeus shaped a copy of Hera out of a cloud, whom Ixion seduced. In punishment, Ixion was tied to a fiery wheel that continued to spin for eternity.

12. See the note to 4.43.

13. In this octave Marinella gathers together some of the most egregious inhabitants of the pagan underworld, with different degrees of precision. Although she refers to one, there were three Eumenides, literally (and ironically) "the benevolent ones," also known as Erinyes or Furies; their task was to punish men committing certain grave crimes. Megaera, who falls in love with Cerberus in the following stanza, is a member of this trio. Sisyphus is the subject of many myths; he is invariably presented as sly and ready to challenge the gods. In the underworld, he is punished by having to roll a heavy rock to a peak, only to see it roll it down again and have to begin anew. The Belides are the Danaids, the fifty granddaughters of Belus and daughters of Danaus. Forced to marry their fifty nephews, all but one

9. While each one got warmer, wicked Megaera turned her fiery eyes to the three-headed dog, which ejected flames and darts from its proud likeness; so she lit up and burned, little by little. The enraged wild animal wandered about and roared, quivering as she was taken by love and could not find peace; the snakes that formed her hair whistled, the fire in her breathed, groaned, and sighed.

10. Then she showed herself crying for her beloved, sad and moaning but with a proud brow; alone, she made murky Acheron aware of the burning affection in her heart. She wanted to burn Dis and wreak havoc and bring shame to it, and awaken quarrels among the people in Tartarus. At last Pluto acceded to her plentiful moans and tied the three-headed dog to her in marriage.[14]

11. At the wished-for news, tears, sighs, torments, and pains soon ended; her clouded face cleared up at those words, and her heart was filled with hope and happiness. Then Cerberus, conquered by joy, wagged its tail and received love in its heart and gave up its wrath, pride, and conceit; taken by love, it loved and appreciated her.

12. It seemed as though handsome Cupid felt all love: he wandered here and there and walked around, but he could not find the one that wounded his heart in that shadowy and untrustworthy place. Hope was dead in his trusty chest, and he made room for desperate pain. At last, laden with painful weights, he arrived at the field that took its name after truth.[15]

13. There Minos, Aeacus, and Rhadamanthus judged souls and bestowed punishment or gifts to them: as they lived with a wicked or holy will, so they received a sentence or forgiveness.[16] There is an open field that took its name from weeping; few small leaves of grass were in it; over there was a forest with green myrtle trees that shaded pretty spirits in love.[17]

---

killed their husbands during their wedding night, and were condemned to carry water in perforated amphorae for eternity.

14. On Acheron, see the note to 3.59. Marinella calls the underworld "Dis" and "Tartarus," two of its classical names, which were later reprised by Dante. Pluto was the god of the underworld; see the note to 1.49.

15. This is a likely reference to the Elysian Fields, which were ruled over by Rhadamanthus (about whom see the note to 5.13 below). The Elysian Fields were bordered by the river Lethe, the river of forgetfulness, whose name was related to the Greek word for truth, *aletheia*, literally, the non-forgetfulness.

16. Minos was the son of Zeus and Europa and king of Crete; after his death he became one of the three judges of the underworld, together with Aeacus and Rhadamanthus, sons of Zeus and Aegina.

17. A reference to the Mourning Fields, or Vale of Mourning, the underworld abode of those who have been unhappy in love. Dido, who leads the attack on Cupid in the following stanzas, is a resident of the Mourning Fields.

14. Once they saw their enemy, the souls, already dead and taken by love, wanted him to pay his old sin with new punishment; they were irked by pain and inflamed by outrage. Dido said:[18] "Here is the unholy one who wounded our chaste hearts with an immoderate flame! With unchaste horrors he darkened the beautiful splendors of our glory from the sun.

15. "Come on, female companions and dear beloved sisters! Let's avenge our ill, take the culprit, and torment him: may he learn from his own predicament what that pain was like he once made us feel! May the Thracian Orpheus have suffered fewer bitter punishments at the hands of the Bacchantes than he will!"[19] Having said this, the cruel crowd rushed on him, who was naked, defenseless, and alone.

16. With the fury with which a lion throws himself toward a timid herd from its hollow cave, or a tall flame rises to the golden stars in the blind air with red bubbles, with the same, pushed by anger and dark hatred, one grabbed him by his handsome tresses, another by a hand; yet another grabbed his wings, one a foot, and they hurt him as much as they could.

17. Cruel and wild hands tied and grasped the beautiful white milk of his tender arms; vexing bruises marked and painted the wretched boy's virgin limbs. Those quick, fast women carried him to a myrtle tree, and to that myrtle tree each one tied and bound him: they wanted to lighten and unburden the pain in their hearts.[20]

18. This one ripped his blond hair, that one (in whose mind the offenses of love were alive) hit his delicate, beautiful face, from which roses and lilies took their

18. Dido was the queen of Carthage. In the fourth book of Virgil's *Aeneid*, Juno and Venus made her fall in love with Aeneas. When Aeneas left, she made a pyre with all of his belongings, and killed herself by leaping on it. Marinella singles her out as the example of all women whom Cupid made fall in love, unhappily.

19. The Bacchantes were female followers of the god Dionysus (whose Roman equivalent was Bacchus), and were portrayed wearing fawn skins, each carrying a thyrsus (a long stick with vine leaves on it). They were also known as the Maenads, literally "the frenzied ones," because, during the rituals in honor of Dionysus, they would reach a state of uncontrolled ecstatic frenzy; they were sometimes depicted on earthenware vessels as dismembering living animals. In a version of the Orpheus and Eurydice myth, Orpheus, after losing his wife the second time, encounters a group of Bacchantes; when he spurns their offers of love, they tear him apart in a frenzied rage. Once dead, however, he is able to reunite with his beloved in the underworld. He is referred to as "the Thracian Orpheus" because in one version of his story he is the son of a king of Thrace.

20. In this octave, Marinella consistently juxtaposes young, helpless Cupid to a throng of bitter women, after having likened their actions to those of a lion, and to fire (octave 16). The repetition of the name of the tree to which Cupid is bound, furthermore, serves to identify it beyond any doubt, creating a sort of Dante-like *contrappasso*: the myrtle, the very tree sacred to Venus, is now aiding the efforts to punish her son, and her intermediary to humans.

colors. One wanted to sever his wings, the other rebellious one had her wishes set on torturing him. A thousand ways to kill him with pain presented themselves to the hearts of those canny virgins.[21]

19. While those wretched women were in doubt as to what harsh pain to inflict on the wicked one, beautiful Venus arrived there, and took it upon herself to give the necessary punishments to the guilty one in their captivity: her soul and will were upset at him, and she had barely had any hope of finding him. Her doves and white swans were tired,[22] and her sweet benevolent thoughts were now harsh.

20. She had asked after him, had called him, and had looked for him on plains and among mountains, in clear and dark air, in vain. She found him where she least thought she would, and she thanked her luck. Her beautiful hand worked for his ill: she gathered many branches from rose bushes, and beat her son in a cruel, strange way, because she too wanted to avenge her damage and the affronts and worries she had suffered because of him.

21. As soon as Cupid lifted his eyes and saw his mother acting like an enemy, he trembled, became pale, and sighed. His heart was almost made icy by fear; sad and pained, he turned his eyes, sparkling with tears, and lifted a quick cry, saying: "Dear mother, you no longer recognize your Cupid, your sweet, faithful son?

22. "So, you move against the one you loved so much, armed with anger and scourges? Whenever did I offend you? What wicked crimes did I carry out, tell me, beloved mother? Where is your old affection? Where are your sweet kisses? Where is your face, friendly and pleasant to me? I die in pain!" She seemed as though she did not hear him, rather rejoicing and enjoying his pain and damage.

23. She did not want to yield to his laments, cries, tears, and begging prayers as long as she could not turn and bend those minds in love, which would abandon their hard hearts. Feeling pity for his torments, they spoke and begged that she would untie and unbind her son: "Pity will find open doors into us, as we never encountered our death in him."

21. In the original, all the terms referring to the attackers are feminine, while the pronouns attributed to Cupid are necessarily masculine. Does this octave close with an ironic phrase? At least some of the women taking their revenge on Cupid are not virgins (starting with their leader, Dido); in addition, if they are presented as "canny" in this episode, this is something that the rest of the description does not fully support: they are prey to their emotions, rather than deliberate in their attack. Cupid seems to embody their emotions, and therefore they take their revenge on him, whom they hold responsible for their feelings.

22. Marinella adds a realistic touch here about the birds involved in Venus's exhaustive search for her son. See her portrayal of the sun as a tired laborer in 8.13.

24. Unfastened, the noble boy left the wood and escaped that free, unchecked fury, like a wild animal from a hunter after its paw had been tied in more than one snare; wretched, it escapes into the forest happy that he had removed the strong snare from its paw, and although it ensconces himself in a dark den, it fears its enemy, and does not feel safe.[23]

25. Finally Cupid rose, pale and trembling, in the roomy fields of air; although he was burning with wrath (he seemed to be in flames), fear added wings to his soles. He turned to see if the enemy crowd, with their cloudy countenances, had imprinted the terrain behind him; despite not seeing them, he did not change his mind, and twice and more times he turned his blazing eyes.

26. Like a weak man who has a sworn enemy—he thinks the latter is nearby, with a sharp iron, although he is far away, and he fears that the sword will fall and hit him, defenseless and naked, so he feels his chest and voice trembling and his coat of mail[24] and shield as weights rather than defenses—Cupid ran so far away that he no longer feared the extreme strength of the enemy fury.

27. Meanwhile earth deposed the black cloak in which it had been hidden when the day died; roses and violets dried up their tears, all flowers dried their weepy cheeks, the previously quiet birds renewed notes of love sung with their kind tongues, and the sky turned off the torches that had adorned it to celebrate the funeral of the dead day.

28. This was because the sun rose burning out of the tomb that was the sea, more alive than ever; it cast a thousand blazing arrows[25] and happily presented a clear, serene, luminous day. As soon as he looked at the rising light, he saw that he had been made ugly by the wicked smoke of that infernal home; thus he did not want to find the one he loved so well, so that she might not see him.

29. There he saw a clear river, its bosom full of trembling, beautiful liquid crystals, running in the clear light of the sun in pretty, winding ways. He saw dainty small birds spread their feathers among leaves and flowers with dear dances; with their sweet words, they seemed to praise the shining eyes of the god with a quiver.

30. Perhaps with such notes they invited him, who had escaped the pitiless virgins: "Come, o happy one, and wash your smoky cheeks and pretty golden tresses:

23. Again, Marinella switches things around. Cupid, who escapes the wild fury of Dido and her followers, and then that of Venus, is himself compared to a wild animal that has escaped the snare of a hunter.

24. "Usbergo" in the original, meaning a hauberk, or tunic made of chain mail, worn in battle.

25. Implicitly, in opposition to and more powerful than Cupid, who does not shoot multiple arrows at the same time.

then you will make the shining star fall in love in the higher spheres, as well as awaken blazing heat in the heart of a mortal woman with your divine beauty."

31. At the sound of that sweet invitation, at the dear sight of that water flowing among flowered banks, Cupid ran and removed that black that hid his beauties from his white face and handsome chest; then the lively colors of his face and the natural gold of his blond tresses appeared. Later he dried his feathers, hair, and happy limbs under the clear rays of the rising Phoebus.[26]

32. Thus the beautiful sun sometimes removes murky mantles of thick clouds, such that later it shows us the pretty flames and dazzling splendor of its face; or a proud snake sheds its old cloak in the hot flames of a beautiful day and it shakes three tongues.[27] Cupid's eyes shone, and, satisfied with his beauty, he joked, wanton and pretty.

33. That woman coiled around his heart more than a wild animal: with bold fury she almost took from his heart womanly rage while he was constrained in that hellish cage. Wherever he saw a trunk, a rock, or sand, he saw her, beautiful as he had welcomed her in his heart, beautiful but so fierce and cruel against him that a tiger is perhaps less bare of pity.

34. More than ever, burning fire grew and took over his chest; it lit him, it cooked him, and with each passing hour the wound that the ferocious arrow had made in his heart was getting deeper and more evident. He looked for her throughout the earth in summer air and in the freezing shadows of atrocious hell, but he could not find her. As he felt pain he expressed his sweet moans in these words:

35. "I looked in the most hidden caves, deep valleys, and high mountains on earth; I scorned labors and the glaring looks and threatening brows of alpine beasts. Still these blind eyes could not admire the famous beauties of my beloved. Where do you make light with your beautiful eyes? Let the world be adorned by you alone.

36. "Now you are not making it beautiful, since you, my sun, have already enriched my beautiful kingdom with your rays! Why won't you make it worthy of

26. Another name for Apollo, the god of the sun. See the note to 1.30.

27. An interesting turn of phrase that appears to draw on Isidore of Seville's seventh-century encyclopedia, the *Etymologies*—the most widely used textbook of the Middle Ages. As Isidore observes (12.4.44): "No other animal darts its tongue as quickly as the snake, so that it appears to have three tongues when in fact it has one." See *The* Etymologies *of Isidore of Seville*, ed. Stephen A. Barney, W.J. Lewis, J.A. Beach and Oliver Berghof (Cambridge: Cambridge University Press, 2006), 258. The *Etymologies* were quoted or referred to by Chaucer, Boccaccio, Petrarch, and Dante, the latter of whom placed Isidore in his *Paradiso*. Marinella herself quotes from the *Etymologies*; see *The Nobility and Excellence of Women and the Defects and Vices of Men*, ed. and trans. Anne Dunhill (Chicago: University of Chicago Press, 1999), 49.

the light of your face, chasing away these sad emotions? You flee, you remove yourself from it, and thus you make me sad, since you deem it unworthy of your beauty, although, as you know, the lightning and rays of my mother shine here."

37. Here he closed his pretty mouth, from which roses took their dear fragrance and beautiful red; with these words he showed his sadness in his faint face and teary eyes. Jupiter's wishes against that noble son were getting harsher and more troublesome every hour, so he made it such that intense pain grew in his heart, alight with too many flames.

38. He lacked hope, and at all moments the desperate pain that crushed his heart grew in his chest. He turned his beautiful eyes to the starry roof and he sighed and seethed as he admired it. He had tears on his face and his divine countenance showed and expressed his extreme pain. He seemed to accuse him,[28] although he did not let his harsh pain express itself without restraint.

39. Because the sun with its chariot burned alight in the middle of the sky, tired from its prior run, pretty birds were quiet in the friendly shadows of a leafy trunk, exhausted by the heat, and the good shepherd[29] spent hours in quiet pleasure near the cold, icy river, singing about his beloved face, and the dear arrows and wished-for fire of his love.

40. Venus's son found himself close to where a leafy plane tree extended its arms all around; no crude herd ever took a noble stop underneath it, or a humble shepherd his sweet rest. Perhaps Apollo enjoyed this grassy plain with his beloved herd in the middle of the day, or the beautiful goddess enjoyed her summer hours in dear delights with Adonis.[30]

41. While there in the shade, he could not give or bestow peace or even a partial truce to his pain. He said: "There is no crying adequate to this pain, or a tongue that could reveal her pride! Though I melt and disappear in water, this alpine rock does not soften;[31] you bind your heart with iron more and more, against my beauty and my prayers.

42. "Why does unhappy fate deny me what heaven bestowed on twin Chiron: vanquished by pain, he prayed and pleaded that his immortal veil become mortal. See, Jupiter heard him and shortly he untied him from his body, made sick by that

28. An oblique reference to Jupiter.

29. This is the first of two occurrences of a phrase that, in an early modern catholic setting, would immediately evoke Jesus; the other, even more emphasized, occurs in 7.16.

30. On the plane tree, see the note to 1.12; on Adonis, see the note to 2.18.

31. On the Alps, see the notes to 1.57 and 3.9. These great mountains are a paragon of hardness and imperviousness, here used to refer to Ersilia's heart.

wicked weapon, and now we see him burn eternal among the golden stars with beautiful features.[32]

43. "Oh, wretched me: I do not ask to become an ornament to the eternal temple, holy seat of the most powerful gods! May death and hell be the prize and reward for my pining. I recognize Jupiter as the author of the great ill that wounds my breast with a horrible whip; he does not want to heal my heart, nor does he want me to relinquish this life, void of any good.

44. "So I moan up to cruel heaven: it enjoys my ill and laughs at my troubles; if I complain to the great lord of Dis, he mocks and jeers my wretched state. Still my sad soul, sadly veiled, sits in pain among its pains; if I don't move heaven to pity, at least I move the breast of rocks, tree trunks, and wild animals.

45. "If I don't move the high pity to pity, I change cruelty to compassion, I make marbles soft, I find pity in a beast, and I make fire cold and ice hot. Still, what good is this to me? If at times I try to heal this wound and to loosen this tie, as an enemy intent on damaging myself I feel the tie tighten and the wound open."[33]

46. He scattered these pained words, and many more that sorrow dictated, that sorrow that had opened his chest and ripped his heart with a cruel hand. No matter how far, every cave echoed the moans and sighs of pining Cupid; the waters flowing from his beautiful eyes created warm springs and rivers around him.

47. So with his pained cry he made wet not just his cheeks and chest, but also the grass and flowers that adorned Flora's green cloak with a beautiful, indeed perfect work.[34] Who could ever tell what the troubled affection of your afflicted breast was like, and how much? I do not believe that you who felt it could tell it, either, but perhaps you would tell it after I prayed that you would tell it.[35]

32. Chiron was one of the centaurs who, in some versions of his myth, was wounded by a poisoned arrow belonging to Hercules; later, the same arrow hit him in the hoof and killed him instantly. The Greeks named the constellation Centaurus after him.

33. Octaves 44 and 45 give the reader an example of Marinella's ability with the redundancy and paradoxes that abound in Italian Baroque poetry. She places four repetitions of the root "pity" in five lines at the end of 44 and the beginning of 45, two of "sad" in 44, and two of "pain" in the same octave (reprised later in 46, 47, 49, and 50). Additionally, we have the juxtaposition of behaviors (for example, beasts and inanimate objects show more compassion than the gods) that point to the power of Cupid's emotions, as set against divine will.

34. Flora (the Greeks' Chloris) was the Roman goddess of flowers and of springtime.

35. In this direct address connected to a first-person verb and a rhetorical question, Marinella ties her authorial voice to the protagonist of her poem by invoking his help to explain his feelings and emotions. At the same time, she indirectly asserts her ability to tell the tale, as the text we are reading answers her question: "Who could ever tell …?"

48. Although hope was dry and shaky in him, endowed with little worth and thus lost and tired, still it stopped and rested on a footing of desire; therefore it seemed more vigorous and confident than ever before, asserting to his tottering heart and doubt that he would see her. His wish was reinforced, revived, and trusted. Hope spoke to the unhappy one with happy countenance and pleasant voice:

49. "So, son of a goddess and of a noble god, eternal offspring of heaven, you allow yourself to fall in the heart of pain? You'd rather not be a god or alive, and you are unkempt and alone like a mortal child deprived of reason. A sad crowd of pains goes with you: do you not remember your greatness, power, and beauty?

50. "Don't you know that you reveal the signs of a gloomy heart if you bend and dip to pain? Dignified souls stand against bad fortune like oaks and mountain rocks against the wind. Sickly voices, deep cries, unkempt hair do not belong to a god who rules and reigns others! Do you harbor so much cowardliness in your chest, where a great, sweet god takes shelter?

51. "Given that you search the world running like a madman, perhaps your enemy, who rules over heaven, has in his envy removed from heat and cold that beautiful, happy face and transported her to heaven. If your heart was struck by such a sharp weapon as you show and a deep pain bothers you, try to go where Jupiter forbids you to, with sly and new manners and ploys."

52. Thus Hope convinced him to hope and repressed the bothersome points of pain, uncovering in his face a light, merry splendor of celestial beauty. There the sun burned and shone with happiness after troublesome clouds left out of fear; with those rays roses sprung in his face, hidden by the winter of fear.

53. He knew he had been banished, and he didn't know how to ascend to the supernal goal, the top of mount Olympus. Good and bad thoughts took turns emerging, making his wishes now happy, now sad. As he thought and thought again, it occurred that his restless mind would rise and fall in the wide sea of doubt; he would follow a thought, abandon it, then pick it up again and abandon what he had picked up, liking and following a new one.

54. He resolved to go where Sleep lay in soft down in eternal shadow, in the inner rooms of his royal palace, where he did not move his face from a soft pillow. Cupid liked those words: he could see all his good gathered in his beautiful breast, and as he enjoyed this and believed himself to be happier than anyone else, he said to himself:

55. "I'll go to Sleep and by way of prayers and gifts I will make it so that he won't deny my ascent to where the highest, Jupiter, sits in eternal happiness on a tall, shining throne. I want Sleep to spray Jupiter's eyes with Lethe's waves: they are

always alert to affronts, fraud, and new tricks. That way my sad hopes will turn to happy ones.[36]

56. "There will be no one, I believe, who will criticize my dear maneuvers! Here, I already take the path, I'll go up the shining back of clear Olympus, and I'll fear no exertion. Already it seems a propitious friend to my wishes. May the god of sleep offer me help! It seems to me that I'll find in the eternal blaze the one I keep in my heart, with happiness."

57. He fell silent and left that embellished lawn full of hope; he spread his golden feathers, and as he went a gold circle opened up around him that was a great sign of his divinity. He did not stop his wings till he had reached that royal place from the path that he had taken. When he arrived he gathered his wings and rested only a little, because love burned him too much.

58. Quickly he slowed down the loving dove and pretty swans attached to his mother's chariot. They rose happy and flew in the clear air, almost foreboding of his will.[37] Meanwhile, the goddess that surpasses all others in beauty and appreciates games and jokes moved her feet away from sad souls, the house full of pain, and the lakes of Tartarus.

59. She believed that her son had fled his beautiful kingdom in wrath to go to her stately royal palace, and that he burned with hatred and indignation against her; she did not know how to behave with him. Quickly she went, and shortly she touched the illustrious abode with her worthy foot; she looked for Cupid, called him, asked after him, and said, as indignation wounded her heart:

60. "Since I snatched him from deep hatred, he flees and avoids this roof, once so dear to him! Against what is right and just he removes his happy countenance and deprives his mother of it! Is his mother perhaps base? Still she is the goddess of beauty, of the graces, and of delight; your brothers frolic in this place; there is laughter, song, dance, sound, and play.

61. "So, for what reason do you flee and fly away from your birth nest and from your mother's love? Come! Is there no pleasure that might not console my pain with sweet demeanor? Is there, perhaps, a greater joy than this one of mine where

36. Hypnos (in Greek) or Somnus (in Latin) was the god of sleep, twin brother of Thanatos (the personification of death). As a son of Erebus (Darkness) and Nyx (Night), he was also a brother of Charon, the ferryman of Hades. Hypnos lived in a cave in the underworld, which was never reached by the light of the sun and through which Lethe, the river of forgetfulness, flowed; see the note to 3.62.

37. Later on in her poem (in 7.51 ff., to be precise), Marinella seems to have forgotten that Cupid takes off in his mother's chariot, since Venus utilizes the same vehicle to look for him.

you wander, stay, or fly? Either you are buying mortal glory in the world, or you are securing and looking for ill, having had enough of good."

62. As she complained, she burned with resentment no less than with tender love in her breast and in her face. The pretty goddess of holy Idalium[38] thought that her son was separated from her, and it seemed to her too hard to be without his sitting by her side all the time; it did not seem to her that men adored and admired her and heaven saw her as a goddess and a beauty any longer.

63. Without Cupid she was like a flower: pretty, but not beloved and held dear; therefore she pined away in suffering and pain, melting her loving heart in bitter tears. Yet, since crying is a sign of a base heart, she stopped the falling clear liquid and gathered the crystal pearls in a beautiful veil; they seemed such when seen on her noble face.

64. Her being resentful, her beauties made resentment beautiful, and her beauty made resentment more beautiful, for her innate sweetness made that harshness worthy of her face.[39] Whether the tired sun was falling or a new one was rising out of the salty kingdom surrounded by warm rays, she wanted to look for the handsome appearance of her fleeing son in the place where Styx flowed.[40]

65. She said: "No other river or harsh beast can stop my progress, no labor, danger, desire for rest, flattery, or prayer. After I find him, he will discover my heart not pitiful but inflexible and harsh. I will imprison him and perhaps place ties on his hands and feet so that he cannot unfasten himself.

66. "I won't let him loose as long as he harbors a crazy desire, a wandering soul, and vague thoughts that are not still and calm. Humble words or demeanors and prudent actions won't sway me: I know full well that he knows how to pretend! I know him, alas, to be light and inconstant, and I know his secrets; although he's shrewd, he won't trick me." Having said this in wrath, she sighed and was quiet.

67. Upset but beautiful, she moved her snowy foot from the sweet home where she was. It was not sorrowful for her to ford rivers and torrents, to pass mountains and rocks, with trouble and labor. Such was her desire to see what her ungrateful son was doing that laboring seemed light. While at times she called him and looked for him in vain, she called him a thankless and insane boy.

38. On Idalium, see the note to 2.18; here Marinella utilizes it to refer to the island where Venus was particularly worshipped.

39. Another accumulation of polyptota and repetitions, in keeping with the prevailing poetical norms and to underscore that circumstances make it possible for Venus to be upset and yet still beautiful.

40. On Styx, see the note to the Argument of Canto 4.

68. As the goddess who could claim the graces for herself was looking for her son with her power, promises, and labors; meanwhile far away her son arrived in the friendly city to sleep, at the very hour when the sun, wearing a shining cloak, left the bosom of the ancient nurse,[41] curbing his brave horses and awakening lilies and roses with his rays.

41. That is, the sea.

Canto 6

Argument of Canto 6

The harsh tamer of souls, in love, arrived in the quiet kingdom of lazy Sleep; Sleep tied Jupiter's worthy senses, and Cupid struck proud Iridio from heaven with his lightning. Full of resentment, wrathful Jupiter struck beautiful Cupid from the supernal empire with lightning, while he moaned and cried with pained and miserable noises in the shade of a mournful yew tree.[1]

Allegory

Sleep, who, acceding to Cupid's prayers, makes Jupiter be taken by the pleasure of sleep, will show us the craving of the senses: at times it blinds and puts to sleep reason, which is right, removing what's right, just, and reasonable with its tricks. Iridio struck by Cupid's lightning indicates the height of our minds, lowered and debased by the wrathful hand of enemy fate. Jupiter throwing a bolt of lightning against Cupid will be understood as our intellect: it sits in its noble seat and debases and punishes the senses, immoderate and unrestrained, which wish to enjoy the sweetness of comfort and the ease of pleasure without any guilt from reason. The soft boy is struck by lightning as he sits under the shadow of a cold yew tree: this will show us that, while man dwells among the feathers of worldly pleasures (understood by the shadows), he is reduced by a higher eternal power that calls him away from laziness and vanity through harsh travails or bothersome illness.

1. In the middle of the ocean lay a big city, safe and surrounded by tall trees; there silence dwelt, there was peace; Jupiter did not thunder and lightning did not fall. The sound of iron and the fury of wind were silent, as only a soft breeze kissed and skimmed branches; among them dark birds, owls, and nocturnal bats slowly flew.

2. Among its deep haze sprang two sources; here the sun never brought any light generating the blind and murky waves that split earth and made rivers. These

1. The yew is an evergreen tree whose Latin name *taxus* comes from the Greek *toxon*, arrow; the connection seems to have been to the fact that the poison extracted from the arils covering the seeds was utilized to make arrows more deadly. Yews were also planted around cemeteries (which might be why Marinella dubs it "cold" in the Allegory below; she describes them as "mournful" in octave 44). An important additional echo here is to one of Marinella's literary inspirations, Torquato Tasso; the Italian name of this tree, derived from the Latin, is *tasso*.

peaceful and propitious waters circled the city devoted to the sleepy god, without ever becoming proud, as rivers do that swell and make tall buildings tumble.

3. The dark royal palace had two big doors: one looked at sunset, the other at the east; one was made of ivory, hence it was white; the other was made of clear, transparent horn, wrought with such art that the rarest, most famous, and most excellent would not match it. If they blazed with gold, even gold would lose its great value in comparison with their craftsmanship.

4. Industrious artists depicted dreams in choice colors on the door made of horn, in a hundred, a thousand, even a hundred thousand guises, some low and base, others sublime and illustrious; they gave an indication of the truth to human minds, as clear as the sun shining and beaming on us. On the door made of ivory there were no earnest images or true semblances of the future.[2]

5. Here, wrapped in black, was the highest temple where Sleep was adored and worshipped; he sat as lord, ruler, and master of the city and of its decorated and refined temple. Around him stood many dreams as servants in a thick group; they could be seen, some white, others black, both happy and sad, and in each one a thousand guises.

6. Inside the temple was a bed, decorated in black, made of ebony and with black curtains; on it the lazy god placed his slow, tired limbs, and never lifted his hair. With him was Silence,[3] who never closed his eyes, whether the sun would give us blazing rays or yielded and declined in tiredness; he was his trustworthy guard, who took care that no sound would be heard within the royal walls.

7. Sleepy poppies grew around that large, shadowy mansion; a very tall plane tree spread its branches before the door of that lethal residence so that the sun might not send a ray inside as it turned and brought the day back.[4] Trees had such thick branches that the light from the sky never assaulted the roof.

2. Marinella derives this feature from Virgil. In the *Aeneid*, the god of sleep, Hypnos, is depicted as living in a house with two doors. One is made of horn and provides people who enter it with true visions of the future; the other is made of polished ivory, and people who enter it experience only illusions and dreams (6.893–898). On Hypnos, see the note to 5.55.

3. This appears to be Marinella's invention, as Hypnos had no such companion and there was no god of silence per se in the Greek pantheon. Harpocrates, a god of silence and secrets in Hellenistic Alexandria, was adopted by the Greeks, but he seems to have been a minor deity.

4. Marinella utilizes "lethal" in its etymological meaning, in connection with Lethe, the river of forgetfulness, mentioned in the following octave; see the note to 3.62. On the plane tree, see the note to 1.12.

8. You did not hear the sharp call of the cockscombed bird,[5] the sinister bark of a faithful dog, the quiver or the rasp of a wolf or a lion, or harsh and bothersome sound of any other wild animal. No savage noise reached the lazy nest of that indolent god, but only the sweet murmur of waves inviting sleep, a river originating only from Lethe.

9. The child archer looked and observed the temples and roofs of that quiet city; they were not very refined, as the eyes did not see excellent paintings or choice marbles. In one of them lay Laziness, who did not even turn his eyes to the shining faces of the sky; in another room he discovered sick Apathy, sitting, slow, unmoved by any praiseworthy works.

10. Cupid saw the wonderful building consecrated to Sleep rise a little toward heaven; alert hearts offered poppies and pale violets to it with pure zeal. The building had few openings, and those few he saw so sealed with black veils that the sun did not enter; Cupid entered and brightened its shadows with the bright light of his golden feathers.[6]

11. He spread and radiated so much light and splendor from his burning, beaming face and hair that the dark and blind palace of Sleep was dazzled and confused by his appearance. As he saw the god that flamed with beauty inside that tall and deep haze, the son of the Night felt amazed, hid from his rays, trembled, and was scared.

12. He placed his hand on his eyes twice and more; he was terrified, he staggered, then he shook; he hid his face from the divine light that he had carelessly glimpsed, then moved in order to flee. Similarly, a nocturnal bird runs in the woods if clear lightning hits its eyes; similarly, a mole accustomed to the dark, hidden and lonely, flees and escapes from the sun's rays.

13. He feared that Jupiter would fling a burning lightning strike from heaven into his dark abode; so he trembled and was shocked by the pure bright strike of his noble face. But beautiful Cupid consoled him with well-conceived words and made his mind rejoice, because he said: "I am the one that wounds gods and mortal men with his arrows.[7]

5. The cockscombed bird is the rooster, which is believed to awake everybody with his song at dawn.

6. Another example of polyptoton; here the root "bright" is repeated three times in close proximity (in the original, all occurrences are in the same line, the last one of the octave, making it even more evident) to underscore the radical difference between Cupid and Sleep's palace.

7. Interestingly, Marinella has Cupid single out "mortal men" (*uomini mortali* in the original), as though women were somehow spared his arrows.

14. "Do not fear: I bring sweet contentment and wished-for peace, for I am love.[8] In my beautiful eyes I harbor my torch, hidden also in my noble heart and blond tresses. I throw arrows from my pretty eyes, I catch daring souls in golden nets, and all that comes from my works is a great marvel: both men and heaven are amazed."

15. Never did a tossed boat, tormented by waves, reach the shore, never did a man defending his reasons while in chains see his foot untied from an unworthy noose with so much happiness, as the brother of the woman who evened the heads of the great and the least worthy at the same time and knocked them down and floored them.[9] He said: "What are you looking for in these shady rooms?" To which Cupid replied in the following manner:

16. "I'm looking for my heart, I'm looking for my life, without whom I cannot live, although I am a god! If I have life, it is more painful and harsher than death, and my living is void of any sweetness. Assist my wretchedness with pious wishes! If my voice hasn't yet moved you to pity, let my hair and unkempt, base face move you: they once were paradise-like!

17. "You do not see these pretty beauties of mine, once so dainty, because they express trouble and pain. The snow of my face barely gathers pale roses in its whiteness, my sad heart lifts sad sighs to the air, and my tongue lifts pained words to heaven. You now see Cupid in love, prey to love, burning and tied.

18. "You, sweet comfort, relief, and peace to afflicted bodies and troubled heart, you alone can extinguish love's torch and the pains and suffering in a troubled breast, god more peaceful than all gods, who enjoys fleeing from light and remaining in blind darkness, rest for souls that comforts chests filled with dark poison and blazing affection.

19. "Forgetfulness of any unworthy fate, deep sweetness over bitter trouble, now listen to me with pity, listen to how this soul, little accustomed to love, is tied by unhappy knots. Neither my power nor my beauty can allow me to catch and bind the one who wounds and flees from me. She flees from me, in fact, like a young woman flees snakes or a lamb a wolf.

20. "Leader of happy hearts, I don't know where to look for her, who doesn't care for my beauty, where to look for her, who is my sun and my light, who flies ahead

8. Given Marinella's use of "Amore" to designate Cupid and the vagaries of capitalization in early modern printing, this sentence could also be translated "I am Cupid," since the original means both.

9. Sleep was the twin brother of Death (Thanatos), who equalized all human beings; see the note to 5.55. Marinella here follows the female grammatical gender of *Morte* (Death) in Italian, and thus transforms it into Sleep's sister.

of me all stiff and harsh! She flies away from me, and perhaps she goes where her cruelty toward me will grow harder. I don't know if she takes refuge among tigers and learns and practices from them to be cruel.

21. "With eyes wet and filled with pain I looked, in vain, for her eyes and blazing hair in woods, plains, countryside, valleys, hills, dark rivers, large ponds, and deep torrents; I could not satiate my eyes or diminish the pain and torments in my heart. Lacking any hope to find her in the world, I looked in Pluto's large and deep kingdom.

22. "There, too, I wasted effort and trouble: I didn't find or even see my noble goddess. Due to her valor and chaste beauty, I believe that she lives in heaven, having become immortal; I cannot climb up there, because Jupiter's wrath is my enemy and he removed me from heaven. He, envious, competes with me and believes he can take away from me the honor that corresponds to my valor.

23. "Offer assistance to one who asks for help! You are his only hope among his many pains! You alone can heal the mortal wound of this heart, if your will be friendly. I wish for you to climb to heaven now, find Jupiter, god of divine heroes, touch him with your staff, and overwhelm his senses with sleep, although they cannot sleep."

24. The one who sweetly held bodies and heart in the waters of quiet replied to him: "God of love, if I spray Jupiter with Lethe's water, I fear harsh punishment, because he is always awake: his noble mind is always awake to the clear light of the world and to the deepest darkness. I was once worthy of heaven and he deprived me of heaven: he threw me into the sea, when I made him fall asleep the one time I was begged to do so.

25. "If it hadn't been for my mother, who protected me from that evil wave with grown up love and took me in while sick and sad, I would have been dead in that surge.[10] See if I have reason to fear! It is my right to fear the one who could have killed me. It's good to flee the one who sits up on royal height and who bears great wrath and severity to those who offended him.

26. "Not long ago you tamed Jupiter's alert senses in heaven with your noble powers; your strength is not deprived of might, so if you were able to, you still can work. If your power is as it showed itself, if you are able by yourself, why do you bother me? It pains me, indeed it burdens me, that I cannot satisfy your wish, beautiful child.

10. Sleep's mother was Nyx (Night), whose kingdom was so fearful that even Jupiter was afraid of entering it.

27. "I have reason to fear the fierce outrage of the ruler of the gods, and I want to fear it. Because he is the greatest god, he harbors more pride than anyone in that high kingdom." Then Cupid replied: "I will take upon myself the evil that his cruel outrage can provoke: I do not fear his wrath! His weak forces have been bound by my ties a thousand times.

28. "To you I will bind with nuptial knot the prettiest and most beautiful among the nymphs whom the kingdom of love holds, and the most charming; no star in the sky smiles with more beauty than her, and she'll be your happy bride in her prime: I want you to have children with her, and I want your whole life and each day to be clear and serene.

29. "I promise you this! Now remove and depose that fearful ice that covers your soul, quickly. Wake up, get up, and make your bodily weight light in flight to the gate on high! Clothe your heart with boldness and don't be afraid of pain. Now that your mother arrives with fame and nobility, you will leave the shady haze with more self-assurance." To this the god of sleep answered:

30. "Although I will endanger and risk my own godliness, still, in order to please you and later to have a woman to delight my senses and my soul with children and her beautiful face, I will go and lull his harsh feelings. He will toss me among sharp, dreadful rocks, but I will quickly flee where my city and kingdom lie."[11]

31. Having heard all this, Cupid left and returned to his royal palace happy and full of hope. Meanwhile, the slothful god sat on his bed, rubbed his eyes, and was keen to leave, but his chin drooped to his chest many times, until at last he stood up using his utmost strength. He quickly flew up to the ruler of heaven and earth and sprayed him with Lethe's waters.

32. Then the one who moved everything without motion, who ruled and governed everything without doing anything, and who gave order and laws to heaven, the stars, and the sun in new ways, with silence and love, Jupiter,[12] who rewards and

11. Marinella appropriates the events concerning Sleep and Hera (the Roman Juno) in Book 14 of the *Iliad*: Hera convinced him to put Zeus to sleep in order to allow the Greeks to enter Troy, having promised him a Grace, Pasithea, in marriage. Marinella's intervention is evident in the description of Sleep's feelings for the unnamed nymph: in stanza 28, Cupid promises to make her Sleep's "happy bride" so that he can "have children with her;" in stanza 30, Sleep replies along the same lines (she will "delight [his] senses and [his] soul with children and her beautiful face"). There is no reference to sensual or sexual pleasure, but rather an emphasis on future generations and companionship.

12. An inherent tension exits in this octave between the phrases describing the deity and his name, as the former typically refer to the Christian god rather than to Jupiter; Dante, for example, utilizes the image of God as responsible for all planetary movement — "the One who moves all things" (*Paradiso* 1.1) — without ever moving himself.

corrects the world with one gesture only, was lulled by Sleep. Through this ploy the son of the beautiful goddess wanted to go to heaven and opened his wings to fly.

33. He unfolded his golden wings toward heaven to find the soul dear to his heart; he could not believe that the one who had given him a mortal blow would live with a mortal body. The goddess of the woods was spending her life in chaste pastimes on Cynthus, in Delos.[13] He looked for her in that first circle and did not find her; this helped his flame little or nothing.

34. He looked everywhere in those vast eternal circles, but he did not find any footprint or trace of his beloved. Then he moved to the noble fields of the highest part of heaven, where the eternal form of beauty resides;[14] it seemed as though the celestial kingdom burned and blazed with love, that divine Cupid made it beautiful and shaped it. There he heard a very sweet song endowed with noble harmony from a siren, to which he paid attention.

35. Then he saw the king of the gods sitting sublime in a proud and lofty seat; his blessed eyes were closed and devoid of their functions, sweetly asleep, and his hand held tight on to the burning lightning that kept fires sharp and lively all around. His demeanor was so proud and joyful that he looked as though he ruled the world even though he was asleep.

36. While the highest ruler of the celestial empire was oppressed and vanquished by a dark sleep, as his heart, senses, and both eyes had been sprayed and dyed by the water of forgetfulness, foolish Cupid moved around him, pushed by too much daring, and teased him. Wretched one, what are you doing? Do you know how the powerful king sends lightning and thunders? Are you out of your mind?[15]

37. He pulled the golden hairs on Jupiter's rosy cheeks and tousled his tresses, then laughed out loud and hit him gently while making fun of him. He took pleasure and effected his revenge at the same time: he pried Jupiter's hand open and removed from it the bolt with which he would shake heaven and earth and bring trouble and pain. He said: "King of noble heroes, strike me, if you can: You hate me so!"

13. In Greek mythology, Artemis was the goddess of the wilderness and twin sister of Apollo. She was also known as Cynthia because her birthplace was Mount Cynthus on the island of Delos, in the Cyclades. As the goddess of the hunt and of virginity, she became associated with the Roman goddess Diana; see the notes to 1.12, 1.18, and 1.67.

14. Marinella refers here to Plato's concept of forms, eternal ideals after which all things and beings on earth take shape.

15. Marinella's direct address to Cupid chastises him for his behavior, as a mother would chastise her son (and more forcefully than Venus does in the poem).

38. Because he felt burning wrath in his chest against the daring youth Iridio, watching him from heaven wander, blazing, to catch a hungry beast with honor, Cupid hurled the bolt like an arrow. Immediately, lo, it thundered horribly, broke, was demolished and destroyed. That famous youth dropped dead on the ground, crushed and vanquished by that terrible strike of lightning.

39. Nymphs cried for you, Iridio, in their sadness, and gave a worthy tomb to your veil of modesty.[16] When celestial Dawn scattered pearls on flowers and gave light to the sky, the following morning, those chaste nymphs came back in drab clothing to honor Iridio in the icy cold, but they discovered that a flower had been born from him, pretty to behold and endowed with a beautiful color.

40. Its shape resembled the lily's, because its petals gathered around its stamens. As far as color, I liken it to the pallor that death spreads on a dead face or to the loving pallor found in a pretty violet. It didn't fear love's cruel clutches, and kept the beautiful name that it had when a mortal body weighed it.

41. Thus the world calls this beautiful flower endowed with pretty appearance iris, after Iridio.[17] This way Cupid took out his cruel wrath with his death and hatred left his chest. Meanwhile the one whose bright star lived and gave light to the eternal roof woke up at the racket and noise of that serious lightning bolt, trembled at the sound, sighed, and felt fear.

42. He realized he had been asleep and blazed with anger; he looked for Sleep, but the latter had fled his impending harm. Jupiter looked to see if the one who shot that lightning-like arrow left his footprint among the stars; he feared that other Titans had climbed up by never-used ladders to where he had set up camp, looking to steal scepter and kingdom from him, full of daring and prideful outrage.[18]

43. As he looked for the one who had flung the harsh bolt from on high in the royal palace without his permission, he saw the son of the one who blazes with too much dear fire in the third heaven.[19] He saw him, again I say, and he burned

16. "Veil" is a metaphor for "body," as it covers and gives shape to one's soul; here Iridio's veil is qualified as endowed with "modesty" to underscore his virtue.

17. Marinella seems to have invented a *Metamorphoses*-like origin for the iris, whose name comes instead from the Greek term for rainbow and the goddess that embodied it (about whom see the note to 3.52). Notably, as well, Marinella postulates a male body mutating into a flower, rather than the more customary female ones in Ovid's work.

18. On the Titans, see the note to 2.25.

19. Again following Dante, Marinella utilizes his division of heaven into nine parts, as devised and presented in the *Paradiso*. The third heaven is that of Venus; there, Dante places the souls of those who loved, depicted as bright and moving in a circle (Cantos 8 and 9).

with anger and flashed, filled with marvel and amazement that he would dare and venture to rise to the fields of light with a trick, while banished as an enemy.

44. Yet the latter left the eternal circles to escape Jupiter's blazing wrath and arrived at the plain below, sitting in the cold shadow of a mournful yew tree to rest and stay a while. But his suffering mind did not enjoy any peace, for what gave joy to others yielded troubles for him: he felt enjoyment in his pains, set the air on fire with his sighs, and seemed to breathe flames.

45. Rocks shed tears of pain and opened up at the sound of his words and laments; birds stopped flying, winds stopped blowing, and fleeing wild animals stopped in their tracks. Grass dried up, torrents paused, the air moaned, and the sun became paler. I know that if you heard him, highest Jupiter, you would have placated the new wrath in your heart.

46. Full of outrage and burning with hatred, Jupiter took his three-tipped weighty bolt[20] and set himself to punish the guilty one, who despised him and did not fear his power. But he remembered it would inflict too harsh a pain on his beloved daughter, endowed with pretty eyes and a sweet face; so he held back the hatred in his heart that led him to be cruel.

47. Therefore he took a less harmful, less strong approach: he would not harm him, but rather give him fear, fright, and scare; he knew Cupid was a god and could not die. Although a great pain or grave fire oppressed him, it was enough to him that his arrow would bring Cupid a terrifying sign of his supreme power. He quickly gathered clouds and opened up the cave of the winds;[21] soon they felled branches and leaves.

48. At once the sun's beautiful clear face clouded, the sea rose, the shored quivered, and the sky rumbled horribly; among thick clouds shone the trusted messengers of his fury.[22] A terrible wind shook, bent on doing harm, and it seemed as though it challenged the earth and the sky to war: it broke, carried, whistled, knocked branches, uprooted trees, and lifted roofs, waging war on everything.

49. At that daunting noise, every wild beast fled and escaped from the open fields. Only Cupid did not move: he moaned and pined without caring for the sky, blackened by lightning. Wretched one! It darkened and roared for you! For you the winds shook and the air was blind and black; lo, Jupiter now turned his burning bolt against you from his heavenly place.

20. Jupiter's thunder was believed to have three prongs; see the note to 1.8.

21. The cave on the island of Aeolia in which the winds were locked up by their keeper, Aeolus.

22. This phrase refers to lightning bolts, believed to be privileged by Jupiter in expressing his unhappiness with humans.

50. The sky lit up with horrible lightning all around, among thick fog and noisy hail. The great thunderer looked with angry eyes, armed, from this noble high dwelling place. Toward Cupid, wandering child, for the humiliation he had received, he shot what the gods called Jupiter's second arrow: it had only lively burning fires around it.[23]

51. That harsh lightning thundered terribly, leaving the parted clouds by force; it made its way to him, who was mixing tears with sighs and did not use armor or shield to protect himself. It enveloped the delicate naked child with fiery heat that grew as it went; he trembled and feared, then he asked out loud: "Jupiter, have pity! Jupiter, have pity and mercy!"

52. The wretch fell, lying on the ground as if dead, his eyes dazzled, and his heart bewildered by the fury of that celestial fire; his beautiful body, though, was little harmed, or not at all. After the loud terror from the sky stopped, he stood up, gripped by fear; the fire of that bolt did not extinguish in him the flame of love that enflamed his beautiful chest.

53. If flame could ever be extinguished by fire, that time it was not; indeed, the torch of love that had lit up his heart when the wretch had discovered her noble beauty came back blazing more. Meanwhile the sky chased thick fog away, the winds calmed down, and the sun offered its light; lilies uncovered their breasts and dewy cheeks to dry up their wet roses.[24]

54. Each stem, happy, opened up its tresses to Phoebus's sweet warmth, which allures every soul; the green grass lifted its wet hair; and flowers laughed when the sky cleared. But you did not laugh when it uncovered a choice light or when it wore a veil of clouds; the wished-for light of your sun and joy never shone and sparkled in you.

55. When will be the day, o wretched one, when you'll go back to your customary pastimes, to singing, and to laughing? When will you adorn your hair with roses? When will your breast be satisfied and your face be smiling? Will you have a sad heart and murky days all the time? Will you spend all hours burning and vanquished? May Jupiter not allow this to happen and may wrath be defeated by pity, so that he may go back to what he was before.[25]

23. Jupiter's second arrow is another one of Marinella's inventions, a counterpart to Cupid's, one of which was made of gold and the other one of lead.

24. The attribution of human features to flowers (breasts and cheeks), and the paradox of the identification of different types of flowers (lilies and roses), is a hallmark of Baroque poetry, which builds on early modern conceits and makes them more extreme.

25. The last stanza of this canto is a disconsolate dirge addressed directly to Cupid, as well as a cliffhanger concerning the plot: will Jupiter deploy his wrath?

Canto 7

Argument of Canto 7

While asleep, handsome Cupid saw the beautiful face of his Ersilia in a dream. Then, awake, he saw her, pretty and lithe, among a hundred nymphs. He became cruel and untrustworthy. Venus searched for him over here and over there, without overlooking any wood, field, lawn, or shore. She found him, threatened him, and scolded him; he felt outrage, pain, wrath, and shame.[1]

Allegory

Cupid saw Ersilia in a dream, and he believed that he could hear her asking for help: this would be for us an example of man in the thralls of hatred or of love; he seems to see and hear what he wishes for and greedily desires, such is his concentration on the core of his imagination. Cupid admiring his woman among a hundred nymphs will be understood to be sensitive man, wholly given to his comforts; he looks at what is reasonable and crowned by a thousand virtues and spreading rays of its glory all around, so he is touched by great envy and would like to pursue it, but he is tricked, like Cupid. This is because the methods he employs to achieve it are faint and weak, in a word, childish. Venus looking for her son Cupid will be understood as the generating virtue, which cannot be complete without heat, understood to be Cupid.

1. Cupid sat, devoid of all joy, his feathers singed and hair scorched by the bolt that had struck him, burning and alive with flames, laden and rich with terror. He was not such that he did not show the angel-like, graceful appearance of a noble god; although pale, he still radiated celestial beauty that anybody would adore and admire.

2. With the water of his tears he completely extinguished the fire and flames in his feathers and hair: then he almost despised his own worthy beauties and blamed them in a faint, feeble sound. He had already lost the lofty banners of love. He no longer had Festival, Laughter, and Play with him; rather, a moaning crowd of sad sighs and a teary mass of cruel pains.

1. This is the second time that Venus goes looking for Cupid and finds him; the very proximity to Canto 5 would make it easy to recall in readers' minds.

3. He seemed like a small, breathless bird burning with love in the grass and flowers; it had followed the burning love of its beloved, which then quickly fled from it. It vented the pent-up ardors to happy breezes with tired notes and a sick, pained voice. Similarly, handsome Cupid looked at the sky, opened up the fire of this trusty chest,[2] and said:

4. "Woe is me, I'm alive and I burn with a lively flame! I am held by ties, I am wounded, I die! While love freezes and enflames my heart, binds, and kills it, still I find some comfort in the hope that a speck of fire should awaken in her, since the same fire is so alive in me! Such is my hope, for in these woods I saw trees and wild animals moved by my pain.[3]

5. "Where should I look for your lively rays, my sun, that can make me blessed? I lived surrounded by tricks and fairy tales because I loved too much, and so I'm not in this pained state, and I cannot stop. My heart aches for this ill-conceived strand of my life! Alas, I cannot bring these many pains to an end or untie my heart, unless that cruel woman unties it.

6. "Where, tell me, idol of my heart, my hope and noble desire, where will I see the shining splendor of your beautiful lights, the only comfort to my unhappy life? Enjoy the sad liquid from these eyes and the sighs that I send your way, since in your cruelty you disdain that I stamp any kisses on your beautiful face and lively eyes.

7. "Breeze that ripples the sea and sweetly caresses the hair of the grass with whispers, you that temper a burning day with sweet drafts and that sit in the green of lovely branches, as you wander and meander in the air, carry these moans from a wounded heart and pained soul to that icy heart for which I melt and vanish, like snow in the sun."[4]

8. As he said this in his sadness, he poured and let stream plentiful liquid from his lively stars.[5] The troubled pains of his heart made his features frail, yet handsome. He stopped talking but not crying, and with each passing hour he gathered harsh and cruel pains in his heart; he wasted away like a flower that languishes on a summer day, deprived of sweet breezes and water.

2. Cupid's chest is in fact not "trusty" (*fido*), as both Canto 6, above, and the ending of this canto make clear.

3. In this stanza, Marinella shows off her awareness of and ability with Petrarchan topoi concerning the devastating and contrasting feelings of a man unrequited in his love.

4. Marinella insists on the paradoxes of ice and fire that recur in Petrarch's and Petrarchan lyrical love poetry. Here the juxtaposition is between a cold heart and its ability to melt its beloved.

5. A complex expression to indicate that he cried copiously.

9. At his tears, cold marbles cried; caves and deep hidden valleys moaned; swift winds stopped their run in mid-air; and rivers stopped their shiny waves. Compassionate Echo replied from her caves to his tears, cries,[6] and loud complaints, while wild animals, rocks, and sense-deprived plants felt pity for Cupid, hated lover.[7]

10. While he complained and moaned, the torch of day quickly descended into Thetis's womb; tired and weary animals took some rest and peace among branches, under roofs, in lairs, and on water. The sky lit lively flames from rays here and there to provide mortals with some light, and Delia scattered clouds of pearl from her pallid face and loose blonde hair.[8]

11. On the hard ground, in the scary blindness of the dark of night, you alone called for death; you wished that a bear or a cruel-eyed lion would come and eat you to its satisfaction, or that the earth would open, accept you in its terrible chasm, and hold you, wretch, after it had closed up. You would rather be a sea rock without senses in order for the harsh pain in your chest to stop.[9]

12. He spent the entire night in sobs, pain, tears, and moans, and he never rested, like a turtledove that fills the sky with cries, sad and pained after losing its beloved. As soon as smiling, dewy Dawn mixed her lively rays to the darkness, a light sleep took him over; he was not alert or awake, but his sleep was troubled and short.[10]

13. Cupid's peace never stopped being disconcerted and troubled by horrible images and false dreams: to his mind, alert in that state of rest, there appeared a wide field; it seemed to him that he saw the roses, lilies, and graces of the one who had captured him, and that the sun was flaming with a serene light, which shone only from her eyes.

14. Happy and thoughtful, she was spending her day pressing the fields with her feet to make them blossom, and looking at the sky in its splendor, with flames and ice of chastity and honor.[11] Then she saw a man covered with a dark veil leave a

6. On Echo, see the notes to 1.35 and 3.3.

7. The polyptoton *Amor / amante* (Cupid / lover) is lost in our translation. It is also a way to underscore the paradox introduced by the adjective.

8. On Thetis, see the note to 1.62. Delia is one of the many designations for Diana, born on the Greek island of Delos; see the note to 1.63.

9. This direct address to Cupid attempts to build pity in the reader for the distraught protagonist.

10. On Dawn, see the note to 2.19.

11. The complexity of the syntax in the original generates the possibility that "flames" and "ice" be in parallel or chiasm with "chastity" and "honor." We have here a classic Marinella move: by exploiting both Petrarchan topoi and the rhetoric prevailing in the lyrical poetry of her times, she suggests

cave, or rather a wild animal, to bring violence and dishonor upon her. Fleeing, she called handsome Cupid to defend her with a terrible yell.

15. Pushed by heavy worry and by the wish to offer help to his beloved quickly, he made it so that while asleep his dream spread his wings and lifted his life. He was startled, opened his eyes, but did not see her pious face. The wound in him deepened; he would have fallen dead, but the lively hope of all lovers kept him alive.

16. The sun's maid was rising, laughing, among privets and roses;[12] perhaps all flowers opened their closed hearts at your beautiful rays and dewy breezes, Cupid. Over here one could see a good shepherd lead his herd to grassy plains; over there a young maiden adorned her brow with braided jasmines by a clear spring.[13]

17. Meanwhile, pretty birds praised rising Dawn with new songs, happy, and wove wandering dances among green branches, filling their chests and the hour with joy. His handsome features motionless, Cupid kept his eyes trained on them: he wished he could do what they were doing, singing about the eyes and shining hair of his goddess with sweet notes among the leaves.

18. Harsh love was already beginning to sap strength and words from his sane mind, which no longer held the bit of reason with as careful a hand as it used to. So he did not hold back the delirious, useless desire coursing through his sick inner senses; indeed he believed in it. He thus enjoyed having the utmost praise for it, rather than blame.[14]

19. He spread his wings and rose among the green leaves of an evergreen bay laurel,[15] then sat and sang about the blonde braids of his beloved, her beautiful face, and her pretty foot. Similarly a little bird asks its beloved for sweet mercy,

---

that "flames" (fundamentally male and dangerous) can be tied to two essentially female qualities like chastity and honor, themselves no longer passive, but a sign of strength.

12. On privets and their symbolism, see the note to 1.64.

13. The startling phrase "good shepherd," utilized in the New Testament to designate Christ, is emphasized by the occurrence of *ancella* (maid) and of *verginella* (young maiden), terms used in the gospels to refer to another soteriologically crucial figure: Mary, the mother of Jesus. Such words apparently went unnoticed by the Dominican friar reading *Love Enamored and Driven Mad* before its publication, or perhaps they did not raise any suspicion of a negative admixture of pagan (as the following octave makes clear, the Sun's maid is Dawn) and Christian.

14. This is a complex stanza, meant to draw the reader's attention to the tension between love and rational behavior and thought.

15. The repetition of "green" twice in quick succession to describe the bay laurel may be sloppy writing, but as a crown woven from laurel leaves was given as a gift to poets winning competition in classical antiquity (and hence in early modernity), it serves to underscore the immortality of poetry in general, and of the poem at hand, in a self-referential gesture. The laurel was sacred to Apollo; see also the note to 1.47.

with loud happy notes; it removes the intense pain and too hot affection from its chest, through its song.

20. As he sang, that handsome boy gave wonder to the world below and to the highest sphere. As he praised her graceful actions and royal deportment, his tired heart revived; lo, he glimpsed a chaste crowd filled with beauty emerge from the wood near him, and little by little he saw the woman who had set his heart on fire appear.

21. Similarly, from high up in the sky, the goddess of laughter and love, happy and charming, watched a welcome, pretty rose open up among snowy privets and other white flowers, making lovely breezes richer with choice beloved fragrances, and so self-content. Dawn wished for the sky to fall in love with her, adding its worth to her own innate beauty.

22. With her were a hundred nymphs in white veils, all with beautiful faces and beautiful manners;[16] similarly blond, cheerful stars woo Delia in the sky, their hearts heated by love. It seemed as though air, the ground, and each stem became happy as her slim feet moved; it seemed as though each stalk wanted a thousand tongues to praise her, whom they wanted to honor and love.

23. One gathered privets and another roses to make her golden tresses pretty and adorned. One stretched nets in a dark, brown spot, hidden among thorns, to catch a flock of birds. One sang about the uncertain and different movements and doubtful ending of love and luck; another looked at herself in the spring, and a third one bedecked her blonde hair with the gathered flowers.

24. One sent dogs after a hare, others raced each other, and some more shot arrows. Ersilia wished to follow the wild steps of a tiger or of a bear, her soul intent on glory.[17] One nymph came to help free birds from tricky nets, and another one vied for fish among the waves: with a thin web she bothered their peace, tossed some bait and small balls.

25. What are you doing? Wretch, what are you doing? Seated in the branches, happy and unhappy at the same time, you admired heavenly paradise in that face, the dear target of your beautiful wishes. Alas, while you stared at her with your eyes, you sent flames and arrows to your own heart from her beautiful face, so that

16. Marinella omits any explicit identification of the woman emerging here. If it were not for the Argument, readers would not know that this is Ersilia.

17. Marinella wastes no opportunity in stressing the fundamental difference between Ersilia's ambitions and the behavior expected of women. The glory she vies for is linked to hunting, physical courage, and strength, in juxtaposition with the glory of love that is extolled; here, the latter belongs to Cupid, in a gender switch.

the fire in you grew and you struck that harsh wound, wounding that old wound with your hit.[18]

26. The noble young man stood still, weary and in pain; he languished due to a harsh wound that had become more excruciating. He moaned and wailed with a pained low sound, and shed tears of blood from his eyes. He watched her beautiful face, her movements, her eyes, and her gait, while he was covered in sweat, pale and bloodless; he praised each action and admired each word of hers: crazy Cupid was delirious because he loved.

27. Pushed by the pain that charred his heart and by the desire that consumed and ate him, he ran fast to wound her with love; yet as he arrived next to her he sighed and fell silent. He placed on his bow a cruel, atrocious arrow, in order to chase peace from her heart, then shot thousands upon thousands to her chaste breast, without wounding her. In the end, it seemed that she felt them,[19]

28. and she got angry and quickly took away bow and golden arrows from him, breaking and destroying them. She let loose her angry wishes on him, made fun of him, derided, and despised him. Thus pains grew in his afflicted breast, since his craft and his handsomeness had no power. He said: "How could it be that the matchless might of my weapons has no might?"[20]

29. Did you not make the hearts of Hercules and Theseus effeminate, and their bosoms weak? Or those of the courageous and great warrior Achilles, or the great priest Orpheus? Did you not make them foolish and crazy? Yet although you tried a great deal, such a woman did not lose her noble virtue: her heart was made of iron, her chest of diamond, and your frail weapons could not turn either into lovers.[21]

18. The root for "wound" (*piaga*) is repeated three times in two lines, emphasized by its being in the last rhyme of the stanza; it then recurs in the following octave as well. This serves to insist on the pain that Cupid is inflicting, for once, on himself.

19. Marinella treats her readers to a short cliffhanger, enhanced by a rare occurrence in which the octave does not end with a period.

20. Another repetition in the crucial end-of-stanza rhyme position. Marinella cleverly utilizes two homonyms (*possa / possa*) that are grammatically different in Italian; in order to reproduce it we have modified the syntax slightly in the English translation.

21. The juxtaposition between four named men from Greco-Roman mythology with the implicit and unnamed Ersilia subtly points out that, in this poem, a mortal woman is better equipped than demigods, warriors, and even poets to withstand Cupid's attacks and stay true to her decision. Despite the regular accusations—especially in misogynist tracts—that women are inconstant and thus untrustworthy, Marinella places a woman ahead of men who are "effeminate" and "weak" despite their power, heroism, and fame. Tellingly, all four find their place in *The Nobility and Excellence of Women:*

30. He said: "Oh cruel woman, listen: wound this chest of mine with the arrow with which you wound happy and dear wild beasts! Take away my pain with extreme pain and bitter agony, as your celestial immortal beauty can help by bringing death. I'm happy if I die by your hand, the hand that I so love and honor.

31. "Since I love you, you hate me. If I hated you, would you love me, monstrous wild animal?[22] Still, I cannot hate you! Even rocks love you, though in their stiff way. An enemy puts an enemy to death, not a haughty soul her beloved. You kill me every hour, and now you refuse to give me life with one of your glances."

32. The beautiful nymph had already been wounded by a leaden arrow, yet she laughed and did not care; like a cowardly boy that people point at, she turned her back on his arrows, feeling safe. She wished to keep herself wholly chaste and pure, silent and apart, recluse among wild animals, in the woods. She wished to climb the tall mountain of honor via an unknown path full of valor.[23]

33. From tall banks he jumped into the nearby river that brought beautiful, moving, pretty waves to the bosom of the sea; he was vanquished by too much pain and aimed to satisfy her wishes. He said: "Why doesn't your mercy spread a sweet liquid in my open wounds? Why don't you chase the heat away from my burning feelings with the breeze of your sweet words?"

34. As he jumped in the water, that beautiful woman and her choice group moved their feet; smiling, they removed their pretty eyes and graceful miens from that beautiful lawn. Soon he emerged from the waters and turned his eyes, looking for his sweet beloved. As he could not see her, he, wretch, almost went mad and hardened like a rock.

Hercules is an example of vanity, Theseus of thanklessness, Achilles of both vainglory and cowardice, and Orpheus of despair for the loss of his wife.

22. Cupid uses a strong and unusual phrase to describe Ersilia, in his laments to her: she is an *immane fera*, which emphasizes her wild nature and large, indeed monstrous size. When Tasso introduces the character of Clorinda in Canto 2 of his *Gerusalemme liberata*, he calls her "fèra a gli uomini . . ., uomo a le belve" ["wild beasts think her a man, men think her wild"] (2.40.8). There is a certain correspondence between the two, but two fundamental differences: first, in Marinella the words are uttered not by the omniscient narrator, but the woman's beloved; second, Tasso emphasizes that Clorinda does not belong to either the human or the animal domain, while Marinella's Cupid stresses her alterity from him, which is obvious to any reader, since he is divine, and she is mortal.

23. Here Marinella underscores that Ersilia's ambitions, already highlighted in octave 24, are the exception rather than the rule for women. As Laura Benedetti has pointed out, Marinella presents herself in the same manner in her last work, *Essortationi alle donne*—"as an Amazon, a phoenix, an exception to the rule, established by God and nature, that women should not waste their time in intellectual endeavors." See Laura Benedetti, "Introduction," in *Exhortation to Women and to Others if They Please*, ed. and trans. Laura Benedetti (Toronto: Iter Inc. and Centre for Reformation and Renaissance Studies, 2012), 32.

35. Thus he was back to being full of sighs and sad, in the cold shade of that mournful yew tree;[24] he made his pain known by crying—a fierce pain that took over his breast and his heart. Every happy little bird vacated the wood at his cry, at his sick and sad yell; with his laments that wounded the air he disturbed the repose of the cruelest of wild animals.[25]

36. While he, brooding, moaned, grieved, complained, and repined at the foot of that green yew tree, his beautiful mother did not stop her steps: she spent both time and words looking for him. Turning her sweet eyes below,[26] she saw shepherds and nymphs playing and caroling; she came lower and asked them if her son were among them, whom she wanted to find.

37. One answered her: "Light, greatest splendor, shining ornament of heaven (for such you seem to me!), show us his face, his mien, and his deportment without any veil. May the goddess of Delos be a truthful witness![27] I'll satisfy your wishes quickly." She formed sweet breezes in notes between the roses of her beautiful lips and replied to him:

38. "I don't know if he was welcomed among you, old with age or looking like a wanton boy, with his sweet tricks; woe is you, if he stops his feet among you: a hungry lion or a wandering bull doesn't take as much pleasure in ripping up things as he does in straining hearts with a cruel whip and intense heat.

39. "Hyrcania and Syria do not harbor such a fierce tiger or deadly snake![28] Beware if he gets mad: he'll spit wrath and poison, you'll feel him hot or cold and bloodless; at times he's so small that he seems to be fainting, at others he runs, a fierce giant; sometimes he languishes, lazy, and sometimes he laughs amid the roses of his handsome face, or he rests and sits in golden hair.

40. "At times he pauses, playful as a child, surrounded by the flashes out of someone's eyes, at others submerged in the frost of someone else's white breast. Sometimes he hides among angel-like and divine words, wounding a loving soul, and sometimes he does the same among the crystal-like falling waves of the dear

24. On the yew tree and its symbolism, see the note to the Argument of Canto 6.

25. Cupid's utterances are primeval yells, an irrational mean of self-expression, not to be confused with poetry. Marinella underscores her craft indirectly.

26. Because Venus is flying, she is above the earth and thus looks downward when trying to discern Cupid and when addressing human beings.

27. Diana's presence in these woods is underscored time and time again. As Ovid points out (*Ars amatoria*, 1.261), she stands in opposition to Cupid, and this location is fundamentally inimical to him.

28. On Hyrcania, see the note to 3.45. Here Marinella adds Syria to deepen the sense of remote and wild places.

tears of a beauty in pain. He doesn't rise as utterly as fire; I know he is in a thousand places trying a thousand things, but I don't know where right now.

41. "In his hand he has a bow, and on this bow is a rough arrow made with opposing metals; with it he wounds soft hearts, filled with heavy worries, keeping them always balanced between hope and fear. He's a disloyal boy, always lying in wait till your heart melts in tears! His back is winged, and a quiver full of weapons dangles from it, with which he strikes souls.

42. "His hands are laden with ties, nets, and torches to strike others; with them he captures, burns, afflicts, and gives bitter pains to lazy chests and useless spirits. He doesn't just bother inexperienced chests and vile wishes, but the wisest and healthiest bosoms. No knowledge, power, coat of mail, or shield has any power against him, although he's young and naked.

43. "His eyes are lively, lit with a sweet fire; purple mingles with privet in his handsome face. His hair is partly wavy and partly straight, his heart is cruel and ever-changing, and his smile is pleasant. His voice, with which he wounds many, is sweet, but what is carved into his forehead is the opposite of what he harbors in his breast. If he laughs, jokes, or coddles, he always afflicts and brings damage to the heart.

44. "His handsome body is infused with a lively fire that attracts and allures; he harbors divine graces, and he scatters a fragrance more precious than ambrosia wherever he directs his flight. Such is the mien, such are the singular actions of my son, the child Cupid! I get angry and I grieve because I can't satisfy my wish for his face.

45. "If he plays or sits among you, may it not be difficult for you to point him out to me, in your kindness! As a generous recompense, I will bestow on the one who will make me aware of him more than a loving kiss."[29] A good shepherd bowed his head and kneeled in reverence, and in a humble and pious voice he answered: "He's not here, goddess, nor do we know where your great son is now.

46. "He often spends time with us: he doesn't eschew pastoral lowliness. With his noble head crowned with flowers, he only goes after youth, grace, and beauty. Although he's not here, still a ray laden with his inborn sweetness stays with us: even cold earth customarily stays warm due to the strength of the sun, after it's gone."[30]

29. We have here a rare explicit sexual reference; please see our Introduction, above.

30. The metaphor that the "good shepherd" utilizes here is both fitting for the "pastoral lowliness" that marks his culture and surroundings, and in keeping with the image of Cupid that Marinella builds

47. Having heard this, the goddess moved her golden chariot, adorned with a thousand decorations, elsewhere. Time and time again she considered in her heart where she might find her beloved son. Meanwhile Night wrapped her tresses in golden jewels and wore her beautiful starry cloak; but she did not stop putting all her care in looking for her son, whether the air was bright or dark.

48. Whether it was day or night, that outraged goddess ran and wandered around to find her son. She looked for him among patricians and plebeians, and she sighed when she did not find him. She immersed herself among shepherds and nymphs, among hoes and rakes. She looked and then looked again in each village and city, and she did not regret to look often in a place where she had already looked.

49. If she saw happy women and maidens in the grass and among flowers, with pretty faces and beautiful features, lower the summer heat with cool breezes, though their hearts were warm with love, she removed wrath and fury from her sweet words, as she wanted to know if her son was among them. She said to them: "May it please you to say if my son Cupid, my only hope, is among you."

50. As she spoke, she radiated a fragrance all around more precious and dearer than a rose, and she flashed a very clear bolt of celestial beauty from her beautiful gaze. From this they became aware that an earthly home was not fit for her, but a unique heavenly one; thus one of them said, with humble heart: "We do not know or are acquainted with Cupid."

51. Without saying anything else, the goddess loosened the bridles on the white necks of her beautiful doves; they spread their wings and soared toward the clear sky following sweet, fluid paths. She tried but did not succeed in bringing happiness to her breast and assuaging her eyes. She wandered here and there, already despairing that she would ever find him; she moved, disdainful and fierce.

52. While the noble goddess from Cythera[31] went about pained and full of wrath against Cupid, a beautiful nymph rose from a river nearby. More than a nymph, she looked like a celestial goddess: the gold of her hair, glistening more than the sun, covered the snow of her back. She said: "Perhaps, goddess, I'll be the one to give you news of your son.[32]

---

throughout the poem: he is a force of nature, the source of all life, exactly like the sun. See also the note to stanza 16, above.

31. On Cythera and Venus, see the note to 1.7.

32. In parallel to the later scene in 9.40–45, here, too, it is a nymph who finally provides Venus with information on her wayward son; the goddess initial reaction, there and here, is to turn deathly pale (see 7.54 below).

53. "There, where the tall trees make the plain shady with their tall heads, I saw a kingly child with a gentle face, a noble mien, and divine gestures; he had wings on his back and filled the sky with many words, scratched his breast, and struck himself with his own hand. With his sighs he seemed to shake pines, beeches, and strong turkey oaks[33] so that their leaves would fall off."

54. Having heard that, the goddess's face lost all color: an arrow laden with harsh pain had struck her chest. As she imagined to see him, she was aware that her beloved son was hurt by some pain; with her heart marked by throes she moved the bridle restraining her choice small group of beautiful birds; quickly they took her where the wood was densest, most impenetrable, and darkest.

55. When her celestial beauty appeared, that horrible forest chased away its fearful darkness, transforming what was harsh into sweet and hard into soft; it covered itself with pretty blades of grass and flowers instead of thorns. Where sad breezes once made fierce and hoarse noises among the tree trunks, Zephyrus sweetly exhaled his breadth, awakening new choice flower shapes.[34]

56. With his melodious murmur taking the shape of intelligible and beautiful words, he seemed to say: "May it not be burdensome for you to bring joy to this darkness with your face, splendor of golden stars! Although unworthy, it does hold within itself your offspring, filled with harsh and nasty pains. Come and console your handsome son's much too hot emotions with your sweet words."

57. He thus invited the noble goddess, adorned with haughty graces, with his sweet murmur, and with melodious noise he pointed out where her handsome son stood and cried. She turned the light of her eyes to a harsh and lonely spot, and she saw him; then, stunned, she watched and observed him. He did not notice, then at last he turned his eyes to her.

58. Like a man who with a trick has stolen a nice cache of jewels, pearls, and gold, or who has wounded a very worthy man and bears full responsibility for his death, he is confused, stunned, and lost if he sees the king's soldiers upon himself; he trembles, his voice is lost, and he shows himself guilty of his worthless misdeeds through a thousand signs,

33. Interestingly, Marinella specifies the turkey oak (*Quercus cerris*) by name, rather than merely "oaks." This tree, which is native to Europe and Asia Minor, produces bitter, bristly acorns that squirrels will eat only if no other food source is available; the tree also provides a home for the gall wasp, whose larvae can infest and destroy other oak species, as happened when these trees were introduced into Britain. Appropriately in this poem, then, the turkey oak thus seems to symbolize both beauty and deception.

34. On Zephyrus, see the note to 1.67.

59. similarly Cupid was at his mother's sudden arrival. He did not know how to hide his tears, his stunned face, his half-burned wings, and his charred tresses. The goddess from Cyprus did not know that he carried a woman's face and her beloved name engraved in his breast. So, staring at him with her eyes, confused, sad, and outraged, she said:

60. "This is how I find you? Alas, I see you so pained and tearful! What wound, pain, or strange illness hurts you and makes your heart sad and pained? Are these the hair and wings with which I made you pretty and full of love? Is this the fire that I lit in your face, now (alas!) turned into the pallor of death?

61. "Who extinguished it? Where did he go? Where is he hiding? Why can't I see him anymore?[35] Woe is me, what do I see? I see your heart, unfaithful boy:[36] why doesn't your lying tongue answer what I'm asking? You wander and rove and you don't know where your pain comes from; what should I think? When I see you in such a state, I regret having given you life and adorned you.

62. "Is this the reverence and love that a respectful son owes his mother? I'll chase you out of my home and I'll exile you for all time! Do you believe that I won't be able to make another son, another Cupid, more courteous in his looks and more grateful in his mind?"[37] At that moment he directed his eyes to her face with a false smile.

63. "Mother, my goddess, from whom the third circle receives motion, light, and beauty, I know that my sense, my soul, and all I see depends on you, my captain![38] Perhaps your heart ignites with deep wrath in seeing my tears and my pain? I'll explain the truth behind them; please believe the truth that I say and that has taken over my breast.

64. "I see you with so much joy, great mother, flame of my torches, iron of my arrows! What can Cupid do without you? His powers are weak! I was on my way

35. The Italian original does not identify by gender the responsible party; we have used the masculine here to underscore Venus's utter inability to consider that love for a woman might have reduced her son to that state.

36. An ironic utterance, since Venus emphatically does not grasp his emotions, as octaves 62 and 67 make clear. The juxtaposition with the repetition of "truth" in stanza 63, uttered by Cupid, could not be stronger. A mother's love blinds her to circumstances.

37. Venus's utterance to Cupid echoes the one Marinella places in 5.60–61, where she similarly berates her son for his trespasses and wanderings. Another instance occurs in 8.22.

38. The word used in the Italian original (*duce*) has both a political and a military valence. It is a strong attribute, in keeping with the tone of reverence that Cupid wants to strike with his mother in this speech.

to my happy kingdom, beating my wings through the moving air; I carelessly flew above the mountain that presses down on the haughty brow of that fierce Titan.[39]

65. "Because of my unlucky fate, quick as lightning a flame emerged, rolling out of that fierce giant; it burned my hair, singed my feathers, blackened my face, and darkened my breast. My heart felt such pain and outrage! I came very close to fainting and came here out of shame; so now you see me at the hard foot of this cold yew tree.

66. "I was not recalcitrant to your will, I didn't think I was, nor did I have the courage to be. Please believe my words! Displace outrage, hatred, and wrath from your white, immaculate, and pious chest! I have always wished to obey you, and I always will, because I recognize that my whole being is from you: not just my life, which I appreciate, but any grace and beauty that have ever been in me."

67. So handsome Cupid hid and concealed his love and his mistake, with a cloak of falsehood. She believed his utterance and did not think what her smart son had revealed to her was untrustworthy. She gave up all wrath and felt pain in her beautiful chest; she anguished and complained, she embraced, kissed, caressed, and consoled him. He hated and despised all that.

68. A sweet and tender emotion, and a dear desire for pity, touched her noble heart. She did not want her son Cupid to leave her once she entered her royal doors, as long as the pretty flower of his beauty had not returned and tears and pains had not left him. She brought him in her arms, climbed on her chariot, and took the bridles of her flying coursers.

39. A reference to mythological events narrated by Aeschylus in *Prometheus Bound*: the Titan Typhon was confined to Mount Etna, causing its eruptions.

Canto 8

Argument of Canto 8

Handsome Cupid tried wretchedly to flee away from his pretty mother, but in vain. She tied him as a prisoner, then left her royal nest, to put some distance between herself and her son. Locked up, he cried, devoid of trust in himself; he struck his chest and became insane with rage. He knocked down walls, broke tall doors, and deprived her beautiful garden of pomp and beauty.

Allegory

Cupid imprisoned by his mother will figure for us the senses bound by reason, or it will represent our freedom taken by the pleasantness and prettiness of a beautiful face. Venus's son breaking, shattering, and knocking down walls, statues, and other adornment in her royal palace will be understood to be those men bamboozled and pushed by wrath or love (both very powerful passions): after they have lost all hope of revenge or of possessing their beloved, they are so afflicted that they break, waste, and use up all their belongings to misery and nothingness, like crazy men. There have been some such men who became so evil and upset that they used weapons not only against their own riches, but against their own chests, hoping to remove themselves from such desperate pains; some even hung themselves. Vulcan's son uprooting bushes and trees and destroying flowers in his mother's garden will be understood as time, which removes and destroys all power and all beauty from our frail nature.

1. Wanton little birds flitted up and flew in the air, racing with each other. Sad in her heart, she turned her beautiful eyes, full of tears, toward her son; she looked and looked again at his partly burned wings and singed hair and at the roses gone from his beautiful face, not without pain. She saw laughter completely banished from it.[1]

2. She said: "Alas, my son, why do you derive happiness and pleasure from staying away from me, in darkness and gloom, through harsh dangers, all splendor

1. Marinella explicitly juxtaposes Venus's mood and demeanor to natural elements, emphasized by the fact that "little birds" (*augelli*) are dubbed as "wanton" (*lascivetti*). Venus is stripped of erotic elements and emerges here as a mother concerned by her son's behavior. This is emphasized by the fact that Marinella does not mention the goddess's name in this first stanza. She simultaneously tests her readers' recollection of the end of the previous canto and generalizes the opening of the present one to a common human situation.

drained from your eyes? Why do I see your handsome innate color disappear from the pretty whiteness of your white lilies? Yes, you used to be handsome, just like a laughing rose when the sun appears.

3. "Now I see you sad, languishing, and in tears! Do you fear, perhaps, that the graces and the beauty that used to dwell in your noble loving face may never return? Don't you know that even if the sun is hidden by clouds, the day will still come back, happy and blazing? In the same way ultimate beauty comes back, although lost from where it belongs.

4. "Chase away from your brow and your eyes the ice and fear that surround your soul! What do you fear? You are in your mother's arms now, and your mother's pity embraces and holds you." The wretched boy, whose breast burned and froze, was afraid to uncover himself, held his sighs, and showed his cloudy face all clear, with a smile.

5. She laughed when he did so, as does a mother who mirrors her son's wish: she cries if he does, she grieves if he does, and she mingles her wails with his; if he unveils and shows joy in his heart with very sweet words, she is satisfied. Love always makes one heart out of two, and one soul out of two.

6. The goddess of love was busy stealing a thousand kisses from his handsome eyes and a thousand more from his beloved face. She looked at him with gentle words and sweet teardrops, as she said: "Cupid, calm the tempest in your heart, rekindle your eyes, push away the glum shadow of sadness and tears from your brow and from the sky!"

7. The sun was setting in the west, its face purple because of its strain, when the tall mass of her royal palace showed itself, nearby; in it was gathered everything that was good and beautiful, beauties lofty and unique. The beloved sight of her dear home brought much happiness and delight to the great goddess, so she said to herself:

8. "May god make you happy, dear and beloved nest, with all my sweetness and peace! May the innate goodness of heaven not scorn that I find rest in your trusted womb, now that I bring in the sad lord that I harbor in my chest from a long and arduous way!" As she said this, her white birds slowly descended to the desired place.[2]

9. There were Aglaea, Euphrosyne, and Pasithea, all similar in goodness and beauty. The first one took sick Cupid in her arms with kind manners and sweet gentle actions; the second one humbly extended her hand to the beautiful goddess

2. The irony implicit in Venus's wish is inescapable, since the Argument and Allegory have already revealed that peace and concord are not going to occur. At the opening of this canto, Marinella presents the readers with a human depiction of Venus, as a mother easily convinced by her son's pretended serenity or as a woman quick to believe her beloved's lies.

so that she might get off her chariot; the third one untied the pretty birds from it and gave them sweet ambrosia to eat.[3]

10. One prepared a bejeweled seat, another set nectar in a golden goblet, and yet another maiden, pretty to behold, flattered Cupid, still anguishing in bitter pain; she created a thousand kisses with her beautiful mouth and nourished his beloved brow with them; with an ivory comb she imparted order on his hair, deprived of art and disorderly.

11. She plunged him in a tub filled with perfumed water, and noble Pasithea washed his arms, back, and blond tresses that shone more than pure gold. Then the beautiful goddess from Cythera[4] welcomed him, wrapped in a clean thin cloth, in her bosom; she dried the dewy drops off his body with pure, utterly white veils.

12. Afterwards she nourished and fed her noble charge with sweet ambrosia and divine nectar; yet he despised the unpleasant taste of worthy food because of the pain that was again surfacing in him. He did not show the flame that was becoming warmer with each passing hour; still, his frequent sighs placed some doubts in the goddess's mind.

13. Meanwhile the sun had set, eager for food and rest, its face wet with sweat;[5] it had already gathered its tired limbs in the wavy bed of the wide ocean, when a base animal started wandering in the shadowy air that harbored fear in its bosom, and gold stars displayed their beautiful cheeks to show themselves off.

14. Among them the pretty moon proceeded, haughty, like a queen among her maids, competing with the sun, making the dark shadow of night light. Sleep rose, adorned with poppies and violets, and with it an untrustworthy crowd of dreams, which troubled the minds and souls of us mortals with good and bad omens.[6]

3. Aglaea, Euphrosyne, and Pasithea were the Graces, minor deities of beauty, splendor, mirth, and fertility. Although they were conventionally depicted as a group of three (typically three beautiful nude maidens dancing in a circle, as immortalized in Botticelli's *Primavera*), there were as many as four or more; Thalia is usually referred to as the sister of Aglaea and Euphrosyne. On the Graces, see the note to 4.6, and on Pasithea, see the note to stanza 27, below; on ambrosia, see the note to 2.9.

4. On Cythera, see the note to 1.7.

5. Marinella provides a human touch here, presenting the mighty sun as a laborer resting at the end of his day's work. This image is carried over into stanza 17 below, in which "beautiful Dawn invited each mortal soul to work and toil, when a new sun made the tall bright mountain peaks golden with its golden light." This evokes the description of Venus's doves and swans as tired after their exertions in 5.19.

6. On Sleep, see the note to 5.55. The deities who ruled over dreams and nightmares were the Oneiroi, brothers of Hypnos (Sleep), of whom the most famous was Morpheus.

15. Exhausted minds had already hidden their daytime worries in Lethe's bosom.[7] Earth, air, the sea, and the winds were silent under the clear night sky. Still you vented your burning desires with sighs, because your heart was touched with a harsh poison, while each soul sweetened its bitter emotions among leaves or in lairs, under water or roofs.

16. You counted the hours and used your ears to notice if the song of the cockscomb bird was heard;[8] you spoke as if Dawn, escort to the new day, in eager enjoyment casting light on to the world, was later than usual in returning with her sounds. He gnawed his heart, because he wanted to leave his mother's kingdom and plumage as soon as new light emerged.[9]

17. When beautiful Dawn invited each mortal soul to work and toil, when a new sun made the tall bright mountain peaks golden with its golden light, he quickly left that soft bed, which seemed to him harder than thorns and nettles;[10] he vented his heart's pain and exceedingly hot passion in a lonely spot.

18. Since his chest harbored a deep wound that he tried to hide, he hated flatteries, comforts, festivities, and pleasures. He hated life, his mother, her leisures and palaces. He wished to be in a lonely, harsh, secluded spot, fitting for his pain, as he hoped still to see the woman who had shot flames and arrows in his heart.

19. He waited for an opportune moment when his mother would be occupied with games, with pretty and charming works, or with braiding and tying beautiful but unkempt hair. She did not want him to be at all removed from her. He wanted to flee to dark and scary woods, to places so far removed from her that she might not see him or hear his name; she would be left only with the bitter weight of pain.

20. One day, when she was gathering the shiny gold of short hair in beloved ringlets, tying and ordering long scattered hair with divine and superhuman work, satisfying her wishes for her own beauty with pretty flowers in a beautiful mirror, Cupid moved his feet and quickly unfolded his wings with a trick, in order to leave.[11]

21. She was close by and noticed that he was stealthily escaping; she ran quickly to him and grabbed the runaway by his white foot, making him captive, though he hated it. "Is this, ungrateful son, the reward and the love that come before all

7. On Lethe, see the note to 3.62.

8. On the cockscombed bird, see the note to 6.8.

9. Uncharacteristically, Marinella here opens the stanza by addressing Cupid in the second person, then closes it by talking about him in the third.

10. Nettles are weeds with stinging hairs filled with irritants, common on the Italian peninsula.

11. We have in this octave a rare marker for the passing of time; typically Marinella is less precise, an approach that enhances the mythical atmosphere of the world in which the plot develops.

other virtues? Is this the recompense that you give me? Is this how you amend your flight and your mistake?

22. "So, faithless one, you pay back my love and my grace with ungratefulness? Oh cruel one, you hate your kingdom and your devoted mother, and even your own royal palace! I'll keep you locked up in sturdy chains in a harsh prison; I'll see your complaints and I'll enjoy hearing your laments, your sad tears, and your sigh-laden words."

23. Having said this, she picked one of the one hundred rooms on which gold and jewels cast light and wrought decorations; their superior craft surpassed all that had been considered sublime and worthy of a king. Its bed was made of citron wood,[12] adorned with the most beautiful treasure and admirable embroidery that she possessed; the floor was made of pearl and corals, with parts wrought of gold and silver.

24. The windows had intertwined iron bars, barring the way to those wanting to leave; the door was made of strong turkey oak[13] with many keys and other irons. There she locked up her son so that he would not stray; that he would test the heavy load of her power; that he might learn to obey her and pay attention to what she liked; and that he might look and reach for what was good.

25. As one feels whose chest harbors and prizes the highest goodness and true innocence, who feels his head spring open and his chest wounded by cruel swords, even though he has not bothered anybody, similarly Cupid felt. His face, devoid of courage, fell onto his chest; vanquished and lost, he regretted that he was immortal and alive, as he wanted to be neither.

26. Right then love renewed the nets, arrows, and fire in his white chest; pushed and wounded by outrage and spite, he wailed, regretted, and could not find space. Noble son, how will you be able to leave the bothersome prison of this royal roof, a little or a lot, if so much iron and craft keep it closed up? Who will now untie you and let you go?[14]

12. Citron wood, or thyine wood, was prized by furniture makers in ancient Greece and Rome. Its name is derived from the Greek *thuon* ("fragrant wood") or perhaps *thuein* ("to sacrifice"), and in fact it was used in the burning of sacrifices because of its fragrance. Thyine wood is also referred to in the Bible as one of the products sold in Babylon before its fall (Revelation 18:12).

13. On the turkey oak, see the note to 7.53.

14. In this direct address to Cupid, Marinella juxtaposes his identity as Venus's "noble son" (*nobil figlio*) and his impossible wish to escape from her palace.

27. Thus the beautiful goddess locked up her beloved son in a strong prison. She brought along beautiful Pasithea as a companion and an advisor.[15] To make her brow happy after those outrages, she moved her foot away from her royal palace and to Cythera; when she arrived, she banished her outrage and cleared her face, in happiness and laughter.

28. Then she went back to the third circle to make heaven smile again with her beauty. She adorned her blonde hair with white flowers, since a dark veil of pain no longer crowned it. There the noble goddess dwelt, satisfied, full of pleasure and far from heat and ice. Meanwhile Cupid agonized and tortured himself: all hope for hope was wholly extinguished.[16]

29. He looked and searched here and there to see if a road were open to his stealthy departure. A desperate pain ate and lashed him when he did not see a way to escape from prison. He no longer hoped to see the beautiful face that held his freedom and his heart; similarly a locked up bird tries to escape from its prison, moves around, jumps, and gets upset.

30. As he cried, he said: "Will I be locked up here, like a wandering man forced to pay restitution? Will I suffer in prison, bound tightly, vanquished by a cruel mother and disappointed? Will I not admire my sweet beloved and her beauty, mingled among flowers and nymphs? May I not be able to break her heart, hard as rock, with teary prayers, alas, uttered next to her?

31. "Intertwined iron bars, locked doors, and walls wage war against my desire, alas! With my powerful and strong hand I'll break this unworthy iron, inimical to my wish; I'll bring to this happy garden and my rich home a wicked and terrible ending! I'll break, I'll shatter, and I'll reduce to naught what goes against my burning mind."

32. After other sick and weak words, he struck his face and breast with his own hand, now his enemy; face and breast became alive with the bright colors that a beautiful rose brings to life in a sunny meadow, or they became red like the white friend of jealous Tithonus in the cold hour.[17] Rooms echoed when he struck his ivory breast and smooth cheeks.

15. "Noble Pasithea," one of the Graces; she helped welcome Venus on her return in stanza 9, and bathed Cupid in stanza 11. Pasithea, who ruled rest and relaxation, was married to Hypnos (Sleep). According to Homer, she was one of the younger Graces, but Statius called her the "eldest of the gracious sisters" (*Thebaid*, 2.285). On the Graces, see the note to stanza 9, above.

16. The repetition of "hope" (*speme*) in such close succession serves to deny its presence even more strongly; again Marinella utilizes the traits prevalent in Baroque poetry to their full advantage.

17. Tithonus was a Trojan man, and the lover of Dawn (the Greek Eos); Marinella here refers to her as "white friend" because she brings light; she turns red in the "cold hour" just before sunrise. Eos asked

33. Such deep anguish and pain squeezed the heart of that young boy in love so that all light in his lively mind became extinguished, so powerful were his torments and pain. Then his face became the color of a dark flame and a lethal light shone from his eyes; he raised his brow with a terrible expression and he threatened heaven with his weapon.[18]

34. Perhaps this is the way in which bombastic Nimrod was seen, full of empty pride, from a high tower, when he thought he was taller than the sun and he could chain the gods in the dark of night.[19] It is fabled that nymphs gave up their songs and carols and no longer spent happy hours with their beloved shepherds as they used to do before, goaded by cruel pain.

35. He yelled: the Hyster, the Rhine, the Euphrates, the Tagus, the Nile, the Hebros, and the Iberian heard him; heaven and the dark caves of Erebus heard him; haughty Neptune in the sea heard him.[20] The world trembled at that yell and wholly understood what a bitter and fierce will was upon it. Nature was shaken up and spilt its milk, then almost dead, from its hundred breasts.[21]

Zeus to make Tithonus immortal, but forgot to specify that she wanted him to be eternally young. Zeus agreed, and Tithonus lived forever but continued to age. When he could no longer move or speak, he was turned into a cicada.

18. This is the crucial octave in which Cupid goes mad. Light is an essential component of rationality in Italian culture, and Marinella here expresses it in three different ways, before moving quickly to Cupid's changed behavior.

19. Nimrod was a biblical character, great-grandson of Noah; he was associated with the foundation and building of the Tower of Babel, which was intended to reach up into the heavens (Genesis 11:1–9). This was interpreted by God as an act of defiance against him. Deciding that humankind had had too much freedom, he punished the people by turning their single language into many, so that they could no longer understand each other.

20. Marinella presents the impact of Cupid's crazed yell with a crescendo of geographic and natural elements. First, she lists several rivers, an inventory that echoes the list of rivers traversed by Cupid as he searches for Ersilia (4.32). She then moves to the two spheres of the afterworld before reaching the sea and the very essence of nature, identified with its nourishing element. "Hyster" (*Istros*) is the Greek name for the Danube, Europe's second longest river, flowing from the Black Forest in Germany to the Black Sea. The Rhine crosses Europe from Switzerland to the North Sea. The Euphrates flows from Turkey to the Persian Gulf. The Tagus is the longest river in the Iberian Peninsula. The Nile is the longest river in the world, and flows northward from Lake Victoria in Africa to the Mediterranean. "Hebros" is the Greek name for modern-day Maritsa, which flows in the Balkans. The "Iberian," which is also mentioned in the list of Canto 4, does not designate any river; it may be Marinella's name for the Ebro, the second longest river in Iberia, or simply a way to mention another recognized toponym. For Erebus, see the note to 4.54.

21. Nature with "its hundred breasts" is a reference to Artemis Ephesia, a mother goddess unique to the area of Ephesus in Asia Minor and not to be confused with Diana/Artemis, chaste goddess of the hunt. Artemis Ephesia was related to the pre-Hellenic deity Cybele, and worshipped at the famous temple at Ephesus; statues depicted her as having many breasts.

36. Woods crumbled and large forests trembled deeply; all beaches shouted. It seemed as though one fear and one terror made their way in the forests, so that each bird left branch and nest. Wild animals were horrified and bewildered at the terrible sound of such a horrible yell. Sad turtledoves wounded themselves with disdain and killed their sweet charges.[22]

37. When the sky foretells disintegration or death to a kingdom or to a king, it shows itself dark and sad, the air troubled, its brow oppressed by an unhappy comet and other inauspicious additions;[23] Apollo deposes his happy golden mantle and wears a different veil, black and ominous, appearing to be weary and tired, as if horses did not bring light but dark and black smoke.[24]

38. All the more so, at that point, the sky revealed signs of harm to come, all around, since a boy adorned with a thousand graces, indeed a great god, showed himself to be in such trouble; he was war and peace for this mortal dwelling place, its leader and its tyrant, who made it so that humid and dry, hot and cold would be at peace, without quarrels, and united.[25]

39. When that beautiful day flew to darkness and to thick shadows of night, wearing a red cloak, nature embroidered its shining mantle with inauspicious decorations and a poisonous flame: shapes of death and future tears, ungodly stars appeared carrying tails and horrible tresses. The whole world was saddened by such a strange sight.[26]

40. The boy archer's anger and wrath grew and deepened with each passing day; that sweet, dear, and noble face of his inspired more terror than the appearance of hell. He jumped, sang, wandered around, danced, struck his handsome bosom, sighed, uttered blasphemies to heaven, cried, laughed, ran like a greyhound, and sat, in quick succession.

22. This stanza continues the reversal of the order of nature already emerging in the previous one, giving more examples of the upheavals caused by Cupid's madness. Turtledoves were believed to mate for life, so the fact that they hurt themselves and their offspring is doubly troubling.

23. On comets, see the note to 4.39.

24. The reference here is to Apollo driving the chariot of the sun across the sky; instead of bringing sunlight, however, his horses bring darkness and "black smoke."

25. "Humid and dry, hot and cold" were opposite principles in the Galenic theory of humors that influenced Western medicine in early modernity. Marinella was presumably familiar with these through her family, as her father, brother, and husband were physicians and natural scientists; see our Introduction. The very essence of all things is turned upside down by Cupid's madness.

26. Another reference to comets, described as "ungodly stars" with tails.

41. Lo, a great fury started; never a similar was or will be! Never high heaven or the dark kingdom heard the same, or the sea of India to the one of Thule.[27] Those who learnedly sang of Orestes and his errors while the Furies bothered him, should be quiet, as well as those who sang of the crazy love of the lord of Anglante: they have nothing on this one![28]

42. He moved with the same movement that forces a fiery ball out of a terrible cannon;[29] wrath awakened and strengthened his forces, so he knocked down anything wherever he moved his hand. His blind fury did not abate at all; in fact, it seemed to grow deeper and fiercer with each passing hour. He broke the iron bars on those rich windows, which bestowed pomp and beauty with their craft.

43. He was furious and enraged: he shredded, broke, and wasted that golden bed, richly adorned with dear jewels, and the canopy embroidered all around by the immortal work of the Graces. One could not see any decorations in that famous dwelling. Are you breaking silk cloth, woven with gold? Do you not stop after so much damage?[30]

44. Still not content that he had annihilated decorations and wasted riches, he moved on to the great hall; roughly, in that large, wide, and open space, he destroyed the great beauty of sculptures, and he broke and shattered vases carved out of ruby, diamond, and topaz, pushed by fury: compared to it, iron and walls seemed frail, and he looked like lightning.

27. As in stanza 35, Marinella names points far apart from each other to indicate the entirety of earth: from heaven to hell, and from the East to the North (on Thule, or "Thile," see the note to 2.61).

28. Orestes was the son of Agamemnon, king of Mycenae and Greek leader of the Trojan War. When Agamemnon returned from war, his wife Clytemnestra and her lover killed him, and Orestes avenged his death by killing his mother. He was then chased by the Furies because of his bloodguilt. "Lord of Anglante" is one of the titles of Roland (Italian Orlando), one of the heroes of the Carolingian epic cycle written in French throughout the Middle Ages. For her implied (contemporary) reader, this phrase would have naturally evoked Matteo Maria Boiardo's *Orlando innamorato* (1483 and 1495) and Ludovico Ariosto's *Orlando furioso* (1516 and 1521); in the latter, Orlando is portrayed as having gone mad because of his beloved Angelica's unreciprocated love. Marinella boldly proclaims that her chosen plot is even more difficult to tackle than two canonical precedents and thus, implicitly, that her work exhibits a higher level of craft than those of Homer and Aeschylus, in one case, and those of Boiardo and Ariosto in the other.

29. The original term (*Bombarda*) meant a bombard, a type of cannon used during the Middle Ages and Early Modern era to hurl stone balls at targets. The usage is now historical, but of course survives in the verb form and in such terms as "bombardier."

30. In this address to Cupid, Marinella reprimands him in ways similar to Ariosto's characterization of his crazed hero, Orlando: both are so out of control that they escape even the governance of their authors. Similarly, in stanza 45 below, Marinella upbraids Venus.

45. What were you doing, beautiful goddess, who fill the third heaven with love thanks to flames and laughter? Did you peacefully spend time on Mount Olympus, crowned with roses and veiled in white?[31] Did you not see how furious Cupid destroyed everything, as though stung by a harsh weapon? Or how he struck his chest and beat his face, oppressed and driven out of his wits by a desperate pain?

46. He took a sword that fierce Mars had left in that unhappy royal palace when he abandoned the highest part of heaven to visit the beautiful goddess of Cythera.[32] With it his unvanquished hand razed to the ground the wondrous art of the eternal maker that you see impressed in breathing marble, such that you would believe that it spoke and breathed if you saw it.[33]

47. He knocked down and broke famous sculptures of noble gods and mortal men, to whom no equal exists or ever existed as far as value, excellence, and beauty are concerned. He stripped all charm away from the royal palace with these and other extreme ills; then, with this powerful and strong sword, he broke the lofty doors to the noble garden.

48. He uprooted beautiful orange trees and a golden citron adorned with white flowers, both replete with sweet smells; till then they had offered sweet gentleness all around and in charming fields with their happiness. If he could have, he would have damaged and brought disdain to the beautiful, serene clear fields of clear air. In his heart he complained that his great enemy, Jupiter, was not in his hands.

49. The strength and craziness of the furious lover uprooted, troubled, stripped, and shook up quiet springs, beautiful meadows, beautiful flowers, and leafy trees; deer and other slim wild animals fled his cruel face and troubled expression. He uprooted ancient pines and green laurel and myrtle trees, devoted to his goddess.[34]

50. Teary and sad, beautiful nymphs emerged naked from waters and springs, their never-ending hair unkempt and scattered to the airs, their faces pale and their expressions sick and gloomy. They lifted their tearful eyes and troubled

31. On Mount Olympus, see the note to 2.23.

32. On Mars, here presented as Venus's lover, see the note to the Argument of Canto 1.

33. The "eternal maker" (*fabbro eterno*) here refers to the artist who created the statues and vases that Cupid destroyed (indeed, Marinella later says, in 9.52, that the palace's "tall columns" had been "raised by a learned craftsman"). The phrase "eternal maker," however, is normally associated with God. Marinella underscores that a visual artist's work is not eternal, precisely because it was just shattered; following Ovid, she also implies that poetry is a more permanent memento of events, more durable than marble monuments.

34. On myrtle, see the note to 1.32. The laurel tree was sacred to Apollo, and out of laurel branches the Greeks fashioned crowns with which they honored winners of the Pythian Games, held in Apollo's honor and including sport, art, and dance competitions; see also the notes to 1.47 and 7.19. Marinella underscores here that nothing is safe and immune from Cupid's fury.

brows to their heavenly home and said: "Alas, are these the effects of love, rather than signs of outrage and fury?"

51. They cried in sadness over the scattered honors and the stripped faith of their beloved woods; pained and disheveled, they turned their feet toward blind caves and dark and shady caverns. Whether the air was clear or murky and dark, pain followed upon pain and cries followed upon cries within them. It is famed that they melted in water and became trees and were turned into springs, in fields and on mountains.[35]

52. Thus gold and deep purple did not shine to make beautiful the noble garden and tall royal palace, pleasing refuge of the highest gods, now deprived of all decorations; no plane tree rose in its greenery to render the garden pretty. Clytia did not lift her courageous face as she was wont to do, in order to admire the sun.[36]

53. He rendered the palace afflicted and the flowers sad, now deprived of all beauty, uprooted, and cut; clear spring waters were murky; and hares, deer, and roebucks lay killed. As he took off, he unfurled the pretty splendor of his wings, decorated with gold; with disdainful laughter, crazy Cupid said: "May the goddess receive this damage as a prize for the outrage that she imposed on me!"

54. He flew so fast that breezes in the air were slower, as was the flight of an arrow. He cut through the clear air, leaving his mother's fields and meadows, and everything in tears and in pain. The air sang as his golden wings parted, while he, cruel, left his native land. He fled like a thief who brings along stolen goods and fears punishment and death.

55. As he handled the moving air with his golden feathers, he saw a meadow adorned with flowers and where round and soft acanthus lay smiling, the envy and shame of the gardens of Paestum.[37] He gathered his unfurled wings and, as a madman does, he uprooted and cut beautiful plants and killed animals, even where many pretty flowers scattered a sweet fragrance all around.

35. Continuing her implicit competition with previous (male) writers, here Marinella offers an alternative mythography to Ovid's *Metamorphoses*, asserting her own creativity and authority. She does the same in 6.41, above.

36. On the plane tree, see the note to 1.12; on Clytia, see the note to 1.35.

37. It is unclear why Marinella makes reference to the gardens of Paestum, a Greek colony in Campania whose apex occurred between 560 and 440 BCE and whose imposing ruins are still extant now. The settlement was famous for its flowers, and its rose gardens were mentioned in Book 15 of Ovid's *Metamorphoses*. The acanthus is a flowering perennial that grows in warm environments around the Mediterranean; it is the plant whose form is widely used as ornamentation on the capitals of Corinthian pillars and other architectural elements.

56. As he wandered, he saw a gentle young shepherdess, her brow serene, her face pretty, and her manners kind; she had male and female lambs to lead to graze with her commanding staff. Since the afternoon burned up that charming area, she made haste as he moved her nimble feet; she went to the middle of a meadow, where the shadows of a plane tree were such that they seemed to expand everywhere.[38]

57. There she sat and sang. A nearby river, the air, and the sky seemed to feel sweetness. Her herd was intent and attentive to her notes and to the light of her eyes. Her kind actions and angel-like demeanor seemed to have extinguished all of Cupid's anger. With rough style, she sang about the graceful gait and pretty face of her lover.

58. The boy heard her and turned his feet toward her. He moved as he used to, not full of irreverence, and sat next to her with charms and flattery, as she shed her sweet song to the air in the sky. The young woman, whose heart fear had already wounded, fled with yells and tears after seeing him. Upset at that, he grabbed her by her blonde tresses and tossed her in the water nearby.[39]

59. Whether the river took pity on her because it remembered her sweet notes or because it was vanquished by her beautiful shining eyes, it displayed a pious soul, like a lover's, and pushed her to the other shore with slow movements; she forgot that great danger. The crazy lover no longer cared for her; he moved on, shaking and yelling.

60. He saw a white doe[40] extinguish the bright fires of its thirst at a clear spring, and playful wishes quickly rose in him. Deposing his customary fury, he ran, grabbed it by its lofty brow, as it eagerly lapped the wished-for water, and said: "Doe, I wish to know if I or you may be a faster runner.

61. "There is no thicket or anything else to stand in the way of our run; the path is well trodden and good. If I win, you will yield me your branched antlers as a gracious gift. If I lose, though I don't believe it, I will give you this decorated quiver and my weapons, with which you'll be able to make harsh and mortal wounds in my stead."[41]

38. On the plane tree, see the note to 1.12.

39. Marinella's simple language belies the violence it conveys, and the originality of including such a direct depiction of male violence against women as perpetrated on a whim.

40. The white doe (*candida cerva*) would have instantly recalled to readers Petrarch's famous poem (sonnet 190 of the *Canzoniere*), in which a hunter follows a hind with golden antlers and then sees the following words inscribed on her jeweled collar: "Nessun mi tocchi; libera farmi al mio Cesare parve" ("Let no one touch me; it has pleased my Caesar to make me free"). Cupid now adds violence against this peaceful animal to the violence against the young shepherdess he has just perpetrated.

41. Cupid is presented throughout as being completely self-absorbed, and the competition he proposes here is no exception: the juxtaposition is not "I win" vs. "you win," but "I win" vs. "I lose," immediately

62. That beautiful wild beast wished to flee, and moved around here and there as much as it could. He yelled at it: "Look, that's the wrong way!" He threatened it and at once shook and got angry; then, vanquished by a pleasant frenzy and hoping for victory, he said to it: "This is not what we agreed upon! You're now afraid and wish for your dark cave!"

63. As he reasoned with it,[42] he held on to it with such strength as would break metal plate and mesh. It would have liked to flee, but the one who wounded and troubled souls and hearts did not allow that. "If you don't go the right way, you'll die in anguish; you'll get to know how powerful my right hand is!" As he said this, he let it go, and it fled in a different direction, quick and slender.

64. "Is this the trust that we share, most evil wild animal? Is this how you despise the beauty of virtue? Is this how you trample on my noble divinity? I see it: you don't appreciate it! Since you had the audacity to flee, certainly if I win I won't waste time! In fact, I'll kill you immediately and cut those antlers that nature adorned you with."

65. As soon as that cruel one realized that it did not follow the trampled path he had indicated, he yelped like a terribly wounded ox. With movements and face outraged and fierce, he went toward it as it stood freezing, trembling, and fearful. He yelled that he had a mind to kill it, took the wretched creature by its neck, and squeezed it in such a way that it could no longer move.[43]

66. As he said: "My beloved, more merciless than hell, resembles you in whiteness, and she too is very evil," he took off in a swift and quick flight, so that in a short while he covered thousands and thousands of miles, pushed by a raw and cruel pain, yelling like a maniac; heaven, earth, the sea, and the shore echoed his yell.

67. He did not stop from the time when beautiful Dawn made the clear light of air purple with her golden feet, scattering flowers on it and uncovering hidden treasures to the lively sunlight, until the time when the sun seemed to burn and blaze with flames at the last hour of the day. Then, vanquished by weariness, he fell onto hard ground, almost dead.

68. Cupid fell on the warm sand of Arabia Petraea, close to death, if death could attack gods, yet laden with a sadder fate and worse pain than death.[44] Where,

qualified by a clause expressing his doubt that the latter will occur.

42. The irony of the language Marinella utilizes here is palpable: Cupid is irrational, and yet he tries to "reason," and with a wild animal to boot.

43. Octaves 63–65 depict another scene of violence, on the heels on the one in stanza 58.

44. Arabia Petraea was a border province on the southeast edge of the Roman Empire, with capitals Petra (the famous "Rose City" of modern Jordan) and Bostra (now a city in Syria). It was conquered

wretch, oh, where is your mother's serene air that could comfort you? There are such comforts where the Graces are! Nectar and ambrosia … Ah, cruel Jupiter,

69. you give him such recompense? Are these the prizes in exchange for the gift that you used to get from him? He was the only reason why you enjoyed the lively snow of beautiful Europa! And when you rained in Danae's womb as a golden cloud and made your desires less harsh, it was he who lightened your pain … Now he was alone, naked and despised in that forest.[45]

70. Instead of comfort and noble help, abandoned and prey to pain, the tyrant of hearts, you inflicted a darker wound in his breast, grew his pain, and made his anguish worse. Still not happy with this, you have taken away his sense and silenced his mind, the ultimate injury. So much wrath and hatred dwell in a heavenly chest, then, in the tallest abode?

71. You lie abandoned, wretch, your noble face stuck in the sand. You do not receive the sweet kisses of your dear mother, or a grace to entice or hold you on her lap. You did not lift your lively eyes from the ground, your heart oppressed by the wrath of love, until the sun chased the thick shadow of night away with its burning flames.[46]

72. Whether his tiredness was over, so that he recovered his senses and his life; or whether the sweet heat of the morning flames awakened his lost soul; or whether the dear liquid of falling frost recalled his fled soul; he revived when he was sprayed, like someone who has fainted revives where clear waters are scattered on him.

73. I would not know the truth: as a rose awakens when the smiling sun appears, perhaps he revived his tormented mind with dewy air. So, sick and pained, he lifted his pale and dark face, once so pretty; like a man wholly stunned and vanquished, he kept his gaze trained on heaven, his enemy.

---

in 106 CE under the rule of Emperor Trajan.

45. On Europa, see the note to 1.46. Danae was a princess of Argos; when her father, Acrisius, consulted an oracle to inquire if he was going to have any male heirs, the oracle responded that his grandson was going to kill him. He locked up Danae in a tower to escape the prophesized fate, but Zeus/Jupiter entered her room disguised as golden rain and seduced her. Out of this came a son, Perseus. The story is told in Ovid's *Metamorphoses*, Book 4.

46. Marinella alternates direct addresses to Cupid (octaves 68 and 71) and to Jupiter (69–70). In the former, she goes back to expressing pity for Cupid, despite the tone at the beginning, which showed understanding for Venus, and the violence against the young shepherdess and the doe closer to these stanzas.

Canto 9

Argument of Canto 9

The most beautiful things that nature had shaped and that great Jupiter had created languished as Cupid languished. He broke pine trees and carried out unbelieved and unbelievable tests with wicked, evil wishes. He killed a young shepherd singing about the stars and the new beauties of a certain face. Beautiful Venus looked for him and saw him wholly filled with fear and unhappy mourning.

Allegory

Venus's son cried, sighed, and became languid and weak because Jupiter was not friendly to him. Similarly, our soul languishes without the food of holy actions and the dew of heavenly grace. Cupid destroying and squandering everything shows us the senses moved by an empty and lascivious desire: it wants to enjoy the sweetness of pleasure, it troubles the clarity of the mind with furious storms, and it annihilates true virtues and knocks down their strong foundations. Cupid wasting, killing, destroying, and reducing the world to evil will be understood as the wars, plagues, earthquakes, and floods that God's fully just wrath sends to chastise pride, sensuality, and other evil works by men, the enemies of true justice.

1. Wretched Cupid languished, and with him the beautiful and graceful works of his power languished. His hair was unkempt, his gaze dark and sullen, which once had the beauty of laughing stars; even more, he was deprived of the sun of his mind, such that he could not tell horses from lambs. His eyes and tresses no longer breathed love; nothing other than the name of love remained in him.

2. Cupid was not to be found: only his wretched tomb in a bright meadow.[1] There he nourished and fed himself with tears and laments among destitution, yells, cries, and pain. He left Arabia's sandy soil, pushed and goaded by an old flame, and went where fierce, wild animals peacefully defended the woods of Hyrcania.[2]

1. In some sense, Cupid is similar to Ulysses, both in his Homeric and Dantean incarnations: he wanders from place to place with no direction or goals, and is condemned not to find a resting place.

2. On Hyrcania, see the note to 3.45.

3. That evil boy uprooted wild ash trees and strong firs from the tangled ground, like tender nettles and fragile dills; he knocked out tall beech trees with a single hit. The woods on wide Erymanthos[3] did not remain happy, either; he unleashed his strength there, breaking ancient pines. His right hand, accustomed to wounding hearts, snapped each tree.

4. He knocked down bears and killed fierce strong lions. Who vouches for this? That such a refined body harbored such terrible strength?[4] He made it patently clear: he ran, crazy lunatic, through those huge fields, winning over agile and swift deer. Like a wounded bull, he happened to carry in his heart the arrow that would kill him.

5. Full of crazy fury,[5] he destroyed and uprooted his blond tresses with his hand, his own enemy; he plucked beautiful feathers from his wings with moans and deep sounds. Burning stars glowed less brightly than them, and the sun did not spread and cast a similar light to the shining golden down that gave light to shadows, till then completely dark.

6. The most hidden spot of those wide woods sadly echoed his frightening yells. Night shadows, winds, and hours trembled. The sky rumbled; valleys and shores did too. With his horrible countenance, his moving eyes, and his shrieks he brought terror to the most beautiful nymphs, the most handsome shepherds, and the gods living hidden in caves.

7. From a hill he saw a pretty young shepherd who calmed down the most evil of hearts in all wild animals with the melodious sound of a sweet cithara; he stopped rivers and sweetened Aethra.[6] He begged his dear beloved for help with his notes,

3. Erymanthos is a mountain chain in Greece, which appeared in one of the labors of Hercules. This is significant because, as we will see, Marinella refers to the madness of Hercules later in this canto.

4. A reference to a witness to buttress the version of events as given by Marinella, the narrator. Here Cupid's own actions give credence to her story, which means that readers have to take it at face value and accept Marinella's authority in the matter.

5. Marinella's original term is *furor(e)*, with which Neoplatonists translated *enthousiasmós*, used in Plato (specifically, in his *Phaedrus*) to designate a state of exultation and of proximity to the gods. One of the possible causes of *furore*, destructive or otherwise, was in fact love.

6. There are four mythological characters named Aethra in classical antiquity. The most likely to be invoked here is the wife of the Spartan Phalantus: the oracle of Delphi had predicted that he would found a city when, after reaching the land of Saturn (Saturnia, to wit, Italy), rain would fall from a clear sky. Upon landing, he passed out; his wife Aethra (whose name means "clear sky" in Greek) started to cry, and her bitter tears became rain, and Phalantus, once revived, founded the city of Taranto, in Apulia. This story is narrated in Strabo, Pausanias, and Diodorus Siculus. The cithara was an ancient Greek musical instrument (the *kithara*) similar to a lyre; the word *kithára* now means "guitar" in Greek. Playing the cithara required considerable skill, and its music was said to evoke strong emotions in listeners. Instruments such as the cithara were associated with Sappho and her lyric poetry (i.e.,

his song, and his handsome face. He took him by the hair, spun him around, and tossed him in the sea six miles away.[7]

8. Perhaps noble Alcides tossed trembling Lichas to the waves when he saw himself full of large, deep wounds and burning with foul-smelling flames.[8] Out of fear, that crazy lover hid in a cave, where earlier he had killed cruel wild animals. Dawn untied her hair to the breeze four times before the sun saw him again.[9]

9. He left that cave, furious, and ran, pushed by the fierce pain assaulting his heart. Similarly a deer tries to remove a poisoned arrow from its side by running. He shook, got upset, and tried to untie that fatal golden arrow from his heart. That fury did not stop: the crazy god reached a river, deprived of his reason.

10. Lunatic, he willingly leaped into the waters from its tall bank; those waves took pity on such a god, and they welcomed and embraced him without hurting him at all. Nymphs lifted his blond head out of the clear waters and he opened his noble eyes. They admired their own mercy and carried handsome Cupid in their arms all the way to the shore.[10]

11. Although he was crazy, of the type of craziness that never affected or bothered any mortal, at times the clear immortal sun uncovered its shining rays in his mind, such that at times he cried and bemoaned his troubles with true reason and in such a way that mountains, plains, nymphs, fauns, satyrs, and silvans cried with his cries.[11]

---

poetry meant to be sung to the accompaniment of a lyre), but of course the musician who can charm nature also recalls Orpheus.

7. This scene of physical brutality echoes the one in 8.58; here Cupid's victim is a young shepherd, there a young shepherdess. It is another potential anticipation of references to Hercules's own madness.

8. Alcides is one of the several alternative Greek names for Heracles (the Roman Hercules). Lichas, one of his servants, brought Hercules a shirt that Deianira had poisoned out of jealousy for Iole. Feeling his skin burning, Hercules grabbed Lichas and tossed him into the sea (Ovid, *Metamorphoses*, Book 9) to form one of the rocks dotting the waters off the coast of Euboea.

9. That is, Cupid remained in the cave for four days.

10. Marinella devotes a few octaves to Cupid's madness, in contrast with Ariosto, who described the paladin's madness in 23.100–136 and 24.1–14 of his *Orlando furioso*. Cupid inflicts his fury on nature and people, similarly to Orlando, who abandons his armor, uproots trees, and kills people. In one small (but telling) detail Marinella evokes Ariosto directly: Orlando slept for three days, resting from his first fit of violence (23.132.1.4), while Cupid hid for four days in a cave (see 8 above). The connection between these two poems is underscored by the fact that Ariosto utilizes "Amore" to designate Cupid in this episode (23.103.4; 23.119.6; 23.121.4; 23.127.5; 23.127.7; and 23.128.8), just like Marinella does throughout her poem.

11. The long list of mythological figures sharing Cupid's pain is meant to be evocative and inclusive: in addition to nymphs, who lived in or near water, we have fauns (minor deities of fields and woods,

12. At the sound of his cries, moans, and sighs, nymphs left their caves, their golden hair untied, with pious words and wishes, sad miens, and teary faces. Compassionate, they consoled his pains and tried to soothe his foolish fury, while other beautiful nymphs left their rivers with afflicted faces and dewy eyes.

13. With kind, chaste, and grateful manners, veiled in black and with sigh-laden words, they said: "Cupid, why do you grieve? Are the eternal wheels perhaps un grateful to your merits? Or did your mother offend you? Are your mighty powers, known to the whole world, scorned? Did you hurt your foot? Or do you love, kind lover, an ungrateful object who doesn't love you back?"[12]

14. Satyrs, fauns, and shepherds reached him, with bold brows and careful and wise words: "Why do you torture yourself, handsome son?" they said; "Why are you in pain among wild oaks and ash trees? Where are your palms and honors? Why are the rays of your glory extinguished? You used to rule over the gods: why are you now slaughtered by the world and a joke for the gods?

15. "The great thunderer doesn't fear the sound of his own lightning, or to be vanquished and interrupted by it. The sun doesn't get blinded, burnt, or damaged by its own rays and flashes. The great god adored and worshiped in the sea doesn't fear the motion and weight of his trident.[13] Mars isn't afraid of his sharp sword, and Pluto of that dog that people fear …[14]

16. "… and yet you, wretch to the world, live burned and wounded by your own arrows and fire? Flee love, noble son: it's a cruel game, the reason for tears and infinite pain! Just as the sea never has enough water, indeed it goes hoarse seeming to invite more, the more it has, similarly love with pains." Sighing, Cupid poured two streams and rivers from his eyes,

17. and he said, leaning against a hard rock, wretched in mien, with terrible face, sad movements, weak and low voice, pale cheeks and unkempt hair: "After I'm deprived of life, sing about the wandering soul and unburied ashes of myself, Cupid; sing about my destiny and the reason for my death.[15]

---

half-human and half-goat), satyrs (the Greek name for the Roman fauns), and silvans (*silvani*, also found in woods and the country); all represented the fertility of nature.

12. These nymphs, minor deities but not biased by their love for Cupid, understand a possibility for his state that Venus cannot see.

13. On Neptune, see the note to 1.8.

14. On Mars, see the note to the Argument of Canto 1. On Pluto (or Hades), see the notes to 1.49; on Pluto's dog Cerberus, see the note to 2.33, as well as the texts of 4.50–51 and 5.9–10.

15. Here and in the following stanza, Marinella bolsters her claims to authority as a narrator through Cupid's own momentous utterance, spoken just when he has given up all hope for the future and believes to be close to death. His last will and testament, in other words, includes the wish for someone

18. "With painful notes, friends, sing not Cupid's triumphs, worth, and weapons; not victories, jubilations, and satisfactions, not my glories, sculpted in bronze and marble. Rather, sing the gloomy story of my death and of my torments with teary poems.[16] Take pity: please bestow rest and peace on my naked bones in a small, shallow grave.

19. "If it ever were to happen that the cruel woman who took my heart from me were to stomp on my pained bones with her haughty foot and mercifully say: 'This wretched boy willed to die solely to please me,' this will be a great reward to my faith and to the love and ardor harbored in my chest. Although I'll be dead, this will give some comfort to my soul.

20. "Still I don't ask for peace or sighs over my ashes in this state; I do not want small, little tears to honor and uncover my pain." While he said this, again he went out of his mind; he was more atrocious and terrible than before, and his right hand, full of noble might, killed men and reduced everything to rubble.[17]

21. Lo, hellish Megaera left the bosom of Tartarus with a hoarse yell; with her emerged Discord and a cloud of Wraths and Brawls, looking dark and wild. A thousand colors embroidered a blazing crowd of hatred around their edges. Wars and shooting lightning strikes of grave illnesses and other terrible evils followed her.[18]

22. Peace fled at that sad appearance; Faith fled to heaven, its wings unfurled; well-liked Justice fled and ascended to be near famous immortal gods; Truth fled, as well as True Friendship of mortal men.[19] Since Cupid no longer infused his deep powers into hearts, Goodness and Beauty hid.

23. The pretty moon refused to pour dewy liquid onto the world from her blonde hair; productive trees shed their fruits; grass was pale and flowers weak. Not happy

---

to tell his story, and the anointed one is Marinella. Given her numerous direct addresses to Cupid, this suggests a type of dialogue between the narrator and her protagonist.

16. One of these "teary poems" (*lagrimosi carmi*) is Marinella's; her word choice here suggests a parallel with Horace, who in Book 3.30 of his *Odes* proclaims that his *carmen* is a *monumentum ære perennius*, a monument more permanent than bronze. This assessment, by extension, applies to the present work as well—as Marinella implies when she describes Cupid's destruction of the sculptures in Venus's palace (see the note to 8.46). The paradox, for Marinella, is that Cupid is a god and therefore immortal; what her poem can and does achieve is to immortalize a specific episode of his existence.

17. The Italian original (*stratio*) implies pain together with destruction, imbuing things with the ability to feel, to reduplicate the impression of powerlessness in the implied reader.

18. On Megaera, see the note to the Argument of Canto 5, as well as stanzas 9–10 of that canto. Tartarus was one of the many names for the underworld in classical antiquity.

19. The verb *fuggire* is repeated four times in the original, adding a sense of inevitable doom to the rhythm of the first five lines of this octave.

or joyful, the sun no longer bestowed light, hiding its splendor in a rust-colored veil. The sky embroidered new wonders in the night-time veil, offering fear.[20]

24. To the eyes of others, nature showed herself languishing in her pretty and beautiful works. Then you would barely see stars burning in the sky when night darkened the world; you would observe Dawn chasing the rebel shadows of day with an impure light, not scattering flowers while wearing a gold and vermilion veil, but unkempt, and her face surrounded by a black veil.

25. A strong herd, a painful pack, bellowed, and their bellows were not dear invitations to loving, as they used to be, but calls to wars and fights from fearful and angry chests. A tender newborn bellowed, asking with moans that someone show it its customary food; but its mother refused and it died of starvation. In vain they called and looked for Cupid.[21]

26. Sad little birds lifted their moans on high with wailing notes, among dry tree trunks. The learned Muses cried and uttered once happy verses, now sad ones, to the winds.[22] You would hear sighs with faint whispers in dry woods and with cruel winds. The world languished, the wide forests moaned, and inside them, wild animals shuddered, devoid of love.

27. The nightingale that lived happily in the shade of a myrtle or of a lively laurel tree and used to unburden its woes from its chest, singing, saying: "I burn, my beloved, and I die loving," now had its chest laden with troubles, torments, and pain, among dry shoots. It no longer sang, and if it did, its singing was sad and afflicted, making the pain in its heart known.[23]

20. The "wonders" (*prodigi*) referred to here are the comets already encountered in Cantos 4 and 8, harbingers of bad luck.

21. After underscoring the turmoil that Cupid's madness creates in the underworld (octave 21), among people (octave 22), and in the sky (23–24), here Marinella turns to the disruption of the circle of life on earth, for animals (25–28). Singling out maternal instincts, she emphasizes how love is a basic force of life, and how fateful is its absence.

22. On the Muses, see the note to 1.2.

23. This octave is filled with references to classical antiquity and a poet's creation. According to Ovid's *Metamorphoses* (Book 6), the Athenian princess Philomela was transformed into a nightingale after being raped by Tereus, the king of Thrace and husband of Philomela's sister Procne (see the note to 3.2). The beautiful singing of the nightingale was likened to a poet's verses. The two trees mentioned here, the myrtle and the laurel, were significant as well: the former was sacred to Venus (Greek Aphrodite), and the latter to Apollo (see the notes to 1.32, 7.19, and 8.49). Again, through them, Marinella connects love and poetry. She also underscores how love poetry, including the type that expresses sadness for unrequited love, is not an adequate utterance of the situation every character faces at this point in her poem. Although the nightingale used to sing about "its woes" (*i suoi guai*), the possibility of love existed; now, however, it no longer does. Moreover, the paradoxical juxtaposition of "dry" (*secchi*) and "shoot" (*virgulti*) reminds readers of the previous stanzas and of the radically different situation that

28. Alas, the swan that sweetly lifted noble sounds and musical accents to heaven, its feathers unkempt and its heart made of ice, cried and rendered long wails with a sick sound. Roses drooped, their beautiful colors already faded; Flora and Pomona cried over fruits and flowers, their dear prizes, their prized honors.[24]

29. The great mother of the gods, hitching noble lions to her chariot, pained and sick, with her hair unkempt and her face dry, wrapped in a black dress, lifted to heaven these words: "Jupiter, what is the reason why heaven denies the bright appearance of its happy looks? Why does it show itself to my eyes decked with terrible, inauspicious ornaments?

30. "Do you not see my tresses, now dry, or this cloak, now dried and once decorated with flowers? Do you not hear the moans and cries uttered by humanity? Do you not see their tears? Pretty birds have abandoned carols and happy songs, because of harsh and evil pains! What did I do that I may be so neglected and that I owe such a great punishment through no guilt of mine?

31. "Yet if I did offend your godliness, if I am guilty, may your powerful and strong right hand shoot your arrow against me, though mother and goddess, taking revenge on your anger with my death! May the world go back to being happy as it used to be and to a more joyful fate through my suffering; it is right that a compassionate mother may die to make her offspring happy.

32. "Still, what did I do? My body is cruelly wounded by hard ploughs every hour; man draws his living from my bosom, not reluctant to giving. If that didn't emerge from my womb, the fragrance did that is lit on your altars. I grieve that I cannot offer food to wretched mortals because of these numerous ills."

33. Thus spoke the great goddess whose hair is bedecked with towers: her face was teary, her brow sad, her arms outstretched, her voice humble, and her knees bent. Having said this, tiredly she hid her face, pushing it into the inner parts closest to her, waiting for Jupiter to offer joy and comfort to such great damages and harsh troubles.[25]

---

every being faces. Indirectly, then, Marinella is asserting that her work is more difficult and novel as compared to that of previous poets: like Philomela/the nightingale, she has taken on a different topic.

24. On Flora, see the note to 2.21. Pomona was the Roman goddess of fruits and abundance.

25. The divinity begging Jupiter is Cybele, the mother-goddess of Asia Minor who remained outside the Greco-Roman pantheon. She was to some extent conflated with Artemis Ephesia (referred to in 8.35), but also with Rhea, the mother of Zeus. Cybele's chariot is drawn by two lions, and her hair is "bedecked with towers," the latter a reference to her mural crown (*corona muralis*, a crown or headpiece representing city walls or towers).

34. But the one who carried his scepter and ruled over the gods, though he bent his heart with pity toward her and was not cruel or strict with her, and though a strong bond did not tie his heart, showed himself fierce against these just moans and teary prayers in order to punish Cupid. Therefore he was believed to be full of rigor and to have his heart full of iron against the world.

35. Cupid, the lunatic lover, kept on, such that it would be long to state thousands of his unseemly acts:[26] wherever he turned his swift feet, he left cruel marks of his fury. He did not kill only wild animals but very many pretty girls and unique intellects. Like a stroke of lightning, he knocked down and broke everything, without regard for youth, grace, or beauty.

36. As he revealed his ferocious heart to plants, animals, springs, and rivers, through his looks, will, strength, and deeds, it seemed as though he roiled and consumed earth and sea. Beautiful Venus turned her loving eyes toward earth from lofty Olympus, from where all deeds could be observed, and she saw the world as murky, dark, sterile, and barren all over.

37. She did not know the reason for this; she turned her face to the beautiful dwelling places within her old royal palace and saw rivers muddied, springs dirty, the once so luscious hills burned up, her dear trees on the ground, and the beautiful flowers that seemed to smile with love even on the coldest days now dry. She sighed. She believed she was dreaming and did not fully trust her own senses.

38. As well as she could, she quickly boarded her shiny chariot, decorated by jewels, and in the blink of an eye she descended to the plain; she made her vacillating heart and her doubtful mind certain. When she saw such damages, she became still and sadder and more pained than any other woman. Then, shedding many tears, she said: "Who thought, carried out, and dared all this?"[27]

39. As she said that, she saw majestic fir trees lying on the ground in her pretty garden, and the cypress uprooted that Phoebus loved so much, the happy lawns dry, golden orange trees uprooted, and not far the citron trees, too, and quiet lakes murky; green laurel trees showed their roots to the sun. She did not hear any small birds, or see grass and flowers.

26. In another nod to the present poem, Marinella begs her readers' forgiveness if she does not dwell on all the details of Cupid's destructive, mad fury.

27. The remark concerning Venus's feelings after ascertaining the extent of the damage inflicted on her palace and garden show that Marinella wants to present the human, rather than the divine, side of the goddess, with an emphasis on gender-based similarities. The destruction of home hits women and goddesses similarly, as she seems to say in this stanza.

40. He had not spared any white breasts or golden heads;[28] he had shredded it all. She scratched and hit her purple cheeks; she was scornful and at the same time tearful and sad. At that moment a sick, gloomy nymph appeared who lifted painful notes to heaven, her hair unkempt and loose, in a black dress, but noble and celestial in her face and mien.[29]

41. "A son, indeed your son, cut, uprooted, and weeded these majestic trees from their very roots; he spread and scattered flowers that once were happy and smiling. Unhappy me! With his wrathful right hand that crazy lover destroyed this happy royal palace. I know you don't know that he's in love with the beautiful and wonderfully pretty daughter of Emireno.[30]

42. "You don't know how much he cried for her, what kind of prayers and moans he lifted to cruel heaven, and how he lit the air with his burning sighs, once his heart had been wounded by his own piercing arrows. You don't know that he looked not only in the kingdom of the mortals, but also among the dead. I heard that once he said such words as to move the sun to pity and many more:

43. "'Extremely cruel tiger, more pitiless and fiercer than a she-bear crushed by injurious pains or than the prideful sea that does not listen to a quiet voice, alas, you're cloaked with impiety! You made your heart harder against me than a jagged, harsh rock! Thus with each passing hour my wound gets more bitter, and still I cannot leave my troubled life.

44. "'I live as a despised lover, as a hated lover: instead of love I reap and gather hatred. Cruel woman, does my crying not move you, or my many torments and my pained and harsh state? A beautiful diamond shatters out of pity, seeing me pale and dark because of pain; and you, my life, my beloved, don't want to give me life and goodness with but one of your glances?'

45. "What didn't he do or say? What laments didn't make the air sing and moan? Every hour he called the cruel woman who could not be placated by promises or prayers. I'm not allowed to bring comfort to the great pain of the highest gods, because I'm lowly; still, stunned, I observed the hidden flame and the unperceived burning within my lord."

28. This could be a reference to the petals and stamens of flowers: the calyx is identified as white, while the pollen is typically yellow. Alternatively, the difference could be between white flowers (the lily and the narcissus, for example) and yellow ones (the daffodil and the sunflower) that Cupid destroys.

29. As in 7.52–53, it is up to a nymph to give Venus information on what Cupid has been up to, and, as in Canto 7, Venus's first reaction is to turn deathly pale. In Marinella's poem, the nymphs are not just maidens who frolic by the water (as the nymph herself says in octave 45 below, "I'm lowly") but keen observers and intelligence agents.

30. That is, Ersilia.

46. The goddess paled and became still at the nymph's words, which she believed. Having become bitter, she kept her tears in check, while a strong trouble beat and wounded her chest. She almost fell because of pain, but her immortal virtue held her up and on firm footing. It seemed novel that he had captured himself with love and offended the whole world.

47. She said: "That grace of mine that heaven admires so, and that the world humbly adores, is sad! He flees and despises me, and he forces me to cry and to despise my own merits, too! May he have to envy frail beauty with pain and tears! This grieves and pains me! If a goddess were in love I wouldn't be so afflicted, and my heart would not be so tired.

48. "Aren't there in heaven goddesses pretty, graceful, and loving, with beautiful manners and faces? They are indeed worthy of making paradise joyful and of pressing shining stars with their feet. It's something fit for a boy and worthy of laughter that he made his desires the servants of human beauty and that he put mortal beauty ahead of immortal beauty, which despises all the rest.

49. "Falling for her is fit for a simple and slight boy, whose wishes are crazy and whose mind is insane; he knows that human prettiness flees like a beautiful flower in the twinkle of an eye and in a short time. Still, he must suffer agony and horrible and strange pain because of it! I'll lock the blasphemous boy up with damned souls in hell, with inner pain."[31]

50. Marvel, pain, scorn, wrath, desire for revenge, and wish for death attacked her; so she sighed up on high, troubled, and called her son ungrateful, cruel, and faithless. She got angry, she struggled, and she wandered; she hated and unloved her decorations and her beauties. She nearly caused trouble and disgrace and nearly went crazy, like her son.

51. Motionless but with upset eyes, she observed the snapped and messed up locks on tall doors, broken hinges, broken golden ties, broken strong iron bars to windows, and shredded precious and worthy cloth. These were the ill effects of outrages too insane! The pictures that adorned and decorated and bedecked the handsome embellished palace were damaged;

52. frames were on the ground, marvelous alabaster figures were on the floor, the tall columns (which had been raised by a learned craftsman) were now ruined and damaged, and the perfumed lights hanging from a golden ribbon were snapped;

31. The irony in Venus's words is clear to a reader, who is well aware that Cupid is indeed crazy. The juxtaposition of the earliest definition of Cupid (octave 47 above) and the conclusion here is stark, but warranted by his state.

other lamps, carved out of precious stones, pretty work, lay scattered, wasted and base.

53. When that beautiful mother arrived and saw all her plentiful beauty reduced to an unhappy fate, she did not know what to do or say, for harsh pain tied her heart with a strong bond. Similarly a shepherd feels who sees his lamb killed by a troubled torrent from a tall mountain; it steals his hope for the year, his fields, and his shelter at the same time.[32]

54. Silent and deprived of daring, her heart in pain, she climbed onto her chariot; that scornful goddess did not cry, as the time made her immovable to tears. She looked for her son by night and by day, in cold or summer air, never resting. Far from here, languishing and tired, he barely took any slow, feeble steps.

55. At last the thick cloud of insane fury lifted through the rays of his mind. He saw his state and was saddened by it; harsh and strong pain clutched his heart. Repentant and aching that he had wanted to offend the immeasurable father of the great gods, he now wanted to ask his forgiveness for his past mistakes, with the sorrowful sounds of his humble voice.

56. Full of deep humility, he stretched his arms, bent his knees, and unleashed vast tears; he said: "Great father, turn your eyes to me with mercy, be so merciful that I might dry off my cheeks, wet with tears, and reduce my pain a bit! Forgive my mistakes! Ruler of the world, eternal Jupiter, may your goodness benefit me!"

57. He was silent, because he could not say anything else. He found himself on Mount Caucasus, which separates India from Scythia; on it winter generates ice and deep snow rests. It was good to observe its top: it shone and smiled like a star in the sky, almost similar to a man who learns by himself the nature, path, light, and movement of the stars.[33]

58. The wretched boy fell in its perennial snow and cold ice, which the sun never melts in water as it circles; he fell where fierce and biting winds blew all the time and thick fog hid the clear air. Cruel Jupiter did not yield to his moans, his love, or his harsh and deep pain; if Cupid had given him love wounds, Cupid had also bestowed sweet mercy on him.[34]

32. This simile reinforces the guidance and nourishments that Venus provides to her son, and the emotions that their lack generates in a mother. Like in 1.24, Marinella utilizes agriculture to render her description more vivid and easier to relate to.

33. On Caucasus, see the note to 4.34; on Scythia, see the note to 3.36.

34. To unpack this difficult sentence: Cupid had inflicted the pangs of love on Jupiter, but had also bestowed on him many opportunities to enjoy the pleasure of love.

59. Neither Stromboli nor Etna nourish and hold as many flames or burning in their bosom, not Phlegethon (whose burnt sands are so hot) has such cruel fire in its lap as he did: his chest, his heart, his bones, and his veins were full of high flames, which made him faint. He shot fire with his looks, and if he breathed, he blew fury, flames, poison, and wrath.[35]

60. How was that, Cupid? You used to breathe immense sweetness of noble gentleness all around, adorning everything with roses, joy, and pleasure, your eyes lit by a divine flame. Now you blow death? I'll say, notwithstanding you, that you have become a dweller of the horrible and thick torches of hell, of that great furnace of plague-ridden flames.[36]

61. Therefore the snow and the constant ice that the frigid cold kept alive and that had brought together their dense matter a thousand times, under a cold sky, then melted into water.[37] The god of Delos admired the harsh slope of that mountain and was stunned to see its face unveiled, once covered by snowy coldness.[38]

62. After thick snow fell down the high, noble mountain as liquefied water, due to the fire and burning rage coming out of crazy Cupid's chest, the most beautiful flower stood, ill and weak, among hard, cold stones. The sky and all elements languished, as if with sad words, at its languishing.

63. Laurel and myrtle trees, woods, forests, fields, and hills cried for you, Cupid; Proteus with his herd and the terrible Syrtes found their eyes wet and shining with pain;[39] sea rocks, the winds, and jagged and rugged boulders never showed

35. Stromboli is a small island to the north of Sicily, site of a volcano. On Mount Etna, see the note to the Argument of Canto 2. Phlegethon is one of the five rivers that flowed in the Greco-Roman underworld, described as a river of flames.

36. Marinella again proclaims the truth of her narrative, here against no less a character than Cupid himself, who arguably should not be believed after having gone mad. The direct address to Cupid here reinforces the difference between his traditional gifts and what he now bestows in his crazed state. At the end of the stanza, Marinella uses the horrifying vision of pestilence and fire—the burning of plague victims in flaming pits—to situate Cupid in the "furnace" of hell.

37. Ice and snow melting signify the first step in the return of nature to its usual state, and the waters now flowing from Caucasus are also symbolic of the power of repentance, much like the water of baptism removes a believer's original sin. As the next stanza indicates, the mountain waters are melting because of the burning in Cupid's heart, so this is perhaps also a baptism of fire. Cupid will ultimately be cured (and therefore saved) by his immersion, or baptism, in Canto 10.

38. The god of Delos is Apollo, on whom see the note to 1.63.

39. On Proteus, see the note to 1.66. Proteus was an early sea-god with the ability to change his shape; like Nereus, to whom Cupid appeals for help in 4.15–21, he became conflated with Neptune/Poseidon. The Syrtes was a desert region in North Africa, covering parts of modern-day Libya and Tunisia, and considered as dangerous and inhospitable.

themselves sated with tears; and the Furies scattered a cloud of great tears in the ample bosom of hell's grotto.[40]

64. Boy, the alpine peaks of tall mountains and ferocious wild animals cried for you; oaks and pine trees with countless leaves cried, as well as Narcissus, in languid ways.[41] Rivers, lakes, seas, and springs, sad light, and dark and black shadows cried; pretty nymphs wearing dark cloth cried for you, and comfort, leisure, and festivities fled.

65. When the sun shot its rays and lightning from its high circle to make the day lively, or when Delia shook clouds of pearls from her blonde tresses and from her beautiful decorated cloak, he never lifted his burning cheeks from those stones or turned his eyes around.[42] The wretch was almost dead. Oh pity! Such power mortal beauty had on him!

66. Beautiful goddess of Cythera, where do you direct your loving doves and white swans? Come to your son: if your heart used to burn with wrath, switch to mercy and forgiveness toward him! If you saw him in harsh and evil pain, you would turn your hard thoughts to amiable ones.[43] I am greatly amazed: how was it possible that her heart could not foretell such harm?

67. How was it? Perhaps the one who wounded your beautiful son's heart with too sharp an arrow[44] did not want your soul to foresee such danger and feel such intense pain! Perhaps he wanted that the wretched remain exiled for long without any consolation, as he did not care about him; perhaps he wanted him to live in an eternal hell of pain, with inner trouble and torment.

40. On the Furies, also called Eumenides, see the note to 5.8.

41. On Narcissus, see the note to 1.35.

42. On Delia, another name for Diana, see the note to 1.30.

43. This direct address to Venus is an invocation, similar to those made to the Virgin Mary to intercede with the Christian god on behalf of humans.

44. A reference to Jupiter, on whom see the note to 1.8.

Canto 10

Argument of Canto 10

The beautiful goddess admired melted snow from the harsh and icy Caucasus; she found her dear son on its summit, and observed him in a wretched state. She believed him dead, so her pained breast exhaled sighs full of suffering and moans. She cried and obtained a genuine grace from Jupiter, so her son was restored his original sanity.

Allegory

Tired, weary Cupid reaching Mount Caucasus, guided by his own fury,[1] then returned mostly to his senses there and asking Jupiter for forgiveness, will be understood to be man: after he is tossed and roiled by the stormy waves of the crazy furies of the senses, in the end he is lifted by the wings of reason to the mountain of rightful thinking and he recognizes that he is tainted and made ugly by a thousand iniquities and perversity, so that repentance is born and he asks the eternal maker for forgiveness. Venus praying to the father of the gods on his behalf will signify the intercession of a male or female saint for any sinner;[2] through his or her prayers God will accept that sinner into his grace, from which his acts of wickedness have separated him. God wants to be glorified many times in one of the springs of the Ardennes,[3] to wit, not simply that man be cleansed by the waters of the sinner's tears, but also by the salvation-bestowing waves of confessions, sacraments, and penance. God then receives him in his grace, where the angels feel glory; and God makes it so that the beauties of Cupid's royal palace and garden, previously destroyed and felled by him, are resurrected, which will be understood to be the dear treasure of virtue, so appreciated and beloved in heaven. Cupid with his eyes covered by a band, because the one who had brought him back to his original greatness liked it that way, will be understood to be man: after receiving divine grace, as he reaps his harvest from it, he has the eyes of the senses covered by a band, so that he might not again fall into the danger of that

1. On fury and *furor(e)*, see the note to 9.5. In keeping with that image, the "wings of reason" (*ali della ragione*) that Marinella utilizes here seem to harken back to the image of the charioteer as intellect or reason driving two horses, one representing moral impulses and the other irrational passions, also in Plato's *Phaedrus*.

2. It is notable that Marinella's original specifies both genders; in other words, ours is not a twenty-first-century, inclusive translation, but a rendering of the Italian, which (differently from seventeenth-century customs) explicitly mentions male and female saints.

3. The Ardennes are a wooded area in northern Europe, originally stretching from Germany in the east to France in the west and located mainly in modern Belgium and Luxembourg. Because Charlemagne has a nightmare taking place there before his crucial battle of Roncesvaux Pass, in *The Song of Roland*, this location appears in many epic poems. See the note to octave 62, below.

eternal chasm, distracted by his senses. He will then be able to enjoy peaceful divine contemplation without the invitations and temptations of the world and of his senses: entirely fixed in God and his eternal beatitude, he will make himself happy and similar to his first principle.

1. The beautiful goddess adorned with all graces was going over wet and damp paths; she saw meadows deprived of flowers, the hills parched, and all pretty decorations taken away from the land. She did not know that her son's crazy thoughts had reduced the world to such shame and contempt. She saw the woods of Hercynia and of Erymanthos[4] uprooted, and everything in pain and tears.

2. She saw the great mountain, the inhospitable and wild Caucasus,[5] rising to the sky higher than all others; neither elm nor beech tree grew leaves on it, among its cruel snow and hard ice. The god of Delos[6] could not boast of melting its snow, nor had he ever done so, and yet she saw its snow wrecked and its ice melted, which were once bound by ties of cold.

3. As she saw the beautiful whiteness of that melted mountain snow, she was vanquished by a deep, strong wonderment; she raised her beautiful eyebrows and felt great amazement in her heart. In order to observe that more closely, she pulled at her doves' gold reins; in a short time she descended on the mountain and she saw (what a sight! what sorrow!)[7] her son made ugly by mud, all naked and alone.

4. She stood like a woman whose dear son has taken off to enjoy himself, who then sees him struck by a mortal wound, her noble pawn having reached his bitter

4. The Hercynian forest was a densely wooded area in what is now southern Germany; it marked the northern boundary of the known world for classical writers. On Erymanthos, see the note to 9.3.

5. On the Caucasus, see the note to 4.34.

6. A reference to Apollo as god of the sun, born on the island of Delos; see the note to 1.67.

7. The closing of this octave (*Ahi vista! Ahi duolo!*) overtly echoes a phrase in Tasso's *Gerusalemme liberata*, down to the location at the end of the stanza: when Tancredi opens the helmet of his enemy, whom he believed to be a man, he discovers she is his beloved Clorinda. The third-person narrator comments: "Ah, thus to see and know his love" (*Ahi vista! Ahi conoscenza!*) to underscore the fact that seeing and recognizing happened simultaneously (*GL* 12.67.8): Tasso, *Jerusalem Delivered*, 244. This recognition leads to pain, indeed to Tancredi's own madness (in Canto 13); for Tasso the first necessary element is rationality, followed by emotion and insanity. Here Venus does not have to go from seeing to recognizing to feeling pain, as Marinella's phrase seems to imply: for a mother, the act of seeing and of recognizing one's offspring are one and the same. As Marinella explains in the Allegory to this canto, there is an inherent danger to human senses: on the one hand, temptation; on the other, findings leading to the realization of an unsettling and painful situation.

end. She felt her soul bewildered and her life getting weaker; agony so struck her senses that she did not feel pain, stunned and confused as she was. She could not move or utter words.

5. Although she knew that a god could not taste the poisonous arrow of death, still she feared that her unhappy son had experienced that ultimate evil. So she poured copious tears from her eyes, feeling a harsh, indeed mortal, pain. Never did Dawn cry over the extinguished stars with such beautiful tears.

6. As deep pain allowed her to strike her face and delicate chest, she struck them, and even the empyrean roof seemed to answer back to her frequent blows. Her whiteness looked as though lively roses were placed on top of choice ivory, or like Delia in the sky, free from clouds, when burning vapor dyes her face.[8]

7. Like privet or lilies when the sun rises, so her noble face immediately showed the great pain that she held in her heart;[9] the rose on her cheeks did not hold beautiful red. Her clothes were shredded and her golden feathers were uprooted. She saw the pale face of her beloved son. Full of amazement she saw him covered and made ugly by mud and bruises.

8. As she cried, with her trembling hand she felt whether his chest still harbored the breadth of life: she did not know if he was alive or had already crossed sorrowful Styx, the utmost damage.[10] Her pain was such that she did not keep in mind the harsh sorrow of her ravaged royal palace; for this strange and novel fate she blamed not her son, but the great thundering Jupiter.

9. She said, as she cried: "Soul and life of my sick chest, indeed of my very heart, I find you thus? I see you thus, beloved object of my soul, which is now sad and lost because of you? Are you my Cupid, my darling son, my beloved, my grateful hope? Are you my son? You are the sweet reason for all my peace; all joy lies within you.

10. "Where are the lilies and beautiful roses of your face, heaven's song and my gift? Where are the pretty loving flames of your eyes, my glory? Where did they go? Where are the rays of your shining hair, which I took from heaven's most sublime throne? I once was a happy mother; now I am an unhappy mother because of this pain and because of unhappy Cupid.

8. On Delia as a name for Diana, see the note to 1.63.

9. Privets and lilies, renowned for their whiteness, show the run rising because they take on a rosy color; similarly, Marinella states here, the whiteness of Venus's face let her pain show.

10. On the Styx, see the note to 4.62. Its crossing was a one-way journey, hence Marinella's phrase "the utmost damage."

11. "I used to be abhorred and avoided, despised by my haughty, illustrious offspring, himself beloved by heaven and earth, although ungrateful! Yes, avoided: the sun barely deigns to show its rays and pleasing face to me, waters seem to avoid slaking my thirst, and plains and airs are deprived of all grace toward me.

12. "Why, father of the gods, do you so afflict my little son with foul torments? What did he do? What can he do that he might live unhappily in pain, tears, moans, and wails? Have pity on him and on me! In the meantime, decrease your burning desire for a harsh revenge: extinguish the fire of outrage with the fire of pity, so that he may have his place among the gods back."[11]

13. Vanquished by great pains, she fell quiet, stopped her sweet words, and kissed the noble breast, languishing lips, and sad mournful face where the clear lightning of love had once dwelt. Sick and sad, she struck her face and seemed to languish and faint with her motions. Who can I liken to you, helpless and wretched mother, wounded by a harsh pain?[12]

14. There was no lonely or strange place that might help her, not even with one word. Neither Mars nor Phoebus removed trouble from your chest or lightened it, consoling you. She did not know in what manner and with what knowledge she, alone and abandoned, might take her son back to her kingdom.[13] In the end she took her own advice and gathered him, half alive and full of harsh pains, in her arms.

15. Dripping liquid added much pity to his pained, afflicted, and sick face, where the gloomy pallor of death had gathered; she let tender affection loose out of her heart. The fog of her many deep pains completely troubled her noble face. As I said,[14] the teary mother gathered Cupid, full of pains, in her arms.

16. She climbed on her chariot and slackened the bridles of her doves; it started its course in the air. In the blink of an eye it reached her kingdom and royal palace, and she promptly dismounted from her chariot. She laid out her beloved son,

11. Venus's speech begins by expressing her sorrow for Cupid's state, then rehearses the recent past, and concludes by assigning Jupiter all blame for the present situation.

12. This rhetorical question has an additional implied answer to the usual, negative, one: the image of the Madonna of the seven pains (Our Lady of Sorrows, or *Mater dolorosa*), whose heart is wounded by piercing swords, was common in early modern (and later) times in Catholic cultures.

13. The original Italian is *arte*, here (and in octave 21, below) translated as "knowledge" because *arte* referred to any specific information used by those belonging to a professional guild in their work. Marinella's use here implies that Venus is completely deprived of any such knowledge, despite her divinity.

14. A reference to what Marinella the narrator had stated in octave 14, above. Readers will notice here, in this canto, the first of an unusually high number of references to the narrator in the first person.

almost dead, on dark cloths in the bosoms of the Graces;[15] she collapsed over him, cried, asked for pity and help, and struck and wounded her beautiful breast.

17. Beautiful nymphs started wailing upon seeing their lord deprived of his sense, bow, and quiver, his shiny hair dirty, his face dark and barely alive. They expressed the emotions in their hearts through feeble utterances, letting loose a river of tears, and pairing their sad wishes with clouds of cries and winds of sighs:

18. "Why do you not move your tongue and reveal the pain and suffering in your heart through dear words? Why do you not let your tongue loose and console these souls, devoid of happiness and goodness? Why do roses not rise to adorn your cheeks and a clear light rise in your shining suns? We would then chase away our trouble and pain at their clear strikes of lightning, you, flower of the heavenly heroes!

19. "Our lord, do you come back to your mother's sweet countenance with such an appearance? Is this your golden hair, this your white chest? Will we not end our days, Jupiter, observing our choice lord in this state? He is our mind, our reason, and our peace, the glory and splendor of this sad circle."[16]

20. Thus spoke the humble, sad Graces, from whose eyes flowed a large river; with it they washed that boy's heavenly hair, dirty breast, and troubled brow. When those honest virgins had done that, his illustrious choice features appeared and the mane of their loving leader showed itself in a less troubled light.

21. More than them, his beautiful mother called him, caressed him, kissed him, and cleaned him; she dampened and cleaned that unhappy man with her white hand and perfumed waters. While tears flowed copiously from her beautiful eyes, such that she almost dove and plunged in them, she tried all knowledge to bring back his lost spirit to life, with merciful help.

22. She was less pained when her hand was wounded by Tydeus's son, whose bold soul was vanquished by pain, abandoned the fight, and lost his soul; it rose to heaven in the chariot of Mars and uttered memorable laments and tears. In the end, other people's suffering and grave pain bestowed some comfort to her heart.[17]

15. On the Graces as caring for Cupid, see 8.9–11, and the note to 8.9.

16. Marinella emphasizes the description of Cupid's appearance by having the Graces echo Venus's questions in octave 10, above.

17. Tydeus's son was Diomedes, one of the Greeks laying siege to Troy. In Book 5 of the *Iliad*, Diomedes is depicted wounding Venus in her wrist after she had rescued her son Aeneas, likewise wounded by Diomedes (297–351).

23. As she saw all her work and effort squandered and scattered to the wind, not knowing what to do or say, consumed and burned by her motherly love, she thought that, once her friend Dawn would rise again, she would go to heaven, not having seen it much; there she would cry so much that she would move the gods not merely to pity, but to tears.

24. A thick cloud of tears hid the light and beauty of her luminous brow; her rosiness vanquished purple and roses, and her whiteness snow and lily. Now tired, afflicted, pale, and in pain, thanks to the evil hurting her noble son, she hid her divine mien, once dear and beloved to heaven, in funereal garb.

25. She removed all beauty, precious pomp, and decorative harnesses from her noble chariot. She despised the whiteness of her white doves and seemed to love and appreciate them with dark feathers; she wanted them to accompany her deep sadness with humble decorations and lowly trimmings. Then she rose to the starry rounds of Olympus with cries and passionate sighs.

26. She appeared in heaven with mournful clothes, plentiful tears, and scattered and disheveled hair. Similarly we see a pale star appear with a dark cloak in the night veil. Play, Laughter, and Song did not accompany her, roses plucked from their native stem did not adorn her; alone, untidy, wretched, and neglected, she stood devoid of daring and closed up on herself.

27. A whisper, a muffled murmur rose among the blessed gods out of immense Aethra,[18] when they saw her with suffering, unassuming shabby brow, pale face, and dewy eyes. With deep and frequent sighs she showed the sorrow and grief that anguished and consumed her. She was quiet and did not look, and even if she looked, her humble, languid, slow eyes shed dew.

28. They said: "She is the one who used to be Cupid's beautiful mother, when celebrating and laughing; with her pretty actions and beautiful face she used to wound all chests and burn all souls. She used to have paradise in her countenance, was the queen and goddess of hearts, and with angel-like words stole Mars's sword and the sun's rays."

29. Meanwhile she arrived at the tall, noble throne burning all around with rays and lightning, on which great Jupiter sat, where he made a luminous and perpetual day for himself with his own flames. Once she saw him, the grieving young woman fell, vanquished by the sorrow she harbored; sighing, she poured springs and rivers of bitter tears from her languishing lights.

18. On Aethra, see the note to 9.7.

30. I cannot liken the pained cries that sorrow sheds from your eyes to pure crystal and shiny diamonds gathered in the most beautiful part of his lightning. The trembling waves of your beautiful crying lit up the hearts of heavenly heroes; such beauty mixed with sorrow seems more beautiful, like a burning star surrounded by dark clouds.

31. That father saw his beloved daughter afflicted by torments and oppressed by harsh grief; her trouble did not allow her to reason, and sighs and sobs took her speaking away.[19] Dearly he asked her to say what she demanded. At last, struggling, she loosened her tongue, her sweet tongue, with these words, with which one would sweeten a heart filled with bitterness:

32. "Great ruler of the gods, you govern the world and with your thunderbolt you scare and shake it; if you were pious, sweet, and happy with me all the time, why do you now show yourself wrathful through well known signs? Why do you strike me, your daughter, and my son with such damage and profound sorrow? We did not try to steal your scepter and the highest empire, as the giants did.[20]

33. "I cannot know when or how I offended you, highest father and lord, to have caused you great pain; I don't know that this heart and these lips offended you with haughty pride. Still, if I did offend you, have pity! May this soul regain the love that you took away from me! Give me your noble grace, so that I might match grace with grace and your goodness may shine more.

34. "It may well be that I made a mistake; yet my misdeeds aren't known to me. The soul shies away from seeing itself; either it doesn't want to, or it can't. Its misdeeds are unknown to it and it seems unable to know itself, so it cannot turn its eyes inwardly and the virtue of sight cannot see itself, although it knows and sees lights, movement, stillness, shadows, and colors outside itself.[21]

19. In this sentence, Marinella seems to state that Venus also loses her mind; this would explain elements like her shredded clothes (octave 7, above). Yet her actions never include the violence and destruction that mark Cupid's madness. If irrationality is a womanly trait, as early modern misogynistic tracts suggested, here it is explained and justified. Importantly, her actions in the narrative that follows are rational, if tinged with maternal love.

20. In Greek mythology, twenty-four giants, sons of Gaia, or Earth, attempted to wrest control of the cosmos from Jupiter and the other gods; after they were vanquished in battle (known as the Gigantomachy), they were buried under volcanoes.

21. In the original, *alma* (soul) is grammatically gendered feminine; it is therefore possible to interpret this statement in a profoundly conservative and anti-woman way. This approach is consistent with the linguistic tradition of allegory, including Prudentius's *Psychomachy*, and in line with Marinella's own figurative intentions. In other words, the soul needs divine grace to save itself; Marinella is not positing that woman necessitating man to save her.

35. "I know that your all-seeing eye saw my furious, foolish son step around the world; can't a little or a lot of pity in your chest stop his foot? Who would believe this? Alas, his mien, his hair, his face are so different, that once were so pretty! Now he breathes death, without movement or life, and he looks as if his young age is over.

36. "Still, as far as I can detect, his unhappy spirit roams in his miserable body. Cut the fatal thread, make him die already, may he not remain in such horrible, painful hell! Son, such is the pity that motherly love can give you in this miserable state." Having said this, she fell silent, as if vanquished by too much pain and colored with pallor.

37. Then she continued: "If the harsh worries of your grandson don't move you to pity, if your justice requires that he cry over his errors with intense harm in unknown places, let this man, now with humble cheeks, unkempt hair, and torn clothes, move you, since he seems to threaten to return the world to its initial chaos, sick and silent.

38. "Highest father and ruler of men and gods, don't you see how everything is sad? Look at murky rivers and troubled seas, and at dark and joyless air; look at all the animals, almost deprived of food and life.[22] Alas, harsh and unhappy fate! My powerful father, I blame you for this, and for the fact that he's in pain, and I in shabby and dark clothes.

39. "I won't just say that you confuse, deny, and destroy nature's seeds and beautiful works. I'll say that you steal the lively rays from golden stars in the clear sky. Look: their pale faces, wretched glimmers, turn away as you enjoy yourself and are silent. Without Cupid, the world is full of horrors, wars, fights, and fury.

40. "I don't cry, complain, and feel pain as much for my harm and inner sorrow; rather, a harsh and cruel grief assails me as I also see the innocent suffer. If my son erred and offended you, I take it upon myself to wash his sin with eternal pain; give him back the splendid flower of his beauty and the stripped away worth of his noble mind."[23]

41. Having said this, she was silent and awaited an answer, in tears; she sighed loudly, wailing by herself. She moved her glance, shining and sparkling with love, over him through the waters of her worry; she fixed her eyes on him, with which she calmed stormy seas just as they became more enraged. It seemed as though the sweet pity in her face was asking for pity among copious dear tears.

22. Indirectly, Venus's words confirm what Cupid was trying to prove, to wit, that he is more powerful than Jupiter, because he perpetuates life through the impulse to love and procreate.

23. As a mother, Venus is profoundly human in her pleading for her son, and also closer to the biblical figure of Mary in her willingness to take on the pains of the world through those of her son.

42. Two and three times did Jupiter turn his eye around; heaven and the elements trembled. Then, pleasantly irate, he moved his blessed tongue with these words: "Will we tolerate that one of the lowliest among the lowly gods, who spent all his hours living in joy and peaceful happiness, will wound, burn, tie, tease, poke fun at, laugh at, and enjoy us?

43. "Will we tolerate, tolerate, that a blasphemous one, who feasts on and nourishes himself with other people's troubles, will afflict and pain us, will massacre us, and will not leave us alone even for a day? He wants the highest temple for himself, haughty boy still fit for breasts and diapers! Still he vies with me and perhaps he believes that he can surpass me in power?"

44. At this point, from his extreme height and his golden throne he saw, with pitiful eyes, the dry earth that was once accustomed to giving birth; the air trembled; seas and rivers were murky; fertile trees had shed their beauty on the ground and resisted producing more; and the elm tree no longer welcomed the beloved weight of his fertile wife in its arms.[24]

45. The great thunderer was vanquished by pain and amazed at this miserable sight, and by the fact that the world would be destroyed, sick, and unraveled only by the languishing of that loving boy. Having seen this, he acknowledged to himself how much Cupid's beautiful countenance was of use; in that moment he became extremely aware that without him the world would go back to its beginning.

46. Therefore, the ruler of the gods told her: "My wish is no different from yours, because I love you, my daughter![25] Stem the rivers of your tears, then, and may your pain stop. Why don't you revive your lost spirits? May vigor come back in your heart, warmth in your face, since I will satisfy you in everything! Who stops me from making him whole, and you happy and joyful?"

47. She returned grace for grace and gave praise to her great father; she discovered that he would forever carry her in his heart, having untied the knots of the pain that had split her chest. Then she gracefully gave rest to the storm in her heart

24. The *topos* of the elm and the vine has a long classical tradition, and is present in Tasso (both in the *Aminta* and the *Gerusalemme liberata*). Marinella utilizes it here and in octave 81, below. For an exhaustive summary of this figure from antiquity to the seventeenth century, see Sergio Corsi, "L'olmo e la vite (*Gerusalemme liberata* XX, 99)," *MLN* 102 (1987), 141–46.

25. Jupiter's acknowledgement that he and Venus (and therefore Cupid) are tied by familiar bonds is at the center of his emotional and rhetorical change, in parallel with Venus's emphasis (itself a clever rhetorical strategy) in octaves 32 and 37, above. In other words, although its cause is the recognition that "the world would be destroyed, sick, and unraveled only by the languishing of that loving boy" (octave 45), he utilizes the same language and reasons as Venus does in his plea to him.

and cleared her face; in this serenity the suns of her beautiful eyes rose, and love seemed to fly in them.

48. With the sweet laughter and graceful fire of her eyes, Cupid's arrows and flames, the trampled flowers of her face revived from the ugly cloud of her tears, with liveliness. Her tears and laughter sent mordant flames of love and desire to all hearts: the warm gods drank them up with their eyes. By themselves they seemed dead, and were only alive with her.

49. After that blonde goddess offered what she owed to her great father with many happy words, again she turned her words and face to him, to ask him what he could do to her son to make him healthy and remove him from the many pains and blame that saddled him. The one who moved the heavenly spheres[26] and shook the foundations of the world replied to her:

50. "You will go to the famous springs in the Ardennes, whose waters are much colder than ice; those waters hide great power against Cupid, for swift desire of love flees all hearts. Before the sun gets back into its golden chariot to chase away the deep shadows of night, you'll set out at first light, and you'll bring boy Cupid along.

51. "In those crystal waters you'll immerse and wash the mad boy three times, and even more, so you'll extinguish the deep burns of my cruel fire; he'll be happy and healthy again, regain his lost color, and become humble, loving, and human again. I want the light of his handsome eyes to cover and cloak the memory of this event in white veils.

52. "In order for an eternal sign to remain in the world of his shames and disgrace, and for him, culprit, to not stomp on the excellent honors of the best minds with his arrogant foot, I want that a white veil stop the worthy rays of his shining eyes, so that he'll blindly tie and blindly wound peaceful hearts and prideful chests.

53. "I want him to light up the icy heart of a lazy old man as much as that of a dainty young one, using his weapons on both without any difference and spreading his flame with generous hand. If I gave it beauty, I don't want it to regain its earlier praise and its lost honor; may it send its flame and shoot his arrow governed by hazard, not by sense or eyes."

54. He fell silent; she bowed to him and descended where her son was spread on a bed as if dead. Not far, the Graces cried for their wounded lord, expressing pain in new forms. At that sight she shed tears from her beautiful eyes and her heart was possessed by a grave pain; she hoped that night would fall, and also hoped that Dawn would bring the morning of the following day.

26. Here Marinella follows Dante's cosmological illustration of heaven as spheres moved by god.

55. Meanwhile, the lamp of day extinguished its beautiful light in the waves of Mauretania.[27] The stars rose and night dyed the air black with its horrid feathers. The cold of night wrung vapor into round drops, as it is wont to do, that then fell in flowers; when they are observed they look like diamonds and precious pearls.

56. When rising Dawn was gathering privets and roses in her pretty garden, when Phoebus offered ambrosia to his steeds,[28] the loving goddess, eager to leave, saw it was the time she strongly wished for. She was ready and did not delay her leaving: she had white swans and doves, pure and kind birds, attached to her chariot.

57. She carried her noble son, wholly deprived of strength and sense, in her lap: similarly a pretty maiden adds roses or lilies to the lively milk of her white chest. She often looked at him with pitiful eyes; she often kissed him, turning her eyes into rivers and leaving the marks of maternal love impressed on his face and handsome chest.

58. As beautiful Cythera[29] washed him with her tears and enveloped her beautiful eyes sweetly around him, she saw the spring that was the target of her wishes and that could extinguish Cupid's cruel and evil flames. She stopped her swift chariot; as she looked at the waters, she sighed and told them: "Do not spurn to quell the fire of love in Cupid's heart with your modest liquid!

59. "Extinguish the harsh flame hidden in my child's soft chest with your ice; annihilate it, so that he may become happy again, and his face may turn clear and serene!" As she said this with a pained voice, she fully pulled the brakes on her doves, dismounted from her chariot, and hid her white foot in those icy waters, her son embracing her neck.

60.[30] Twice, four times did she plunge and wash his face, hair, back, and wings in those waters; thus she removed the atrocious wicked flames that had given deathly pain to his heart. The harsh fire was extinguished that had burdened him and caused so much pain; the pain removed from his chest, he opened his eyes without a veil and saw the goddess and the sky.

27. Mauretania was a province of the Roman empire in North Africa, along the Mediterranean and north of the Atlas Mountains, that stretched from the Atlantic shore in the west to the border with Numidia in the east; it occupied the coastal areas of modern-day Morocco and central Algeria. Marinella uses it to refer to the western reaches of the Mediterranean Basin.

28. On Phoebus (Apollo), see the note to 1.30; on ambrosia, see the note to 2.9. Marinella's phrase means that the sun was about to rise.

29. On Cythera, see the note to 1.7.

30. This stanza is numbered 61 in the original (i.e., there is no stanza 60) and those following are misnumbered. We have corrected all from here to the end of the canto.

61. The evil poison that had been gathered in Cupid's heart spread and mingled in the waters, which had been demure and clear and pervaded by the ice of virginity. Those pure waters became sick and infected that should have worked to a better end. The other waves, untouched by those limbs, had infused the spring with chaste ice.

62. His flame did not die through the power of water; rather, it set those waves on fire with its fire: the warm power of those burning flames remained scattered among the icy liquid. I do not know how those springs had such huge blessings of chastity and praiseworthy honors; I will say what antiquity states about them, since it was friends with the truth.[31]

63. One day, Delia burned with deep thirst, after the heat of a tiring hunt; all covered with dust, her beautiful face was wet with proper sweat. She explored paths here and there to find water to satisfy her wishes; at last, tired and with unkempt hair, she arrived to the famous springs of the Ardennes.

64. There she slaked her thirst and made her unblemished limbs clear from dust and sweat, such that it appeared like snow spread on a meadow, or like curdled milk in a beautiful baskets made out of rush. Since she enjoyed those pretty waters close to the shades of dense thickets, she wished that a friendly memory of her demure virtue might remain in them.

65. She wished that anybody who had been wounded by love and would drink there would have his or her side healed. She wished that this dear and pleasing

31. Marinella devotes two octaves to explain the changes in the temperature and nature of the water of the springs of the Ardennes. She is aware, it seems, that what she is trying to explain can be confusing; furthermore, she knew that these springs had both literary antecedents (as she explains in the octaves below) and successors. The earliest literary precursor is Matteo Maria Boiardo's *Orlando innamorato*. In Book 1, Canto 3, octaves 32–42, Rinaldo chances upon the spring at the same time as Angelica; he drinks from the fount of hate, changing his love for her into indifference, while she drinks from the fount of love, and her hatred for him turns into love. Both fountains are described as having been made by Merlin. In Ariosto's *Orlando furioso*, which ostensibly starts off where the incomplete *Innamorato* leaves off, again Rinaldo drinks from one and Angelica from the other (1.78). Toward the end of the poem, the magician Malagigi hears about what happened (42.34–38, a section which serves as a summary of events narrated at the beginning of the poem). He sends Sdegno to save Rinaldo from the only attack in which he feels fear (42.48–61), and then to guide him to drink from the spring that erases love (42.63), so that the knight can rejoin the rest of Charlemagne's paladins. Marinella uncharacteristically invokes antecedents to support the details of her plot, going as far as to remind her readers that "antiquity … was friends with the truth" (*l'antica / età … del vero amica*) (octave 62, misnumbered as 63 in the original). It is notable that soon after *Amore*'s publication, Andrea Salvadori wrote *Fonti d'ardenna festa d'arme e ballo fatta in Firenze dagli accademici Rugginosi l'anno 1623*, essentially a libretto for entertainment set to music by Marco da Gagliano, and performed during Carnival season in honor of the visit of Henri, prince of Condé.

favor would continue to offer a shield and protection against love. Those springs kept that chaste rite within in an inviolate, untarnished, and firm fashion, until Cupid relinquished his fire and the too hot affection from his body at once.[32]

66. Cruel poison now permeated the spring in whose water Cupid cleaned his body; the other one that did not touch his limbs kept its waves chaste and demure. The ice of the former turned to fire, while the other one hid the opposite trait within: those who drink from one gather the fire of love, and those who taste the other chase love from their heart.[33]

67. I said that Cupid saw his beautiful mother and the bedecked sky upon opening his eyes;[34] out of his closed lids he happily showed the rays that dwelt in his eyes. Similarly, the sun allows shiny gleams among the thick clouds to make the day clearer. Soon he sweetly hugged his mother, who did not know what to say or do because of her joy.

68. A flame grew among the icy snow of his handsome and pretty face; thus we often see a burning rose grow in winter snow. His merry, light brow shone brighter than the dazzling sun under his golden hair. The gold feathers on his back were more beautiful; they shone and gave light to the shadows.

69. I do not know if the happy goddess felt as much bliss in her chest as the pain before, not if her bliss won over her harsh pain, nor if she continued her loving affection. I believe both could be greatly evident because of her beloved: the highest joy and harsh and mortal pain for her beloved son were the same.[35]

70. Her white breast did not hold the joy she felt, born and risen up from the springs in her heart;[36] because of it pleasure spread from her chest and covered her sweet, clear face. Similarly, a vessel full of shiny liquid is lifted and raised

32. The myth of the springs of the Ardennes is not included in either Boiardo's or Ariosto's poems (see *Orlando innamorato* 1.3.34 and 38; and *Orlando furioso* 1.78). It seems that this is Marinella's own creation, another indication of her creativity and fearless contribution.

33. After her explanation of the mythology associated with the springs in the Ardennes, Marinella goes back to her plot, reiterating what she had written in octave 61 (misnumbered as 62 in the original), and utilizing some of the same terms.

34. A reference back to the description at the end of octave 60 (misnumbered as 61 in the original), accompanied by another reference to the narrator in the first person (see octave 15).

35. Utilizing two first-person-singular verbs (*non sò* and *credo*), Marinella cleverly underscores, simultaneously, both her limitations as a narrator (Venus's emotions are impossible for her to measure—but not to discern) and her crucial role and authority as creator of the plot and of her characters.

36. Utilizing a Baroque poetic *topos*, Marinella here conflates the springs of the Ardennes (which freed Cupid from his love and thus gave him back to his mother) with the springs of her emotions, in her heart. The reader is left to figure out whether she means two different sources or only one.

because of great thirst, but it does not hold it and it pours its hot fluids out in great quantity.

71. In the same manner the happiness that she felt in her chest quivered and breathed out of her eyes and clear brow. She hugged and kissed him, and she observed and noticed his famous beauty, more beautiful than ever. She eagerly admired the heavenly lights from his swift and ready eyes. Her sight, full of his sweetness, made the face of the sky happy and clear.

72.[37] The air adorned and dressed itself with purple whiteness, and the sky laughed and burned with joy. Wraths and storms had stopped that used to come from Cupid's royal palace up on high. Having deposed the harmful garb of pain, now filled with sweetness, the world exulted and celebrated; among much rejoicing that worthy son returned to his beautiful kingdom with his mother.

73. At that great sight heaven and earth gathered new graces and beauties: trunks once dry showed leaves and flowers, meadows smiled and put on green garb, clouds fled, and marble and cold ice welcomed loving warmth. It seemed as though love breathed in everything and everything showed itself adorned by Cupid's pretty name.

74. Rhea's noble son, who inherited the sovereign empire of the gold starry kingdom,[38] relinquished wrath and outrage from his heart that had been so cruel and harsh with his grandchild. He willed that the world, tormented by him, fierce and crazy, would go back to its original state, and that her daughter's garden and royal palace return to their happiness. He took great pleasure in doing this.

75. Therefore the palace, which had been deprived of jewels, gold, and every noble frieze, oh wonder, richly shone with the most beautiful treasures and singular works.[39] There the most highly praised and lavish excellence existed with majesty,

37. This stanza is already numbered incorrectly because of the earlier omission of stanza 60; now the error is compounded by another mistake in which our stanzas 72, 73, and 74 are numbered 70, 71, and 72 (a repetition of the numbers on the previous page). As a result, Canto 10 ends at stanza 89 in the original, at stanza 91 in our text.

38. In Greek mythology, Rhea was a Titaness and the mother of Olympian goddesses and gods. Marinella's long phrase serves to identify Jupiter.

39. The interjection "oh wonder" (*O maraviglia*) opens a series of octaves devoted to the reawakening of nature after Cupid recovers his sanity. Deictics and verbs involving the implied reader are scattered throughout: "see" (*ecco*) appears twice in octave 77 (misnumbered as 75 in the original) and once in octaves 80 and 82 (misnumbered as 78 and 80); "behold" (*mirasi*) appears once in octave 78 (misnumbered as 76). It is a miraculous change, underscored by terminology usually found in *descrittioni*; on a similar example in Marinella's epic poem *Enrico*, see Maria Galli Stampino, "Fantasmi di genere in *L'Enrico, overo Bisanzio acquistato. Poema eroico*," in *A Portrait of a Renaissance Feminist: Lucrezia Marinella's Life and Work*, ed. Antonella Cagnolati (Rome: Aracne, 2012), 125–48.

pomp, and dignity. The pretty, lovely garden became green again, which before had been stripped, wasted, and lowly.

76. Of their own volition, the citron, the alder, and the chaste laurel trees stood tall in their previous spots; orange, pine, fir, and mulberry trees rose on each side by themselves; grapevines wore their leaves, flowers, and beloved fruit, looking green here and gold there. Each tree showed its fruit growing, fully grown, or ripe, a sure harvest.

77. They were safe and did not fear outrage, wrath, or any damage from the sky. See, the breath of life already coursed through them, and graceful May smiled in them. See, the flowing ash sighed for love for another ash, a beech tree for another, and crocus lifted its green mane toward the sky, while hyacinth laughed, adorned with its name.[40]

78. Behold, the meadow, whose dry green grass used to barely cover the dry soil, was now green and alive again! The sky, having yielded its cries and pain, flattered the grass, scattered through with flowers; once infected with dark poison, that grass was now extinct from one pole to the other. Wrath-laden snakes no longer hissed in it; now they were only lit by Cupid's fire.

79. Among green leaves, a pretty little bird filled with the flames of love seemed to say: "My beloved, I burn for you!" To which his faithful friend replied: "I burn as well!"[41] The latter did not hide from her dear beloved the old flame in her warm chest. It seemed as though each stone and each tree trunk wished for love, and Cupid enjoyed and loved everything.

80. See a strong, cruel, wild lion that had abandoned wrath from its courageous heart; now, pushed by the love burning in its breast, it ran and wandered to find its beloved. A stag went quickly through thick wood after its doe, sighing for love. Upon first feeling love, a noble steed despised the once wished-for honors and glory.

81. Dearly, grapevines grew all around, lifted themselves, and enjoyed their elm tree;[42] a pear tree, decked with beautiful flowers, desired that another loved and praised it. Fraud quickly went back to its hellish place with Treason, her friend.[43]

40. The hyacinth, a flower, shares its name with a beautiful young man, lover of Apollo, killed by accident when a discus thrown by Apollo struck him as he ran to catch it. His story is told in many Greek poems, starting in Book 2 of the *Iliad*.

41. As what follows clarifies, the grammar in the original specifies that the first bird is gendered male, and his friend is gendered female. Marinella gives her readers a simple example of requited love.

42. On the elm tree and the vine, see the note to stanza 44, above.

43. Following the grammatical gender of the abstract nouns she is embodying, and in keeping with the *Psychomachia* and, more generally, allegorical tradition, Marinella identifies Fraud and Treason as

Then, too, the cruel temple of Janus was locked up, where pitiless Fury was chained.[44]

82. See, Peace returned, and haughty Mars fled, his face still horrible because covered with steaming blood; Discord, a wild monster, fled with him, her tresses wrapped in bloody cloths, and descended to hell. That valiant knight[45] turned his steps toward the loving goddess, and he gave a thousand kisses to the white and clear face of the goddess from Cyprus, though he was covered in blood.

83. Meanwhile the Graces adorned noble, rich tables with white embroidered linen cloths. One of them hid precious wine in gold and crystal clear glass, happily. Beautiful Venus placed the finest sugar, crushed almonds, and perfumed water in a pot, then on low heat she made thin breads and knowingly cooked them little by little.[46]

84. She would make that food when Mars, cruel and fierce, returned from noble wars in his most tired state; therefore the noble goddess, empress of Paphos and Cnidos, gave it the name of "bread of Mars."[47] Quickly the Graces removed weapons from that cruel knight, from his head down to his feet; he washed his chest and terrible brow in a spring nearby to remove the dust.

85. That beautiful goddess adorned the snowy white privets of her body with precious cloths, which enclosed the beauty and craft of famous and illustrious masters, indeed immortal works. She satisfied her wishes to adorn her neck and hair with gold, pearls, and other noble decorations. Lastly, she took her belt of choice beauty, with which she lured the wisest and most prudent men.

---

women; Fury is gendered female, as well, in what follows, as are Peace and Discord in the octave below.

44. In Rome, the doors to the temple of Janus were closed in times of peace, and open during war. This is why Marinella dubs it "cruel" (*crudo*). The reference to Fury, imprisoned in chains behind these doors, is from Virgil (*Aeneid*, 1.294–295).

45. That is, Mars, on whom see the note to the Argument of Canto 1

46. The image of Venus in a domestic setting, baking for her son, stands in stark contrast with the goddess presented until now, determined to find him and nurse him to health and to his senses. Yet while her actions are different, the message is the same: she is, first and foremost, a mother in this poem. Her influence carries over the rest of her family, as illustrated by the convivial meal in octave 87 below, and in contrast with the banquet of the gods that concludes Apuleius's narrative.

47. On Paphos, see the note to 4.23. Cnidos was first a Greek settlement and then a city on the Turkish coast, boasting a temple to Venus and thus believed to have been especially connected to this goddess. The "bread of Mars" appears to refer to the confection of ground almonds and sugar that we know as "marzipan." Marinella alludes to an etymology that may have been in place before it was picked up by the English lexicographer John Minsheu (1560–1627). Minsheu noted that the word came from "*Martius panis*," so named because it could be molded into the shapes of "towers, castles and such like." Several other suggested derivations of "marzipan" exist, but this one fits neatly into the story line here.

86. On it laughter, slow leisure, and sweet disdain had been depicted by the hand of an immortal artist, as well as sweet kisses, dear love, and dignified actions, laughing cries tied to interrupted sighs, and flattering words that would vanquish and triumph over the highest intellects. Satisfied, she encircled her royal hips with it, admirable ornament to her virtue and beauty.

87. Mars and the boy Cupid sat at that noble table, full of sweets, with the noble goddess with serene eyes, who deserves the first place as far as beauty. They enjoyed wished-for goodness, the precious liquid of sweet nectar, and together, with kindness and happy words, they quelled parched thirst in their hot chests.

88. After those happy gods had enough dear ambrosia,[48] they left that royal table and, without any care, went to admire the immense riches of that large royal palace: how diamonds flashed and how garnet burned in its lit flames! Cupid enjoyed himself, without remembering the great damage that his angry arrows had wreaked there.

89. His mother now prepared him a new bow, new arrows, and new torches, then hid his eyes with a white veil, so that he would not turn them to golden stars and poke fun at heaven. Thus thereafter he always mixed and confused beautiful flames with the ice of love, and he seemed to wound old and young and pretty chests, without any difference.[49]

90. Everything was convivial; pretty flowers smiled with their purple and white in his face, and joy and laughter took up his heart, where wrath and fury had finally quieted. Sometimes, sitting by a river and joking, he would temper the hot flames of his arrows in its waters and repair broken nets; at times he prepared ties, at others he made ice, and yet at others he stirred his flames.

91. Now, satisfied with that, he enjoyed it as a pretty sight, removed from dark and sad pain; he knew how humility conquered heavenly grace through harsh torments. Let man rejoice, then, when he enjoys a little peace mixed with long and harmful pains: humility and travails make him worthy of eternal glory and of the heavenly kingdom.[50]

THE END OF *LOVE ENAMORED AND DRIVEN MAD*

48. On ambrosia, see the note to 2.9.

49. In contrast to octaves 51–52 above, here Marinella adds another reason for the need to cover Cupid's eyes with a white veil: to avoid a repeat of the recent events ("pok[ing] fun at heaven"). She goes beyond Jupiter's pronouncement, it seems, to protect her son and herself.

50. Marinella reserves the last four lines of her poem to address the topic of her work outside its allegorical frame. It is the only time in which she breaks her narrative mode, presumably to remind her reader of her goal and message.

Bibliography

Primary Sources

Albertus Magnus. *Compendium theologicae Veritatis*. Venice: Ioannes Antonius Rampazettum, 1588.

Apuleius. *Cupid and Psyche*. Edited by E. J. Kenney. Cambridge: Cambridge University Press, 1990.

———. *The Tale of Cupid and Psyche*. Translated by Joel C. Relihan. Indianapolis: Hackett, 2009.

Boccaccio, Giovanni. *Genealogy of the Pagan Gods*. Edited and translated by Jon Solomon. 2 vols. Cambridge, MA: Harvard University Press, 2011.

Dante Alighieri. *The Divine Comedy. Digital Dante* edition. New York: Columbia University Libraries and Department of Italian, 2014. <https://digitaldante.columbia.edu/dante/divine-comedy/>.

———. *Vita nuova. Digital Dante* edition. New York: Columbia University Libraries and Department of Italian, 2014. <https://digitaldante.columbia.edu/library/la-vita-nuova/>.

The Etymologies *of Isidore of Seville*, ed. Stephen A. Barney, W.J. Lewis, J.A. Beach and Oliver Berghof. Cambridge: Cambridge University Press, 2006.

Lucretius. *De Rerum Natura = The Nature of Things: A Poetic Translation*. Translated by David R. Slavitt. Berkeley: University of California Press, 2008.

Marinella, Lucrezia. *Amore innamorato, et impazzato. Poema*. Venice: Giovan Battista Combi, 1618.

———. *Exhortation to Women and to Others if They Please*. Edited and translated by Laura Benedetti. Toronto: Iter Inc. and Centre for Reformation and Renaissance Studies, 2012.

———. "Lucrezia Marinella's *Life of the Virgin Mary, Empress of the Universe*." In *Who is Mary? Three Early Modern Women on the Idea of the Virgin Mary*. Edited and translated by Susan Haskins, 119–246. Chicago: University of Chicago Press, 2008.

———. *The Nobility and Excellence of Women and the Defects and Vices of Men*. Edited and translated by Anne Dunhill. Introduction by Letizia Panizza. Chicago: University of Chicago Press, 1999.

Marino, Giovan Battista. *L'Adone*. Edited by Giovanni Pozzi. 2 vols. Milan: Mondadori, 1976.

Minturno, Antonio. *Amore innamorato*. Edited by Gennaro Tallini. Rome: Aracne, 2008.

Ovid. *Art of Love. Cosmetics. Remedies for Love. Ibis. Walnut-tree. Sea Fishing. Consolation*. Edited and translated by J. H. Mozley. Revised by G. P. Goold. Cambridge, MA: Harvard University Press, 1929.

———. *Metamorphoses*. Edited and translated by Frank Justus Miller, revised by G. P. Goold. 2 vols. Cambridge, MA: Harvard University Press, 1977.

Petrarca, Francesco. *Petrarch's* Songbook = *Rerum Vulgarium Fragmenta*. Translated by James Wyatt Cook. Binghamton, NY: Medieval and Renaissance Texts and Studies, 1996.

Plato. *Republic*. Edited and translated by Chris Emlyn-Jones and William Preddy. 2 vols. Cambridge, MA: Harvard University Press, 2013.

Ricciardo, Antonio. *Commentaria symbolica in duos tomos distributa*. Venice: Francesco de' Franceschi senese, 1591.

Tasso, Torquato. "Allegoria della Gerusalemme liberata." In *Tutte le opere*, edited by Amedeo Quondam, n.p. Rome: Lexis progetti editoriali, 1997. Reproduced on the *Biblioteca dei Classici Italiani* website at <http://www.classicitaliani.it/tasso/prosa/Tasso_allegoria_Gerusalemme.htm>.

———. *Jerusalem Delivered* = *Gerusalemme liberata*. Edited and translated by Anthony M. Esolen. Baltimore: Johns Hopkins University Press, 2000.

Tertullian. *The Apparel of Women*. Translated with an introduction by Edwin A. Quain. In *Disciplinary, Moral, and Ascetical Works*. Edited and translated by Rudolph Arbesmann, Sister Emily Joseph Daly, and Edwin A. Quain, 109–49. Washington, DC: Catholic University of America Press, 1959; reprint 2008.

———. *Q. Septimii Florentis Tertulliani de habitu muliebri liber*. In *Q. Septimii Florentis Tertulliani Opera Volumen Tertium*, edited by Johann Salomo Semler, 28–37. Halle an der Saale, Germany: Johann Christian Hendel, 1770.

Trissino, Giovanni Giorgio. *La Italia liberata da Gotthi*. Rome: Valerio e Luigi Dorici, 1547.

———. *L'Italia liberata dai Goti poema eroico*. London: n. p., 1779.

Udine, Hercole. *Avvenimenti amorosi di Psiche; poema eroico*. Venice: Ciotti, 1617. <http://bdh-rd.bne.es/viewer.vm?pid=d-3609178>.

Secondary Sources

Altieri Biagi, Maria Luisa, Clemente Mazzotta, Angela Chiantera, and Paola Altieri. *Medicina per le donne nel Cinquecento: Testi di Giovanni Marinello e di Girolamo Mercurio*. Turin: Strenna UTET, 1992.

Baumbach, Manuel. "Cupid." In *The Classical Tradition*, edited by Anthony Grafton, Glenn W. Most, and Salvatore Settis, 244–46. Cambridge, MA, and London: The Belknap Press of Harvard University Press, 2010.

Benedetti, Laura. "Introduction." In *Exhortation to Women and to Others if They Please*, by Lucrezia Marinella, 1–38. Edited and translated by Laura Benedetti. Toronto: Iter Inc. and Centre for Reformation and Renaissance Studies, 2012.

———. "Saintes et guerrières: L'héroïsme féminin dans l'œuvre di Lucrezia Marinella." *Écritures* 1 (2005): 93–109.

———. "Tradurre Marinella in America: opportunità e pericoli di una nuova frontiera." In *Conflitti culturali a Venezia dalla prima età moderna ad oggi*, edited by Rotraud von Kulessa, Daria Perocco, and Sabine Meine, 207–19. Florence: Franco Cesati, 2014

Cavallo, Jo Ann. *The World beyond Europe in the Romance Epics of Boiardo and Ariosto*. Toronto: University of Toronto Press, 2013.

"Chiesa di San Pantalon." <https://it.wikipedia.org/wiki/Chiesa_di_San_Pantalon>

Corsi, Sergio. "L'olmo e la vite (*Gerusalemme liberata* XX, 99)." *MLN* 102 (1987), 141–46.

Cox, Virginia. *Women's Writing in Italy, 1400–1650*. Baltimore: Johns Hopkins University Press, 2008.

———. *The Prodigious Muse: Women's Writing in Counter-Reformation Italy*. Baltimore: Johns Hopkins University Press, 2011.

Crouzet-Pavan, Elisabeth. *Venice Triumphant: The Horizons of a Myth*. Translated by Lydia G. Cochrane. Baltimore: Johns Hopkins University Press, 2002.

D'Alessandro Behr, Francesca. *Arms and the Woman: Classical Tradition and Women Writers in the Venetian Renaissance*. Columbus: Ohio State University Press, 2018.

De Armas, Frederick A., ed. *Ovid in the Age of Cervantes*. Toronto: University of Toronto Press, 2010.

Dionisotti, Carlo. "La letteratura italiana nell'età del Concilio di Trento." In *Geografia e storia della letteratura italiana*, 183–204. Turin: Einaudi, 1967.

Edden, Valerie. "Prudentius." In *Latin Literature of the Fourth Century*, edited by J. W. Binns, 160–82. London: Routledge and Kegan Paul, 1974.

Fenlon, Iain. *The Ceremonial City: History, Memory and Myth in Renaissance Venice*. New Haven, CT: Yale University Press, 2007.

Ferraro, Joanne M. *Venice: History of the Floating City*. Cambridge: Cambridge University Press, 2012.

Fletcher, Angus. *Allegory: The Theory of a Symbolic Mode*. Ithaca, NY: Cornell University Press, 1964.

Fontaine, Jacques. *Naissance de la poésie dans l'Occident chrétien: Esquisse d'une histoire de la poésie latine chrétienne du IIIe au VIe siècle*. Paris: Études augustiniennes, 1981.

Franceschetti, Antonio. "Ancora su Amore e Psiche: la molteplicità delle fonti." In *The* Sense *of Marino*, edited by Francesco Guardiani, 35–52. New York: Legas, 1994.

Giorgetti, Leonardo. "'Colei che 'l mondo e 'l cielo empie di luce': Mary's Glorification and Poetic Fame in Lucrezia Marinella's Spiritual Poetry." In

Genealogías. Rewriting the Canon: Women Writing in XVI–XVII Century Italy, edited by Stefano Santossuosso, 193–217. Seville: ArCiBel, 2018.

Giorgi, Rosa. *Angels and Demons in Art.* Edited by Stefano Zuffi. Translated by Rosanna M. Giammanco Frongia. Los Angeles: The J. Paul Getty Museum, 2005.

Guthmüller, Bodo. "Amore e Psiche a Mantova: Sulla *Psiche* di Ercole Udine." *Rassegna europea di letteratura italiana* 14 (1999): 25–40.

Hankins, James. *Plato in the Italian Renaissance.* 2 vols. Leiden: Brill, 1990.

Haskins, Susan. "Vexatious Litigant, or the Case of Lucrezia Marinella? New Documents Concerning Her Life (Part One)." *Nouvelles de la république des Lettres,* 25, no. 1 (2006): 80–128.

———. "Vexatious Litigant, or the Case of Lucrezia Marinella? New Documents Concerning Her Life (Part II)." *Nouvelles de la république des Lettres,* 26, nos. 1–2 (2007): 203–30.

Keith, Alison and Stephen Rupp, eds. *Metamorphosis: The Changing Face of Ovid in Medieval and Early Modern Europe.* Toronto: Centre for Reformation and Renaissance Studies, 2007.

Kenney, E. J. "Introduction." In *Cupid and Psyche,* by Apuleius, 1–38. Edited by E. J. Kenney. Cambridge: Cambridge University Press, 1990.

King, Margaret L. *Women of the Renaissance.* Chicago: University of Chicago Press, 1991.

Kolsky, Stephen. "Moderata Fonte, Lucrezia Marinella, Giuseppe Passi: An Early Seventeenth-Century Feminist Controversy." *Modern Language Review* 96 (2001): 973–89.

Kristeller, Paul Oskar. "Marsilio Ficino as a Beginning Student of Plato." *Scriptorium* 20, no. 1 (1966): 41–54.

Lavocat, Françoise. "Introduzione." In *Arcadia felice,* by Lucrezia Marinella, vii–lxvi. Introduction and notes by Françoise Lavocat. Florence: Olschki, 1998.

Lazzari, Laura. P*oesia epica e scrittura femminile nel Seicento*: L'Enrico *di Lucrezia Marinelli.* Leonforte: Insula, 2010.

Lewis, Jessamyn Eva. "Gender and Violence in Prudentius' *Psychomachia.*" PhD diss., University of California, Los Angeles, 2000.

Lines, David A. *Aristotle's* Ethics *in the Italian Renaissance (1300–1600): The Universities and the Problem of Moral Education.* Leiden: Brill, 2002.

Maggi, Armando. "Introduzione: Lo sperimentalismo di Lucrezia Marinella." In *De' gesti eroici e della vita maravigliosa della serafica S. Caterina da Siena,* by Lucrezia Marinella, 7–38. Edited by Armando Maggi. Ravenna: Longo, 2011.

Magnanini, Suzanne, with David Lamari. "Giuseppe Passi's Attacks on Women in *The Defects of Women.*" In *In Dialogue with the Other Voice in Sixteenth-Century Italy: Literary and Social Contexts for Women's Writings,* edited by Julie D. Campbell and Maria Galli Stampino, 143–94. Toronto: Iter Inc. and Centre for Reformation and Renaissance Studies, 2011.

Malpezzi Price, Paola, and Christine Ristaino. *Lucrezia Marinella and the "Querelle des Femmes" in Seventeenth-Century Italy.* Madison and Teaneck, NJ: Fairleigh Dickinson University Press, 2008.

Martelli, Daria. *Polifonie: Le donne a Venezia nell'età di Moderata Fonte (seconda metà del secolo XVI).* Padua: Cleup, 2011.

Martini, Alessandro. "Marino, Giovan Battista." In *Dizionario Biografico degli Italiani,* vol. 70. Rome: Istituto della Enciclopedia Italiana fondata da Giovanni Treccani S.p.A., 2008. <www.treccani.it/enciclopedia/giovan-battista-marino_(Dizionario-Biografico)/>.

Micocci, Claudia. *Sondaggi sull'*Adone *di Marino.* Rome: Aracne, 2009.

Panizza, Letizia. "Introduction to the Translation." In *The Nobility and Excellence of Women, and the Defects and Vices of Men,* by Lucrezia Marinella, 1–34. Edited and translated by Anne Dunhill. Chicago: University of Chicago Press, 1999.

Panofsky, Erwin. "Blind Cupid." In *Studies in Iconology: Humanistic Themes in the Art of the Renaissance,* 95–128. New York: Oxford University Press, 1939. Reprint, New York: Harper and Row, 1972.

Paxson, James J. *The Poetics of Personification.* Cambridge: Cambridge University Press, 1994.

Pozzi, Giovanni. "Commento. Canto quarto." In *L'Adone,* by Giovan Battista Marino. Edited by Giovanni Pozzi. 2 vols. 2: 262–299. Milan: Mondadori, 1976.

———. "Le fonti." In *L'Adone,* by Giovan Battista Marino. Edited by Giovanni Pozzi. 2 vols. 2: 89–102. Milan: Mondadori, 1976.

Pullan, Brian. *The Jews of Europe and the Inquisition of Venice: 1550–1620.* London and New York: I. B. Tauris, 1983.

Ray, Meredith K. *Daughters of Alchemy: Women and Scientific Culture in Early Modern Italy.* Cambridge, MA: Harvard University Press, 2015.

Ross, Sarah Gwyneth. *The Birth of Feminism: Woman as Intellect in Renaissance Italy and England.* Cambridge, MA: Harvard University Press, 2009.

Russell, Rinaldina. "Margherita Sarrocchi and the Writing of the *Scanderbeide.*" In *Scanderbeide: The Heroic Deeds of Georg Scanderbeg, King of Epirus,* by Margherita Sarrocchi. Edited and translated by Rinaldina Russell, 1–43. Chicago: University of Chicago Press, 2006.

Schnieders, Laura. "La polemica dei sessi: Lucrezia Marinella e Giuseppe Passi." In *Conflitti culturali a Venezia dalla prima età moderna ad oggi,* edited by Rotraud von Kulessa, Daria Perocco, and Sabine Meine, 191–206. Florence: Franco Cesati, 2014.

Stampino, Maria Galli. "Fantasmi di genere in *L'Enrico, overo Bisanzio acquistato. Poema eroico.*" In *A Portrait of a Renaissance Feminist: Lucrezia Marinella's Life and Work.* Edited by Antonella Cagnolati, 125–48. Rome: Aracne, 2013.

———. "Poema eroico alla veneziana: il problema retorico ed ideologico della Quarta Crociata e la soluzione marinelliana." In *L'Enrico, ovvero Bisanzio acquistato, poema eroico*, by Lucrezia Marinella. Edited by Maria Galli Stampino, 5–33. Modena: Mucchi, 2011.

———. "A Singular Venetian Epic Poem." In *Enrico; or Byzantium Conquered: A Heroic Poem*, by Lucrezia Marinella. Edited and translated by Maria Galli Stampino, 1–66. Chicago: University of Chicago Press, 2009.

———. "The Woman Narrator's Voice: The Case of Lucrezia Marinella's *Enrico*." *Italian Studies* 69 (2014): 75–94.

Stanivukovic, Goran V., ed. *Ovid and the Renaissance Body*. Toronto: University of Toronto Press, 2001.

Steiner, George. *After Babel: Aspects of Language and Translation*. 3rd ed. Oxford: Oxford University Press, 1998.

Taylor, A. B., ed. *Shakespeare's Ovid: The* Metamorphoses *in the Plays and Poems*. Cambridge: Cambridge University Press, 2000.

Ussia, Salvatore. *Amore innamorato: Riscritture poetiche della novella di Amore e Psiche secoli XV–XVII*. Vercelli: Mercurio, 2001.

"Virtue." In *The Concise Oxford Dictionary of English Etymology*, edited by T. F. Hoad. Oxford: Oxford University Press, 1986.

Zatti, Sergio. *Il modo epico*. Rome: Laterza, 2000.

Index